# Applied Psychology

!
Ser

# Applied Psychology

## Current Issues and New Directions

Edited by

*Rowan Bayne and Ian Horton*

SAGE Publications

London ● Thousand Oaks ● New Delhi

SAGE Publications Ltd
6 Bonhill Street
London EC2A 4PU

SAGE Publications Inc
2455 Teller Road
Thousand Oaks, California 91320

SAGE Publications India Pvt Ltd
32, M-Block Market
Greater Kailash - I
New Delhi 110 048

**British Library Cataloguing in Publication data**
A catalogue record for this book is
available for the British Library

ISBN 0 7619 4149 5
ISBN 0 7619 4150 9 (pbk)

**Library of Congress Control Number: 2002114568**

Typset by Pantek Arts Ltd, Maidstone Kent
Printed in Great Britain by Cromwell Press, Trowbridge, Wiltshire

# Contents

## PART II: GENERIC ISSUES

# List of Contributors

The editors would like to thank the following for their contributions to this book: Martyn Baker, Jane Gibbons and Neil Rees (Chapter 1); Alan Labram (the trends and career development section, Chapter 2); Mary Robinson and Mark Turner (the training issues section, Chapter 2); an anonymous trainee occupational psychologist (case study of becoming a chartered occupational psychologist, Chapter 3); Kasia Symanska (Chapter 4); Ian Horton (Chapter 8); Niru Williams (a day in the life of a counsellor, Chapter 8).

All the writers of Chapters 1–13 were members of the School of Psychology, the University of East London (UEL), at the time of writing.

**Bipasha Ahmed** PhD is a lecturer in social psychology. Her current research interests are in critical and narrative approaches to psychology, especially 'race', gender and class issues. She has published and presented research on the social construction of racism and feminist psychology and is currently involved in research into experiences of sexual abuse within the Asian community and how it is dealt with by service providers.

**Irina Anderson** PhD is a senior lecturer in psychology. Her research interests include issues in sexual violence, attribution and counterfactual reasoning theories (particularly in relation to rape), and discourse and conversation analysis.

**Martyn Baker** PsyD is a senior lecturer in clinical psychology and Deputy Director of the Doctoral Degree in Clinical Psychology. His interests are in personal construct psychology and the impact of religious commitment on the clients and staff of clinical psychology services.

**Rowan Bayne** PhD is Reader in Counselling and a chartered occupational psychologist. His main interests are in the Myers–Briggs Type Indicator (MBTI) and assertiveness. He has written, co-written and co-edited several books, including *New Directions in Counselling* (Routledge, 1996) and *The Counsellor's Handbook* (Nelson Thornes, 1999, 2ed.).

**Jenny Bimrose** PhD was Head of the Centre for Training in Careers Guidance for over 20 years. Currently she is Principal Research Fellow at the Institute for Employment Research, University of Warwick, and has also been a practitioner in careers guidance. She is also Chair of the Research Committee for the Institute of Career Guidance and a member of its Ethics and Standards Committee. Her research interests include guidance practice in the UK and women's career development.

**Mary Boyle** PhD is Professor of Clinical Psychology and Director for the Doctoral Degree in Clinical Psychology at UEL. As well as having a strong interest in training and education (she is a past Chair of the BPS Committee on Training in Clinical Psychology), she is an active clinician and researcher. Her main research interests are in critical and feminist approaches to women's health and clinical psychology. She is the author of *Schizophrenia: A Scientific Delusion?* (Routledge, 2002) and *Rethinking Abortion: Psychology, Gender, Power and the Law* (Routledge, 1997).

**Brian R. Clifford** PhD is Professor of Psychology and was a founder member of the DCLP, now Division of Forensic Psychology. He has published over 200 peer-reviewed research papers, chapters and monographs and four books, two in the area of forensic psychology (eye-witness psychology). His main research interest is in the application of memory research in real-life situations, especially children's and adults' recall and recognition abilities. He has taught high-level research methodology to postgraduates for many years. He has served as an expert witness in several cases within the UK where issues of testimony and identification have been in dispute.

**Paul Curran** MEd is an associate tutor and senior educational psychologist.

**Christine Doyle** PhD is a chartered occupational psychologist who has had many years of experience as an educator in the university sector. She has acted as a facilitator on management development programmes in the NHS and local government. She specializes in selection, assessment, appraisal and management development, but also contributes to other areas in occupational psychology such as the design of environments and of work and occupational stress and gender issues at work. She wrote *Work and Organizational Psychology: An Introduction with Attitude* (The Psychology Press, 2002).

**Irvine S. Gersch** – see roundtable contributors.

**Jane Gibbons** PhD is a clinical tutor.

**Ernie Govier** BSc is Deputy Head of School. He was co-editor of *A Textbook of Psychology* (Sheldon Press, 1980) which was the first general textbook produced in the UK for advanced level psychology. His research interests lie in the field of psychological sex differences and occupational choice. He was the UK consultant for the Channel 4 television series 'Why Men Don't Iron' which has been shown world-wide.

**David Harper** PhD is a senior lecturer in clinical psychology. Having worked as a clinical psychologist in NHS adult mental health services since 1991, David is currently Year II Academic Year Tutor on UEL's Doctoral Degree in Clinical Psychology. He is interested in critical and social constructionist perspectives in mental health and psychosis generally, specifically discourse analytic research into user and professional perspectives on 'paranoia'. He has published widely and is a co-author of *Deconstructing Psychopathology* (Sage, 1995).

**Ian Horton** MA, FBACP is Principal Lecturer in Counselling and Psychotherapy. He has been a chair or member of several British Association for Counselling and Psychotherapy committees and is particularly interested in the practical and theoretical integration of counselling. He has co-written and co-edited five books, including *Issues in Professional Counsellor Training* (Cassell, 1995), *The Needs of Counsellors and Psychotherapists* (Sage, 1997) and the *Handbook of Counselling and Psychotherapy* (Sage, 2000).

**Alan Labram** MSc is a field tutor and educational psychologist.

**Nelica La Gro** MSc is a lecturer in careers guidance. She has worked in the voluntary, local authority and private sectors, in addition to higher education. Her research interests and publications include evaluation studies of career guidance delivery systems, contribution to transnational projects and investigation of exchanges of meaning in the careers counselling interview.

**Mark R. McDermott** PhD is a chartered health and clinical psychologist. His recent publication topics include: psychosocial antecedents of coronary artery disease; individual differences in resistance to social influence ('rebelliousness'); social cognition variables as predictors of risky single occasion drinking; and defining health psychology.

**Gladeana McMahon** Dip. Couns. FBACP was a part-time senior lecturer in counselling and is a BACP senior registered counsellor and counselling supervisor and a BABCP-accredited cognitive-behavioural psychotherapist who is UKCP, CBT and UKRC Ind. Couns. registered. She has edited, co-edited, authored or co-authored several books including *The Handbook of Counselling in Britain* (Routledge, 1997) and *Confidence Works – Learn to be Your Own Life Coach* (Sheldon Press, 2001).

**Tony Merry** MA is a senior lecturer in counselling and has a private practice as a counsellor and supervisor. He has a special interest in person-centred counselling, and is author and co-author of a number of books on the person-centred approach. His most recent book is *Learning and Being in Person-centred Counselling* (2nd edn) (PCCS Books, 2002).

**M. Rachel Mulvey** PhD is Head of the Centre for Training in Careers Guidance. She is a full member and registered practitioner of the Institute for Careers Guidance and a NICEC associate (National Institute of Careers Education and Counselling). Her research areas are managerialism and professionalism, the role of ethics in practice and strategy, distance working and the transnational element of applied research in careers.

**Jill Mytton** MSc is a chartered counselling psychologist. She is a senior lecturer and current Course Director for the MSc Counselling Psychology course. Previously she has worked in primary care and in an Employment Assistance Programme at London Transport. Jill is currently the Honorary Secretary for the Division of Counselling Psychology. Her research areas are trauma and its treatment, and the relationship between mental health and religion.

**John Radford** – see roundtable contributors.

**Neil Rees** PhD is a clinical tutor.

**Anne Ridley** BSc is a final-year PhD student, studying the effects of anxiety on eye-witness testimony.

**Mary Robinson** MSc is an associate tutor and senior educational psychologist.

**David Rose** PhD is the Head of the School of Psychology. Before he joined UEL in 1994 he was Reader in Psychology at Goldsmiths College. His main research interest is in rehabilitation following brain damage and, in particular, virtual-reality applications to rehabilitation.

**Kasia Symanska** MSc is a part-time senior lecturer in counselling psychology and a UKCP registered counsellor.

**Mark Turner** MSc is an academic and professional tutor in educational psychology.

**James J. Walsh** PhD is a senior lecturer in psychology. His research interests are in health psychology and personality. Recent publications include work on the predictors of risky drinking, the role of identity in health behaviour and the relationship between perfectionism and statistics anxiety.

**Christopher Whiteley** D. Clin. Psych. is a clinical tutor in clinical psychology and is currently Year I Clinical Tutor on UEL's Doctoral Degree in Clinical Psychology. Christopher is also a clinical psychologist in the NHS working in a specialist addictions service with an inner-city trust. He is interested in associations across drug use, mental health and criminal justice problems in inner-city populations.

**Niru Williams** PG Dip. Couns. is Acting Head of the Counselling and Advisory Service.

**Sheila Wolfendale** – see roundtable contributors.

## The Roundtable

**Ian M. Cockerill** PhD is an honorary senior research fellow in the School of Medicine, University of Birmingham and, for more than 20 years, taught in the School of Sport and Exercise Sciences at Birmingham. He is Chair of the British Psychological Society's Sport and Exercise Psychology Section and is now working in private practice. He has published six books in the areas of sport and exercise psychology, the latest of which is *Solutions in Sport Psychology* (Thomson, 2002).

**Cary L. Cooper** is currently BUPA Professor of Organizational Psychology and Health in the Manchester School of Management, and Deputy Vice Chancellor of the University of Manchester Institute of Science and Technology (UMIST). He is the author of over 80 books (on occupational stress, women at work and industrial and organizational psychology), has written over 400 scholarly articles for academic journals and is currently founding editor of the *Journal of Organizational Behaviour*, co-editor of the medical journal *Stress and Health* and the President of the British Academy of Management.

**Michael W. Eysenck** is Professor of Psychology at Royal Holloway, University of London. He has published 25 books and approximately 130 research articles and book chapters. These publications cover a wide range of topics. However, his main research area is anxiety and cognition. He was the founding editor of the *European Journal of Cognitive Psychology*, and he has been Visiting Professor at the University of South Florida.

**Colin Feltham** PhD is Reader in Counselling at Sheffield Hallam University. He has been co-editor of the *British Journal of Guidance and Counselling*, has had 17 books published in the area of counselling and psychotherapy and edits three book series for Sage Publications. His latest book is *What's the Good of Counselling and Psychotherapy? The Benefits Explained* (Sage, 2002).

**Clive Fletcher** PhD is Emeritus Professor of Psychology at Goldsmiths College and Managing Director of Personnel Assessment Ltd. He is the author of nearly 200 publications and conference papers, mostly in the field of selection and assessment in work settings. He is a former chairman of the BPS Occupational Psychology Section and serves in varying board capacities for a number of UK and international companies.

**Irvine S. Gersch** PhD is Professor of Educational Psychology and Course Director of the MSc in Educational Psychology at UEL. He has published widely in the areas of listening to children, systems work, behaviour management, conciliation in SEN, educational psychology practice and training. He co-edited *Meeting Disruptive Behaviour* (Macmillan, 1990), and his latest book is *Resolving Disagreement in SEN: A Practical Guide to Mediation and Conciliation* (Routledge, 2002). He is a member of the government's working party on the future role and training of educational psychology.

**Nicky Hayes** is a fellow of the British Psychological Society, a honorary life member of the Association for the Teaching of Psychology and the 1997 recipient of the BPS Award for Distinguished Contributions to the Teaching of Psychology. She is an experienced researcher and consultant, with specialisms in both social and organizational psychology as well as in the psychology of exams. She is also the author of several well-known psychology textbooks and lectures in psychology at Bradford University.

**Chris Lewis** is a consultant, a chartered occupational psychologist and a partner in Aver Psychology. He was Course Director of the MSc in Occupational Psychology at UEL for 17 years and is a past chair (three times) of the BPS Occupational Psychology Division. His main interests are assessment and psychometrics and he is the author of over 100 papers and technical reports and of *Employee Selection* (2nd edn) (Hutchinson, 1992).

**Geoff Lindsay** is Professor of Educational Psychology and Special Educational Needs at the University of Warwick, where he is also Director of the Centres for Educational Development, Appraisal and Research. He is a past president of the British Psychological Society and is currently chair of the Society's Working Group on Statutory Registration and convener of the European Federation of Psychologists Association Standing Committee on Ethics. His latest book is *Researching Children's Perspectives*, co-edited with Ann Lewis (Open University Press, 2000).

**Sue Llewelyn** PhD is Course Director for the Oxford Doctoral Course in Clinical Psychology and Supernumery Fellow of Harris-Manchester College, University of Oxford. She was a member of the Mental Health Act Commission and has been involved in clinical psychology training since 1989. She is currently Chair of the Committee on Training in Clinical Psychology which accredits all British clinical psychology courses. She is the author of over 65 book chapters, academic and professional papers, 4 books and over 40 national and international conference presentations.

**Stephen Newstead** PhD is Professor of Psychology at the University of Plymouth and currently holds the position of Dean of the Faculty of Human Sciences. He was a member of the Psychology RAE Panel in 1992 and 1996, has been a QAA subject reviewer, chaired the Psychology Benchmarking exercise in 2000–1, and currently chairs the ESRC Psychology Panel for the recognition of postgraduate programmes. From 1995–1996 he was President of the British Psychological Society.

**Paula Nicolson** is Professor of Health Psychology at the School for Health and Related Research (ScHARR), University of Sheffield. Her research interests are in women's reproductive health, including sexual behaviour and post-natal depression and gender/power relations at work. She is the author of several books, including *Post-natal Depression: Facing the Paradox of Loss, Happiness and Motherhood* (Wiley, 2001) and *Having it All: Choices for Today's Superwoman* (Wiley, 2002).

**John Radford** PhD is Emeritus Professor of Psychology at UEL, where he led the Department of Psychology from 1965 to 1982, later becoming Dean of Science and Assistant Director of the then polytechnic. He introduced psychology as a subject for GCE A-level and founded the Association for the Teaching of Psychology. He was chair of the Psychology Board of the CNAA for six years. He is a fellow and honorary life member of the British Psychological Society, of whose Award for Distinguished Contributions to Teaching Psychology he was the first recipient. He is sole or joint author of 17 books, some of which have been translated into Finnish, Hebrew, Japanese, Portuguese, Romanian, Serbo-Croat and Spanish, and of numerous chapters and articles.

**Sheila Wolfendale** PhD is Professor of Educational Psychology in the School of Psychology at UEL, and is Course Director of the Doctorate in Educational Psychology for practising educational psychologists. She has had 22 books published, as sole author, editor and as co-editor, in the areas of educational psychology, special educational needs, early years and child development, and parental involvement. Her latest book is *Parent Partnership Services for Special Educational Needs: Celebrations and Challenges* (David Fulton, 2002).

# Preface

In 1962 Glenys Turner, a young lecturer at what was then called West Ham College of Technology, began teaching psychology to four students who were studying for a general degree of the University of London. Forty years later, within the School of Psychology in a much expanded institution, now called the University of East London (or UEL for short), over 50 full-time academic staff and numerous part-time staff are teaching psychology to over one thousand students on 3 undergraduate and 12 postgraduate programmes. Our postgraduate programmes span educational, clinical, occupational and counselling psychology, counselling, psychotherapy and careers guidance. Of these, three are professional doctorates – a development in psychology education nationally and one in which the School of Psychology at UEL has played a leading role. Through university validation arrangements the School of Psychology has links with students from three external organizations, the Psychosynthesis and Education Trust, Relate and the London Marriage Guidance Council.

We therefore have a strong emphasis on applied psychology. A crucial factor in the successful teaching of applied psychology is the active involvement of the staff of the School of Psychology at UEL in those activities for which they seek to train their students. The school now offers a wide range of consultancy services and short courses through its recently established Psychology Services Centre, and has a proud record and an extensive portfolio of research on applied psychology. More generally, we seek to give equal weight to teaching, research and professional practice as a basic principle of development.

The School of Psychology, within the institution's various incarnations as West Ham College of Technology, North East London Polytechnic, the Polytechnic of East London and, since 1992, the University of East London, has always been in the forefront of educational developments in psychology. This is perhaps unsurprising. Professor John Radford, its head from 1967 to 1982, is internationally known for his work on the teaching of psychology. We are proud to have worked with him on some of his numerous publications on the subject: Ernie Govier as joint editor of the text *A Textbook of Psychology* (1980), for A-Level psychology, and David Rose as joint editor of *The Teaching of Psychology. Method, Content and Context* (1980), *Teaching Psychology: Information and Resources* (1984) and *A Liberal Science: Psychology Education, Past, Present and Future* (1989). The British Psychological Society's award to John Radford of its inaugural prize for outstanding contributions to the teaching of psychology in 1996 was richly deserved. Subsequent heads have made their own particular contributions, of course, but John Radford had already 'set the scene'.

The range and diversity of our teaching and professional activities within the School of Psychology at UEL provide the impetus for this book. Its purpose is, partly, to celebrate the inspiration, innovation and achievement of both current and former staff. However, we also wish to discuss and to share our experiences and our thoughts about a range of issues which we have encountered during our development. For example, early on in this process of development, colleagues debated the distinction between 'pure' and 'applied' psychology, the relative merits of theory-driven vs. non-theory-driven research, and the appropriate boundaries between 'academic' and 'professional' psychology, or between 'scientific' and 'practitioner based' psychology. A useful framework for discussion of many of these issues has been John Radford's distinction among the *subject* ('the organization of content and resources for teaching purposes'), the *discipline* ('an inquiry into certain problems that seem to be related, and the associated body of method and knowledge') and the *profession* ('a set of people who devote much of their working time to such a group of problems and to trying to find practical solutions to them') of psychology (see Radford and Rose, 1989).

Three issues, in particular, have exercised us in recent years. All are to do with boundaries. The first concerns the external boundaries of professional psychology, the second the boundaries between areas within professional psychology and the third and most challenging issue concerns the cultural boundaries of professional psychology.

First, we run postgraduate professional programmes in mainstream areas of psychology side by side with programmes in counselling, psychotherapy and careers guidance. While a large majority of our staff have qualifications accredited by the British Psychological Society a significant number have, instead, qualifications accredited by the British Association for Counselling and Psychotherapy and the Institute for Careers Guidance. Yet the overlap among the expertise of these staff, the areas they teach and the professional activities they support is striking. For us this mixture of qualifications, experience and approaches within the school is very positive and enriching. We supported the introduction of the Register of Chartered Psychologists by the British Psychological Society, for all the reasons presented at the time but particularly in order to protect the public. However, our experience suggests that the effectiveness and vibrancy of professional training in psychology are greatly enhanced by an eclectic and inclusive approach: too rigid an approach to external boundaries will ultimately be to the detriment of the profession. The 'issue' is to manage the tension between, on the one hand, protecting both members and non-members of the profession and, on the other, the open mindedness, eclecticism and inclusivity which we believe are essential to the development of our profession in a rapidly changing world.

Similarly, there is an issue relating to boundaries between different specialist areas within professional psychology. This is not new, of course, and in *The Psychologist* over the years there have been numerous discussions of whether or not, or the extent to which, we should formally recognize the significant overlaps between the main areas of professional psychology and work towards recasting the boundaries within the profession. Importantly, should there be a generic core training for all? Given the range of our applied courses at UEL we are especially well placed to form a view about generic core training. Already there is significant collaboration between our programmes and there is little doubt it could be greatly extended. The issue here is where lies the balance between the need for generic skills and high-level specialist knowledge? How far should generic core training extend, and when and how should more specialist training be introduced? How much of the specialist training requirements should come before the award of a formal qualification, and how much of it should be provided on a continuing professional development basis? A related sub-issue concerns the boundaries between the activities of chartered psychologists within the current specialist professional areas of psychology and less qualified 'assistants' in those areas. Recent years have seen a proliferation of assistant psychologist posts in clinical psychology and there have been suggestions that a somewhat similar system within educational psychology may be the only way to maintain an adequate service to children, parents and teachers. Needless to say this is intricately related to the issue we have just discussed and has important implications for those who provide the professional training.

The third issue we should like to highlight, the cultural boundaries of psychology, we believe to be the most challenging. It also has particular relevance to the context within which we teach psychology at UEL. An important part of our university's vision is to 'Support social, cultural and economic inclusion, diversity and development'. The ethnic and cultural diversity of our student community in the School of Psychology is a source of great pride, therefore. Yet with diversity comes a responsibility to develop the subject, the discipline and the profession of psychology both to reflect and embrace this diversity. We are making progress: see, for example, the recent and highly acclaimed book by a member of our clinical psychology team, Nimisha Patel and her colleagues (Patel et al., 2000). However, we have a long way to go. This challenge is one which is faced by the whole profession of psychology if it is to have as much influence in the first half of the twenty-first century as it has had in the last half of the twentieth century. As we have said, it is again a question of boundaries but also inclusivity and a desire to embrace change.

These issues and many others are considered in the present volume. We hope you will find it enjoyable, thought provoking and useful. Within these pages the editors, Rowan Bayne and Ian Horton, include a detailed list of thanks and acknowledgements. It only remains for us to thank them for all their hard work and to congratulate them on the result.

*David Rose*
*Ernie Govier*

# Introduction

This book is intended for three groups of people:

1 Third-year psychology students who are considering a career in applied psychology and wondering which of the many possibilities is the most attractive and practical for them.

2 Students on MSc psychology courses who want an overview of issues and new directions in one or more branches of applied psychology.

3 Tutors on those MSc courses who, by definition, are shaping and developing their subject.

The book is organized into two parts. The first reviews nine branches of applied psychology, and the second contains discussions of four generic issues and a roundtable of eminent psychologists commenting on trends and new directions. Each chapter in part one has a broadly similar structure: summary, focus on what practitioners actually do, focus on training, questions for reflection and discussion and suggestions for further reading.

## Part I

Part I of the book reviews practice and training in the three traditional branches of applied psychology (clinical, educational and occupational psychology), three relative newcomers (counselling, forensic and health psychology) and three areas not always regarded as applied psychology (careers guidance, counselling – rather than counselling psychology – and lecturing). Careers guidance and counselling (psychotherapy) are examples of disciplines which are intrinsically psychological but which do not require a psychology degree to study them or for a career in them. Other disciplines in this category, though perhaps to a lesser extent than careers guidance and counselling, are teaching, nursing, social work and management.

A further rationale for the choice of topics in Part I was outlined in the Preface. However, the nine areas chosen clearly provoke the question: 'Well, what *is* applied psychology?' There is no definitive answer, but the British Psychological Society (BPS) publication, *The Directory of Chartered Psychologists and The Directory of Expert Witnesses* (2002), makes a detailed, brave though probably quixotic attempt. It distinguishes 14 broad areas in which chartered psychologists offer services and 108 specialist services within those areas, discussing each area and service briefly (pp. 3–16). The broad areas are represented in this book, with three main exceptions: clinical neuropsychology, psychological services in social service settings, and market, social and consumer research.

There are also two appendices to Part I: extracts from a PhD student's diary and notes on continuing professional development (CPD). Extracts from a PhD student's diary are included to give some flavour of this particular career, or pre-career, choice. Wider-ranging discussions and advice are readily available (for example, Phillips and Pugh, 1994; Bearman, 2002; Murray, 2002). The subject of the second appendix, continuing professional development, seems a clear new direction. The BPS decided in 2002 to make it mandatory (*The Psychologist*, May 2002: 219), and procedures and requirements were being developed at this time by the Standing Committee on CPD. Psychiatrists, for example, in an approach adopted in 2001, are expected to meet in groups of four to six to review their individual plans. We include an example of a psychologist's plan for her own CPD, though this approach, and structured CPD generally, will suit some styles of working much more than others, when quite different styles can be equally effective.

## Part II

Part II first discusses some generic issues for applied psychology in four areas: research as an art and science; evidence-based practice as a recent development with strengths and limitations; sexism as an example of the forms of oppression psychology has been accused of; and higher education as the troubled context for the training discussed in this book.

A special feature of Part II is the concluding roundtable of 14 eminent applied psychologists, commenting on current trends and desirable new directions in their own fields or generally. The branches and areas represented are clinical, educational and occupational psychology, life–work balance (which, like many specialisms, would be claimed by various branches), counselling, sport psychology, health psychology, lecturing in psychology, higher education, ethics, personality and, finally, a view on the dynamism of modern applied psychology generally.

## For Careers Information

The BPS is the authoritative and up-to-date source of information on becoming a chartered psychologist and other aspects of careers and training in applied psychology (www.bps.org.uk; phone: 01162 549568). They will also give details of conversion courses for people who want to be eligible for postgraduate training in psychology but who do not have a recognized psychology degree.

*Rowan Bayne*
*Ian Horton*

# Acknowledgements

David Rose suggested the initial idea for a book. A committee worked on the idea through its earliest stages: Liz Attree, Brian Clifford, Paul Curran, Susan Goodrich, Ian Horton, Ros Java, Nelica La Gro, Sarah Lewis, John Radford, James Walsh and Sally Wilden. A subgroup then developed the resulting outline further: Ian Horton, Paul Curran and Sarah Lewis.

The authors did magnificently to keep (roughly) to schedule in the face of increasing work pressures (see Chapters 9 and 13). Susy Ajith, as before, word-processed calmly and swiftly. Very warm thanks to those named above, and to the many other people who contributed.

# Part 1

## PRACTICE AND TRAINING

# Clinical Psychology

*Mary Boyle and Christopher Whiteley*

## SUMMARY

*This chapter describes the structure and content of clinical psychology training, the main settings in which clinical psychologists work and the types of work they do. It also discusses some of the major issues relevant to training and practice and some current debates. These include the challenges to training courses of expanding numbers of trainees; appropriate models for training and the links between theory and practice; identifying the key contributions of clinical psychology; the transition from trainee to qualified professional; the relationship between the personal and the professional; and the potential impact of government policy. Clinical psychology is arguably at a crucial stage in its development where it is seen as a key profession in the NHS yet is still reluctant to engage with the public, and where its relationship with other branches of psychology in the area of healthcare is likely to become a major source of debate.*

## What is Clinical Psychology?

'What exactly is clinical psychology?' is one of the predictable responses when members of the profession 'confess' to their occupation in social circumstances. Other typical responses often show confusion with the roles of other professionals such as psychiatrists, psychoanalysts, counsellors and psychotherapists. The British Psychological Society's Division of Clinical Psychology (DCP) estimates that there are between 3200 and 4000 clinical psychologists currently practising in the UK and the relatively small size of the profession almost certainly plays a part in the knowledge gap in the general public. Furthermore, in comparison with other groups, the profession of clinical psychology has done little to promote itself and enhance understanding in the lay community. Perhaps the most visible recent face of clinical psychologists has been as commentators to reality TV shows such as 'Big Brother'.

*The Core Purpose and Philosophy of the Profession* (BPS/DCP, 2001: 2) defines the purpose and aims of the profession as:

> to reduce psychological distress and to enhance and promote psychological well-being by the systematic application of knowledge derived from psychological theory and data

and

> to enable service users to have the necessary skills and abilities to cope with their emotional needs and daily lives . . . to make informed choices in order to maximise independence and autonomy; to have a sense of self-understanding, self-respect and self-worth; to be able to enjoy good social and personal relationships.

Many clinical psychologists would not disagree with these as broad, headline statements although they do not perhaps capture the variety and breadth of work of some clinical psychologists such as those who work more exclusively with physical health problems or who work at the level of organizations and service planning. And, as we will discuss in more detail in the section on training, the idea that clinical psychology promotes well-being by 'the systematic application of knowledge derived from psychological theory and data', while a desirable ideal, is not without its problems. The *Core Purpose and Philosophy*, with its strong emphasis on the autonomous individual, could also be seen as de-emphasizing the relational nature of people's lives (and problems) and the necessity of changing environments and contexts in order to reduce distress. Nevertheless, the importance of these statements lies in their firm move away from a medical language of diagnosing and treating illness or psychopathology and in their emphasis on the necessity of links between research and practice. Describing how the DCP statements translate into professional practice is further complicated by the wide diversity of models, settings and client groups covered by the profession. In the late 1980s, however, a review commissioned by the NHS/Department of Health Manpower Planning Advisory Group (MPAG, 1990; see also *The Psychologist*, October 1989) attempted to answer (among others) the key questions: 'What is clinical psychology' and 'What do clinical psychologists do that others cannot?' The review, based on extensive fieldwork and comparisons with other professionals, concluded that clinical psychology operated on three levels (see Box 1.1); Levels 1 and 2 are shared with other health professionals, but only psychologists routinely operate at Level 3, or 'formulate and respond to complex problems in terms of broadly based psychological knowledge'.

---

**Box 1.1 Levels of psychological skill derived from job analysis**

✦ *Level 1*: Skills in establishing and maintaining relationships, simple and often intuitive techniques of counselling and stress management.
✦ *Level 2*: Undertaking circumscribed psychological activities (e.g. behaviour modification) – may be defined by protocol.
✦ *Level 3*: Thorough understanding of varied and complex psychological theories and the ability to apply these to new problems to generate interventions.

*Source*: Manpower Planning Advisory Group Report on Clinical Psychology

This rather abstract statement of 'Level 3' activities can be broken down into the four activities of assessment, formulation, intervention and evaluation, although clearly it is a gross oversimplification to suggest that the process of trying to understand and ameliorate someone's life problems can be divided into four stepwise tasks. A brief description of these processes, however, will help convey how they may be used to try to capture some of the complexity of psychological problems.

*Assessment* involves collecting information about specific problems and the context in which they occur, along with some ideas about desired changes or outcomes. It may involve interviews, self-monitoring, observation, psychometric tests, rating scales and questionnaires. It is crucial to gain a clear description of the problem from the client's (and, if relevant, parents', relatives', partner's or carers') perspectives. For example, people who complain of anxiety or depression are using culturally available language to convey what may be very varied forms of distress with very different meanings for them. The assessment phase also aims to clarify the circumstances surrounding the onset of the problem and its present occurrence as well as its impact on the life of the person and those around him or her. In the second, *formulation*, phase, this information is linked to the observed problems using relevant psychological theory with the aim of providing hypotheses about the factors contributing to and maintaining problems. For example, it may be hypothesized that a client's auditory hallucinations are an understandable response to past sexual abuse, that the negative content of the voices relates to the client's thoughts about him or herself following abuse and that the voices are more likely to happen in situations where negative thoughts about the self are activated. These hypotheses guide the clinical psychologist when planning an *intervention* aimed at reaching a desired outcome. The final stage of this process is one of *evaluation* in which a more or less systematic attempt is made to assess whether or how the problem has changed following intervention. These processes of data gathering and hypothesis formation are not linear; additional important information often becomes available at a later stage and is incorporated into reformulation as the utility of initial hypotheses and thinking is continually tested out and evaluated. The aims of this process are perhaps best conveyed by saying that the clinical psychologist is trying to make the client's (or staff's, or carers', or family's) problems *understandable*, to articulate what brought these problems about in the first place, what maintains them, what is their function and meaning, and how this 'knowledge' might help in alleviating them. This may sound straightforward but it is surprising how very different this kind of analysis is from that traditionally encountered in mental health settings (compare, for example, the very brief formulation above of auditory hallucinations with the claim that these are a symptom of schizophrenia).

Within this general framework, the nature of the work done by individual clinical psychologists is likely to be influenced by three broad factors: setting, client group and theoretical orientation. The vast majority of clinical psychologists work in the NHS in settings which include primary care, community multidisciplinary teams, general hospitals and specialist hospitals and clinics; others work in social services, prisons or private practice. In addition to working directly with service users, who will include adults of all ages with physical and mental health problems, children and families and people with learning difficulties, the majority of clinical psychologists also undertake indirect work, for example, with staff, relatives and carers, using their knowledge of relevant literature and theory to bring a psychological perspective to issues relating to individual clients or wider service delivery. Indirect work also includes service planning, consultation/supervision to colleagues, teaching and training, research and audit. To complicate matters further, clinical psychologists may adopt a particular theoretical model which will influence the type of service they offer. For example, those who adopt a cognitive-behavioural model will tend to work on a one-to-one or possibly group basis while, for those who use a systemic model, much of the work will be with families, organizational or other systems. For many, the potentially diverse ways of working to achieve the core purpose of the profession is a substantial part of the attraction to training and working as a clinical psychologist. This diversity may also add to the difficulty of communicating the key elements that link members of the profession.

Perhaps the most stereotyped perception of a clinical psychologist is in a psychotherapy role with individual clients in an outpatient setting, where clients attend appointments for an hour a week over a period of time. For some members of the profession, however, this is only a small part of their job and for others such an image would bear little or no resemblance to their working week. Table 1.1 provides some examples of the kinds of work carried out by clinical psychologists in various settings; some of the work would be done in collaboration with other professionals, but the problems are typical of those presented to clinical psychologists.

## Current Issues and the Future of Clinical Psychology

### Changing theory and practice

Clinical psychology is not demographically representative of the population it serves. Not only that, but psychological theory has traditionally neglected the role, in the development and maintenance of distress, of those very experiences of disadvantage and disempowerment which clients so often 'bring' to their consultations. In this sense, clinical psychology has never fully represented those to whom it provides services. That this is the case has recently become much more apparent, for three reasons. First, theoretical developments in the human sciences have both highlighted psychology's androcentric and Eurocentric traditions and provided analytical tools for examining the implications of this and for constructing alternatives; secondly, the UK population has become more diverse, especially in terms of ethnicity because of immigration and asylum seeking, so that (at least partly because 'race' has been constructed as a primary marker) the differences between psychologists and their clients are increasingly difficult to overlook; and, thirdly, social changes have increased the visibility and sense of entitlement of other disadvantaged groups such as homosexuals and people with disabilities who are no longer willing to occupy the marginal social status previously assigned to them. As a result, there has been much discussion of how clinical psychology can become more representative of the population it serves and how its services can become more accessible. It is not simply a matter of 'educating' a wider public about clinical psychology services or of offering services in a wider variety of settings, but of more fundamentally examining the nature of these services and the theories which inform them (a point we shall return to in the section on training). In this way we can hope to avoid the traps of continuing to locate 'difference' in clients, rather than in relationships, and of replicating in services the experiences of disadvantage and injustice which may have contributed to clients' problems in the first place.

## Statutory registration and continuing professional development

As noted elsewhere in this volume, the Register of Chartered Psychologists maintained by the British Psychological Society (BPS) is a non-statutory register which is open only to members of the society who are in possession of the necessary qualifications and experience in psychology. Its non-statutory nature means that there is no legal requirement to join the register in order to practise as a psychologist in the UK. Consequently, many of the NHS trusts employing clinical psychologists do not require BPS chartered status from their employees, but merely require eligibility for chartership (i.e. to have completed a recognized postgraduate course in clinical psychology). This means that, in principle, a clinical psychologist who has been removed from the register for serious professional misconduct could still obtain employment as a clinical psychologist although in practice most employers would not condone this. Statutory registration, which remains the goal of the BPS, would certainly prevent re-employment in the NHS as a clinical psychologist, but it remains to be seen how far it would prevent the offering of services as a private practitioner. The BPS has recently announced the setting up of a Register of Psychologists as Psychotherapists from 2003 which will be open only to chartered psychologists (BPS, 2002b). This development has come about partly because of the efforts of (mainly non-psychologist) psychotherapists to achieve statutory registration through bills introduced in the House of Lords, and because of psychologists' concerns that their role as psychological therapists would be obscured. The proposed register was also the subject of much debate, not least because of concerns that an emphasis on psychotherapy did not acknowledge the very diverse roles of clinical psychologists and that this could privilege specialist schools of psychotherapy at the expense of the flexible and inclusive use of theory which clinical psychology training courses encourage.

Both voluntary and statutory registration require a commitment to the maintenance and development of professional competence (see elsewhere in this volume). In 1998, the BPS's Division of Clinical Psychology produced a more detailed framework for monitoring the professional development of clinical psychologists and its use is likely to become a condition of continued registration.

**Table 1.1 Some examples of the day-to-day activities of clinical psychologists in various specialities**

| Child and family | Adults | Primary care | Learning disabilities | Older adults | Forensic |
|---|---|---|---|---|---|
| Design and facilitate a group for children who have lived through parental divorce and separation | Assessment and intervention with a man who is threatened with loss of his job because of poor timekeeping due to prolonged checking rituals at home | Supervise a research project on the training needs of GPs on screening for domestic violence, in particular looking at why they find it difficult to ask screening questions in consultations with patients | Devise and run a training course for people with learning disabilities working for an advocacy organization involved in quality monitoring of services | Work with family of man in the early stages of Alzheimer's disease to devise strategies to minimize impact of his memory problems on day-to-day functioning | Assessment with a 19-year-old man from Bosnia currently on remand in a young offenders institute, where staff report daily attempts to hang himself; potential admission to medium secure unit |
| Conduct a cognitive assessment of a girl who has been referred for school avoidance and who may have a specific learning disability | Teaching session on psychological analysis of self-harm and its implications for clinical practice given to staff from accident and emergency departments | Make a presentation to European visitors on psychologists' involvement with primary care services | Carry out an assessment and intervention with a man with mild learning disabilities who is afraid to go out following an attack | Provide an assessment of a 75-year-old recently bereaved women who is refusing food, as part of a referral asking whether psychological intervention could be an alternative to ECT | Weekly consultation session to probation staff, on risk assessment and risk management for people with psychological problems |
| Undertake assessment and intervention with a boy and his family where a diagnosis of attention deficit hyperactivity disorder has been suggested | Assessment of suicide risk of woman with long-standing intrusive thoughts of suicide, and who hears voices telling her to kill herself | Devise and deliver a training and education course for health visitors on postnatal depression | Undertake an assessment of a woman with moderate learning disabilities who reports sexual abuse by male staff, as part of official investigations | Devise and deliver a training programme to staff on a unit for people with dementia aimed at helping them assess possible meanings and functions of residents' 'challenging behaviour' | Assessment of motivation to engage in psychological therapy for a man with longstanding psychosis and sexual offending against women, to be presented at his Mental Health Act review tribunal hearing |
| Teaching session on the development of sexuality and sexual identity for staff of the local adolescent in-patient unit | Participate in support group for staff in a unit for people with a diagnosis of borderline personality disorder | Provide weekly clinic at GP surgery, including, e.g., assessment and intervention for a man referred for 'depression' and who is very ambivalent about seeing a psychologist | Work with the family of an adolescent boy with mild learning disabilities who is reported to be increasingly aggressive | Assessment and intervention with a couple where the man reports sexual problems following recent coronary by-pass surgery | |

Form part of the team for a regular family therapy clinic

Intervention with a toddler and her mother using behavioural management because the girl has severe 'tantrums'

Provide group supervision for a team of community psychiatric nurses working in a child and adolescent mental health service

Intervention on a one-to-one basis with a 15-year-old boy with depression and suicidal thoughts

Assessment and intervention with a woman with a severe fear of driving

Supervision of research project on effectiveness of referral practices in multidisciplinary team

Long-term intervention with a woman with recurrent depression who was sexually abused as a child

Meet with senior health visitor to discuss request to set up a support group for newly qualified health visitors

Provide management supervision to counselling psychologist, including appraisal and planning of continuing professional development

Carry out assessment of organizational and other aspects of hostel accommodation for six adults where there are a high number of reports of 'challenging behaviour'

Devise an education and support programme for a pregnant woman with moderate learning disabilities

Run workshops for care staff on the provision of sex education to people with learning disabilities

Contribute to group intervention for older people whose mobility is impaired by fear of falling

Carry out assessment of family situation of 85-year-old woman where 'elder abuse' is suspected

Assessment and intervention with a women with a history of serious interpersonal violence who has beliefs that agents from the Vatican wish to harm her

Family work with a man, his father and sister in preparation for his moving from medium secure ward to a community hostel, main themes being understanding psychosis and relapse prevention

Work with ward staff in designing and implementing a graded programme for a man who feels too anxious to come out of his room on the ward

Risk assessment with a man previously convicted of sexually abusing his step-child. Requested by the local authority to contribute to discussions of his request to be allowed to live with his new partner and their young child

## Relationships with other applied psychologists

The last ten years or so have emphasized the degree of overlap between the work of clinical and other applied psychologists, through the development of post-graduate courses in health, counselling and forensic psychology, and clinical neuropsychology. So far, these groups do not have the clear funding and career structures which clinical psychology enjoys but the next decade or two is certain to see the increasing employment of these specialist groups within health and other public settings and see also no doubt vigorous discussion of the roles each group can and should play.

## Accountability and relationships with the public

In an interview, the author of the MPAG report (1990) discussed earlier expressed his disappointment at clinical psychologists' reluctance to state assertively what they could offer the public, and their reluctance to address questions such as 'does clinical psychology work' and 'what criteria would you use for judging the service?' (see Kitzinger, 1989). Arguably, the profession has become somewhat less reticent in both these spheres; for example, the publication and wide dissemination of a report on *Recent Advances in Understanding Mental Illness and Psychotic Experiences* (BPS/DCP, 2000b) provided a proactive statement of psychology's contribution to an area where psychological theory has not been very visible, while the issue of evaluating psychological interventions has received much attention (see Roth and Fonagy, 1996). But there remains a need for much wider engagement with the public on topics such as conceptualizing and responding to psychological distress, evaluating psychological interventions and the contribution of service users to the design and implementation of services. The alternative to such debates may be a defensive oversimplification of the issues in an attempt to 'educate' the public, rather than real engagement which reflects the complexity of what we do and tries to convey assertively how it is different from what is offered by others.

## The political context

A number of policies and proposals issued by the Department of Health spell out a changing NHS as a whole as well as mental health services in particular. Proposals to update mental health legislation include the possibility of clinical psychologists taking or being assigned new roles in compulsory admission and treatment. There has been considerable debate within the profession about this with some seeing it as an acknowledgement of the different approach and expertise that the profession could bring and others as fundamentally in opposition to clinical psychologists' therapeutic role. There are also objections to the conceptual framework of the proposed legislation (for a wider discussion, see Cooke et al., 2001). This issue remains unresolved and could leave the profession looking very different and undertaking very different functions with clients and colleagues.

As we will see in the next section, training places have been increasing year on year for some time as the demand for clinical psychologists continues to increase. The resulting growth in the profession presents opportunities for using our skills in creative and innovative ways within new and existing services. For example, the National Service Frameworks for mental health identify an increasing role for 'talking therapies', although these are not the exclusive remit of clinical psychology. Some proposals have given rise to concerns – for example, the delivery of 'manualized treatments' by 'graduate therapists' and attempts to restrict interventions to those favoured by a traditional view of evidence, focusing on economically driven outcomes (see also Chapter 11 in this volume). More widely, the government has signalled that the 'modern NHS' will be characterized by more flexible professions, removing rigid demarcations, and the idea of 'skill mix' has become a recurring part of discussions on workforce planning. The challenges are to influence the shape and delivery of these proposals and to respond to them in a way that maintains an effective and supportive role that attracts new recruits, while providing services that meet the needs and expectations of the population in a rapidly changing society.

## Training

Perhaps surprisingly, the present standard structure of UK clinical psychology training courses (see Box 1.2) only came about in the mid to late 1990s. Previously, courses lasted two or three years and were based in universities or the NHS (called inservice training); university courses offered a masters degree while those based in the NHS were examined by the BPS and offered a Diploma in Applied Psychology. This situation reflected the historical development of clinical psychology training and, indeed, clinical psychology itself, in which there had been a marked researcher/practitioner split, with university courses supposedly focusing more on academic and research aspects of clinical psychology and inservice training focusing more on practice (see Pilgrim and Treacher, 1992, for detailed discussion of these issues in Britain and Edelstein and Brasted, 1991, in the USA). By the 1980s, and certainly the early 1990s, it had become clear that the application of identical accreditation standards by the BPS Committee on Training in Clinical Psychology had greatly reduced whatever differences might have existed in the two types of course and that it was difficult to justify either different time periods for training or different awards. The requirement that courses provide training of three years full time in order for their graduates to be eligible for registration as chartered psychologists also encouraged moves to a standard structure. At the same time, some academics (e.g. Carr, 1990) were questioning whether a masters degree was the appropriate award for three years of full-time postgraduate study and, by the end of the decade, all courses were of three years duration and awarded a doctoral degree.

---

**Box 1.2  The structure of clinical psychology training**

✦ *Course level*: Postgraduate (requires first degree in psychology giving the Graduate Basis for Registration).
✦ *Duration*: Three calendar years full time.
✦ *Base*: University or affiliated to/validated by university.
✦ *Award*: Professional doctorate (Clin. Psy. D/D. Clin. Psy.)
✦ *Elements*: Academic teaching (20%); supervised practice (50%); research and private study (30%).
✦ *Funding*: Largely NHS through 'local' workforce planning confederations. Registered students become NHS employees of 'host' trust designated by confederation. Small minority overseas funding.

---

## The aims of training

At the most general level, courses aim to provide trainees with theoretical knowledge and systematic opportunities, in both teaching and placements, to link that knowledge with practice so as to be able to gather information about, conceptualize, and plan and implement interventions for the wide range of psychological problems and issues presented in the various settings in which clinical psychologists work (see the section on practice below). Courses also aim to teach trainees how to evaluate critically both their knowledge and practice, including the ethical issues raised by them, and how to communicate their ideas and practice to clients, carers and other professionals. Finally, courses aim to build on research skills gained on undergraduate courses and particularly to facilitate trainees in devising and carrying out research in applied settings. These aims raise important issues which will be discussed later, not least the relationship between theory and practice, the role of research in practice and the types of critical reflection which should be fostered in trainees.

## Selection for training

As Table 1.2 shows, the number of applicants for clinical psychology courses has been falling, and the number of places rising, over the last few years. The latter is due to a vigorous programme of expansion led by increasing NHS demand for clinical psychologists and which has created five new courses in England and Wales since 1996. It is not clear why applications for training should be falling, although a wider variety of jobs for psychology graduates, as well as the perception that it is very difficult to obtain a training place, may have contributed. Nevertheless, the number of applicants still far exceeds the number of places and most applicants in any one year will be rejected. As Roth (1995) has noted, the fact that good-quality applicants may be rejected can lead to the suspicion that entry criteria are arbitrary or perversely difficult to achieve; it can also lead to 'a set of hunches about the magic combination of experiences which will gain entry to training' (p. 589). Course staff are well used to receiving calls from prospective applicants asking: 'If I do *this* or *this*, then will I get a place?'

**Table 1.2  Training numbers 1996–2001**

| Year | Number of places | Number of applicants | Ratio applicants/places |
|------|------------------|----------------------|-------------------------|
| 1996 | 285 | 1645 | 1:5.8 |
| 1997 | 327 | 1642 | 1:5 |
| 1998 | 347 | 1597 | 1:4.6 |
| 1999 | 377 | 1556 | 1:4.1 |
| 2000 | 392 | 1538 | 1:3.9 |
| 2001 | 454 | 1486 | 1:3.3 |

*Source*: Clearing House for Postgraduate Courses in Clinical Psychology.
1996: 23 courses in clearing house.
2001: 28 courses in clearing house.

The answer, inevitably, is more complex and has more to do with what is learnt from experience than with simply 'getting' the experience. In a survey of selection procedures, Roth and Leiper (1995) concluded that, although courses might differ in the relative emphasis placed on particular characteristics, there was good overall agreement on what was being looked for in applicants. The major characteristics included motivation and commitment; academic ability; previous relevant experience; evidence of ability to link theory and practice and to use theory in solving problems; knowledge of clinical psychology and the NHS; and personal qualities such as confidence, interpersonal and communication skills, empathy and sensitivity. Courses use a variety of selection procedures, conducted over several phases involving course staff and NHS psychologists. Most courses specify their criteria for each phase, use ratings and rankings and rely on individual interviews (often more than one) in their final selection. Some courses, however, use group interviews, group tasks, oral presentations or written tasks such as responses to clinical vignettes as part of their selection process (Roth and Leiper, 1995; Phillips et al., 2001).

Although Roth and Leiper (1995) were able to conclude that a good deal of thought and care went into the selection process, there are at least three areas of concern. The first is demographic. Clinical psychology is numerically dominated by white females (although this is much less so at higher levels – for example, the majority of course directors are male). There is no evidence of direct discrimination against other groups (and it is worth bearing in mind that undergraduate psychology students are predominantly white females), but there is concern about indirect discrimination or, at least, concern about factors which might discourage applications from more varied demographic groups or make them less likely to be selected. For example, in relation to ethnicity, Boyle et al. (1993) found that applicants to the University of East London (UEL) course from minority ethnic groups were significantly less likely to have had previous experience as an assistant psychologist. Although such experience is not a selection requirement, this job is the most likely to provide the kind of experience and knowledge which allow people to present themselves well to selectors. Similarly, the demands of travelling to placements with varied standards of access and amenities might discourage applicants with disabilities, while the tendency of mental health professionals to view their clients as 'other' (Sampson, 1993) and their reluctance to discuss their own experience of psychological problems can discourage applicants who have experienced mental health problems. Courses, however, will have to take account of the recent Disability Discrimination Act, and the Special Educational Needs and Disability Act, and there have been wide-ranging discussions of their implications for clinical psychology training.

The second area of concern identified by Roth and Leiper was the limited amount of audit on the selection process, although few courses do no audit and the situation is likely to have improved since the survey was conducted. Audit would include obtaining feedback from candidates and selectors, analysing inter-rater agreement, comparing demographic characteristics of successful and unsuccessful applicants and relating course outcomes to selection panel ratings. Finally, there is concern about the validity of selection procedures. Roth and Leiper note that there is little evidence that expertise from other areas of applied psychology, particularly occupational psychology, is being used in clinical psychology's selection process. A similar point is made by Hatton et al. (2000) who highlight a number of challenges to the validity of the selection procedures. These include the use of an application form with a high proportion of open-ended responses; reliance on relatively unstandardized references; lack of evidence of inter-rater agreement at each stage of selection; over-reliance on interview as a selection method; and lack of criterion-related measures so that selection criteria, even if clearly specified and reliably assessed, may not be demonstrably related to job performance.

In order to address at least some of these concerns, the Clearing House for Post-Graduate Courses in Clinical Psychology set up a research project in 1999, in four phases: first, a job, task and role analysis to identify core-competencies; secondly, the development of criterion measures of job performance; thirdly, the development of measures of applicant potential; and, fourthly, a prospective cohort study of the 2000 intake whose aim is to assess factors associated with positive job performance during and immediately after training, as well as factors associated with non-completion and failure, trainee stress, work satisfaction and immediate job destination. Although some initial results from the first phase of the project are available (Phillips et al., 2001) it will be some time before the data can be translated into usable selection procedures. It is not clear how the success of the project will be assessed or how far results which will inevitably rely on aggregated data will facilitate the kind of fine discriminations which courses have to make among individuals. There is also the question of whether statements of competencies should rely on judgements of those who do the job, rather than including judgements from, say, those to whom the job is done (i.e. service users). Nevertheless, any attempt to evaluate and improve on present selection procedures is welcome, and the project provides a good example of one branch of applied psychology drawing constructively on the resources of another.

## Models of training

There has been much discussion recently of a 'competency model' of training and recent draft revisions to accreditation criteria have been informed by the model in the sense that they involve attempts to 'clarify the desired output from Courses – what it is that newly qualified psychologists should be able to do, with the underlying knowledge and values to support this' (BPS/DCP, 2001: 2). This approach has become increasingly popular with more general attempts to set occupational standards for 'vocational' education and training (BPS, 1998) and, as we saw earlier, it underlies the most recent research on selection for clinical psychology courses. Of course, the idea that training courses should be able to specify what it is they are training has always informed clinical and other branches of applied psychology but its recent greater explicitness within clinical psychology can be attributed to two main factors. The first is the large increase in trainee numbers with consequent pressure on placements and supervisors; the second are the organizational changes which have disrupted the traditional division of placements into discrete core areas such as adult, child, learning disabilities and older adults. Instead, one psychology department might offer experience in an extremely diverse range of service settings while others are increasingly offering highly specialized services. Both these developments have made it difficult to plan training in the traditional way, which tended to emphasize specific experiences which had to be gained in specific settings, rather than emphasizing the outcomes of those experiences. On the other hand, organizational developments have provided the opportunity to plan training much more flexibly as well as creating the demand that we look more fundamentally and explicitly at what it is that training is trying to achieve and how these goals might be met through a variety of training experiences. The result is a model which combines statements of learning outcomes which demonstrate competence with statements of client problems, service delivery systems and modes of work through which these outcomes will be achieved. Although very specific in parts, the model is sufficiently flexible to allow trainees to take a variety of placement routes in order to achieve training goals.

Although it is clearly important that we often examine what we are trying to achieve in training clinical psychologists, the current popularity of the language of skills, competencies and, indeed, training,[1] can create the impression that the role of courses is to teach a discrete set of actions whose implementation will have predictable outcomes. And, as 'the training of clinical psychology is rooted in the science of psychology' (BPS/DCP, 2001: 4) then it may also be assumed that these actions are dictated by an established body of knowledge. Indeed, this is made explicit by the core purpose and philosophy of the profession, to which trainees are expected to be committed, of 'decreasing psychological distress and promoting psychological well-being *through the systematic application of knowledge derived from psychological theory and data*' (BPS/DCP, 2001: 4, emphasis added). Similarly, the learning outcomes of training courses include the acquisition of 'knowledge required to underpin clinical research and practice' (BPS/ Committee on Training in Clinical Psychology, 2001).

This stance involves the explicit adoption of what has become known as the scientist-practitioner model; the model is also discussed in Chapter 11 but its implications for training are important enough to merit further discussion here. The term scientist-practitioner refers both to those who draw on research to inform their practice and/or to those who conduct research as part of their practice (Barlow et al., 1984). The idea that applied psychologists should draw on scientific research and themselves conduct research is as old as applied psychology itself, and a model of clinical psychology training which balanced research and practice was endorsed by the American Psychological Association in 1924 (Edelstein and Brasted, 1991). The scientist-practitioner model was more explicitly endorsed and developed by the influential Boulder conference in 1949; as Clegg (1998) notes, most course directors in both the USA and the UK still regard this model as the most appropriate for training and practice (see also Kennedy and Llewelyn, 2001). The implications of the model for training seem straightforward: the task for courses is to provide trainees with the scientific knowledge base which will, in effect, tell them what to do; to provide them with guided opportunities to apply this knowledge; and to provide a research training which will enable trainees both to carry out research and to interpret the research of others to inform their future practice.

In principle, these aims seem appropriate and desirable; in practice, they appear to be an unrealized ideal, for two major reasons. The first, which we will be less concerned with here, is that the large majority of clinical psychologists do not carry out research, although there is some disagreement over how 'research' should be defined in this context (Barlow et al., 1984; Milne et al., 1990; Agnew et al., 1995). The second and more serious issue is that clinical practice appears not to be strongly informed by research (Long and Hollin, 1997). In a survey of British clinical psychologists by Milne et al. (1990), for example, only 16% of respondents said that research had 'a lot' of influence on their practice. For trainees, this situation can present itself as a lack of 'fit' between the academic content of their courses and what they observe or is expected of them in practice. Burley (2001: 5), for example, described himself as 'a clinical psychology trainee coming to the end of a 3-year training whose academic component has for the most part been largely incongruent with my own experience as a human being'. And while this may be a rather extreme instance, it is not an isolated example of the problems trainees can face both in matching their academic teaching to their real-world experience and in finding psychological theories which seem relevant to the problems they are trying to solve (Adcock and Newbigging, 1990; Pilgrim and Treacher, 1992; Jones, 1998).

This situation may arise because courses do not place enough emphasis on how the theories they teach can be applied in practice or supervisors do not articulate the theories on which their practice is based. Certainly, teachers and supervisors need to be aware that making such links explicit for trainees is a major and challenging task. There are, however, three further possible reasons for the lack of perceived fit between theory and practice. The first is the narrowness of psychological theory. It is not simply that psychology has given little prominence to factors which appear to have profound effects on people's lives and well-being, such as gender, class, ethnicity, economics and power; it has insisted that human behaviour and experience can largely be accounted for through the operation of intra-psychic attributes and that change can be effected through the manipulation of these attributes. The result can be theories which are difficult to match with people's accounts of their relationships or lived experience; it can also be that attempts to change people via their intra-psychic attributes founder on those very 'realities' of life about which psychology has little to say (Ussher and Nicolson, 1992; Fox and Prilleltensky, 1997; Smail, 2001).

The second factor which may account for the mismatch between theory and practice is the narrowness of psychological methods. Psychological research has relied largely on quantification and statistical inference from group data. Danzinger (1985) has called this psychology's 'methodological imperative' and emphasized that, because method is primary in psychology, theory has had to be restricted to that which fits the method – i.e. people have to be conceptualized in ways which allow measurement. Moreover, a reliance on quantification limits what we can know about a person, not least because data-gathering techniques must produce information (e.g. scores on tests or rating scales) which can be handled by statistical techniques. It is not accidental that there should be a lack of fit between theories which rely on restricting or predetermining what a person can 'say', and practice which relies on encouraging people to speak freely, to give an account of their problems in their own way.

A third reason for the theory–practice mismatch is clinical psychology's traditional, if now lessening, reliance on psychiatric categories as a means of conceptualizing people's distress and 'abnormal' behaviour. Yet such categories lack scientific validity and, like quantification, involve overlooking or de-emphasizing many aspects of people's lives and relationships which may be relevant to their problems (e.g. Kutchins and Kirk, 1997; Boyle, 1999; Johnstone, 2001). Thus, Halgin's (1999) comment on US clinical psychology, that the lessons of real-world clinical practice have yet fully to penetrate professional training, can perhaps be rephrased to say that a good deal of the psychological theory which informs training has been developed in such a way as systematically to exclude much of the 'real world'.

Experienced practitioners may be confident enough to recognize these problems and to seek or produce theoretical accounts which seem relevant to their clients' experience. For trainees, however, the mismatch often translates into fears of personal inadequacy if they are not able to do what they are supposed to – apply theory to practice – or if their 'results' with individuals do not match the group data reported in journals.

In a related vein, Schön (1987) has strongly criticized models of training and practice, such as that of the scientist-practitioner, which tend to present human problems as technical problems capable of technical solutions, and present training as the process of instilling the required technical knowledge. As he points out, experienced practitioners engage in reasoning at many levels. In solving problems, they draw on research but also on knowledge from previous, similar cases together with subjective impressions about relationships and context. Schön argues that, while peers can easily identify expert' practitioners, it is much more difficult to articulate, and therefore explicitly teach, the qualities which contribute to this. Schön's model of the 'reflective practitioner' is an attempt to guide both the articulation and transmission of the qualities of the 'expert' practitioner and the development in trainees and teachers of the ability to reflect on the processes of learning and practice (see also Chapter 11 in this volume).

The reflective-practitioner model provides a valuable counter to the idea of practitioners as transmitters of technical knowledge and of training as the process of learning 'what to do'; it does, however, have limitations. As Clegg (1998) has pointed out, in describing skills-in-action rather than knowledge, the main value of the model is also its main limitation since it does not distinguish practitioners in different branches of applied psychology or indeed psychologists from practitioners in other disciplines. The model therefore requires 'the addition of discipline specific knowledge to be combined with the reflective practitioner's artistry in action' (Clegg, 1998: 9). Such knowledge is also crucial if the model is not to slide into personalized and unaccountable reflection with no criteria for choosing between one sort of perceived expertise and another.

These debates have a number of implications for training. First, courses need to provide a broader-based academic programme than has often been the case, and one which distances itself from a reliance on psychiatric diagnosis and takes full account of the social and environmental factors repeatedly shown to be associated with psychological distress. This teaching, however, can also show how traditional theories which do not explicitly acknowledge factors, such as power or social inequality, can still be very relevant – Seligman's learned helplessness theory of depression is a good example. Secondly, teaching on research should include both quantitative and qualitative methods but in the context of their epistemological assumptions. This is important because, not uncommonly, qualitative methods are taught in this way, with quantitative methods still presented as a taken-for-granted way of developing psychological theory. Thirdly, courses should provide a structure for trainees to reflect on their learning and experience as practitioners (a point we shall return to later). Finally, courses should provide trainees with the conceptual means to analyse psychology and clinical psychology as 'enterprises'; in other words, with the means to turn their analytic gaze on their discipline and profession. Such analyses are now well developed within 'critical psychology' but do not yet form an integral part of most training courses. Analysing oneself, so to speak, rather than one's clients can of course bring doubt and confusion as well as important insights (one UEL trainee described the process as 'like scuba diving – you discover a fascinating world you never knew existed'). But this component of training can also act as a counter to the doubt and confusion trainees feel at being unable to find the certainty they are sure must lie somewhere just beyond their reach as well as encouraging the development of creative and innovative practice (Clegg, 1998; Cheshire, 2000; Harper, in press).

## Professional development and support systems in training

It is widely acknowledged that clinical psychology training makes significant personal demands on trainees (Cushway, 1992; Scaife, 1995), and two major sources of demand are often identified. The first is practical and material – for example, extensive travel to placements, moving placements every six months, time management and meeting multiple assessment deadlines with limited study time. While there is a limit to how far such demands can be reduced, courses' organizational and feedback systems can help ensure that the demands are often reviewed and kept to a realistic level.

The second source of demand on trainees stems from the nature of clinical psychologists' work. Nichols et al. (1992: 29) note that psychological therapy involves 'continual exposure to the distress, frustration, defeat and heightened emotional functioning of others', together with the demand to empathize with the perceptions and feelings of another person *and* reduce his or her distress. Carrying out psychological therapy can therefore be seen, Nichols et al. suggest, as a source of continual exposure to low-key stressors.

Clinical psychology, however, does not have a strong history of recognizing the impact of such demands and providing support to its practitioners, although the situation has improved in the last ten years. Discussing obstacles to the development of adequate peer support systems, Walsh et al. (1991), Nichols et al. (1992) and Walsh and Cormack (1994) have highlighted a reluctance to reveal what might be seen as personal vulnerabilities; the desire to convey to colleagues and employers an image of strength and productivity and fear of becoming or being seen as a client (compare our earlier remarks about clinical psychologists constructing their clients as 'other'). And if these are obstacles for qualified practitioners, they are even more so for trainees who may see themselves as risking their qualification by revealing what they fear might be seen as ignorance and weakness.

One result of this is that 'support' has often implicitly been seen in terms of pathology or crisis management. Walsh and Scaife (1998) have argued instead for systems of 'personal and professional development' (PPD) within training courses which move away from a focus on trainees' internal psychological needs towards a culture which acknowledges PPD as an ongoing process of learning. Such systems would include teaching sessions which encourage reflection on the process of training and its emotional implications, covering topics such as stress and time management, dealing with violence in the workplace and using supervision. The systems would make available to trainees personal mentors or advisers who do not have an assessment role and also provide a facility for group discussion – possibly using the reflective practitioner model mentioned earlier – of issues such as the impact of values, expectations and life experiences on practice (and vice versa). A recent informal study of Clearing House and alternative handbooks (Gillman, pers. comm.) showed that most courses now have at least some of these elements in place, suggesting that there is a move away from the idea that 'support' is something occasionally required by the vulnerable, to a recognition of the ways in which the relationship between the personal and the professional can be constructively reflected on and used during training.

There is, however, a third source of demand on trainees which is much less often discussed and which may not be systematically addressed by many systems of PPD. It is the issue we discussed earlier of psychology's narrow theoretical and methodological base, which has limited our potential for understanding and alleviating distress. When we add to this the lack of discussion of this issue in mainstream literature, together with the relatively uncritical promotion of 'evidence-based practice' and the scientist-practitioner model, it is almost inevitable that trainees will feel inadequate (and fear that their inadequacies will be discovered) if they are not always able to do what they are supposed to – i.e. apply psychological knowledge to remove or alleviate people's problems. This situation can also lead to demands on staff to teach more and more 'clinical skills' in the almost magical belief that if only the trainee can learn to do therapy properly, all will be well. Or, as Rudkin (2000: 48) – writing as a trainee – has put it, trainees often have a fantasy 'in which, graduating from clinical training, we shall be presented with an envelope inside of which The Secret will be written, and for ever more we shall be sure we are doing the right thing'.

PPD programmes may well include discussion of these issues but they are not systematically designed to do so, and the emphasis on the 'personal' in such programmes, as in psychology itself, could divert attention from the social contexts which shape clinical psychology's theory and practice. We would argue that PPD programmes need to exist alongside curricula with the features we mentioned earlier – teaching which acknowledges the role of social and environmental factors in psychological distress and its alleviation and which provides a conceptual framework for critically examining psychology's own theory and practice.

## The transition from training to (qualified) practice

Most courses provide teaching in the final year whose aim is to facilitate the transition from trainee to qualified practitioner status. The content might include updating on key professional issues; reflecting on learning and development throughout the course and on how this might continue; and criteria for job choice, writing CVs and preparing for interviews. Many courses involve recent graduates in the teaching to discuss key aspects of the transition and how they might be managed. Courses have developed this teaching without the benefit of systematic research on graduates' experience of working as qualified practitioners. Recent research by Cheshire (2002), however, has highlighted some of the major rewards and challenges of the transition. Her respondents had been qualified for 13–18 months and, while the major benefits were seen as greater autonomy, improved pay and the release from constant evaluation, the extent to which these graduates found the transition difficult was striking: only 2 of a sample of 14 reported that the transition had been unproblematic; the majority reported that they had become significantly stressed during these first months post-qualification to the point where 28% of the sample had considered leaving the profession although none had actually done so. The major stressors included increased workload and controlling the volume of referrals accepted; lack of time to prepare for clients; greater complexity of cases; increased responsibility; inadequate supervision; and the strain of being perceived as an expert while seeing oneself as inexpert. Not surprisingly, respondents reported that it was only in retrospect that they saw how protected they had been as trainees; the transition also highlighted some of the advantages of the sometimes resented dual role of student and professional. Cheshire notes that good supervision either from senior colleagues or peers emerged as the most significant determinant of the quality of the immediate post-qualification experience. Such supervision provided support and guidance on decision-making and on negotiating and managing workloads; it also provided reassurance that senior colleagues were not omniscient and, particularly in the case of peer supervision, normalized and validated respondents' experiences.

This research provides some guidance to courses on teaching content and Cheshire suggests sessions which aim to normalize trainees' anxieties about the move to qualified status as well as to encourage discussion of stresses they are likely to experience and assist them in identifying personal and professional sources of support they can use. She also suggests that placement supervisors should raise trainees' awareness of their personal responses to their work and assist them to develop appropriate coping strategies. These are indeed constructive suggestions and some are already incorporated into course content. What is notable about them, however, is that they focus largely on the individual, on the trainees' responses and their coping skills. Yet the major sources of stress mentioned – inadequate supervision, heavy clinical and administrative workloads which allow little time to prepare for or reflect on work with clients – can be seen as organizational. Not only that, but the 'more complex cases' which challenge new graduates may refer to people with multiple and severe life problems which clinical psychology cannot realistically be expected to solve; yet, as we noted earlier, psychological theory may encourage us to conceptualize such problems in ways which make it look as if we should be able to solve them, thus contributing to new graduates' feelings of being deskilled and inauthentic. Preparation for employment, then, needs to balance an emphasis on what trainees can contribute to the transition with an analysis of the social and organizational contexts in which they work and how these might, or might not, be influenced.

## The future of clinical psychology training

Reviewing training in the last decade from trainees' perspective, Cheshire (2000) commented that clinical psychology is an increasingly segmented profession, with a growing number of subdivisions representing different client groups and theoretical orientations. The challenge for training courses, she suggests, is to reflect this diversity and avoid promotion of a defensive orthodoxy. There are encouraging signs that this is already happening but the challenge will need to be met within an increasingly complex and demanding organizational context, some of whose key elements include expansion in trainee numbers which places heavy demands on supervisors to provide placements and on teachers to develop appropriate curricula and teaching methods; difficulties in recruiting appropriately qualified teaching staff (Thomas et al., 2002); acknowledging directives from the government on health care structures and priorities (e.g. the NHS Plan for England, 2001, and National Service Frameworks) so that trainees are prepared for their future responsibilities; and meeting the requirements of educational stakeholders responsible for funding, validation and accreditation.

## Note

[1] It is interesting to note that the official NHS language for what courses do is 'education and training' but that the term 'education' almost never appears in course or the wider professional literature.

## QUESTIONS FOR REFLECTION AND DISCUSSION

1  The term 'training' is almost exclusively used when referring to the process leading to the award of a degree and qualification in clinical psychology. What impact might this have on the process itself and on those involved in it?

2  Clinical psychology is becoming increasingly concerned with the relationship between the personal and the professional. Why might this be and are we overconcerned about it?

3  It has often been remarked that clinical psychology does not 'market' itself very well. Why is this the case and what should be done about it?

4  Clinical psychologists traditionally train and practise separately from other applied psychologists. Should clinical psychologists be more closely allied to other branches of applied psychology and less closely allied to medical-related professions? Is this alliance likely to increase in the next 20 years?

## Suggestions for further reading

Clegg, J. (1998) *Critical issues in Clinical Practice*. London: Sage.
   An excellent example of the application of postmodern theory to the analysis of clinical psychology's theory and practice. The book provides a critical analysis of key issues and discusses ways in which practice might be changed.

Marzillier, J. and Hall, J. (eds) (1999) *What is Clinical Psychology?* Oxford: Oxford University Press.
   A good source of information on what clinical psychologists do. It covers the major settings and types of work and discusses some of the main issues which apply to each.

Patel, N., Bennett, E., Dennis, M., Dosanjh, N. Mahtani, A., Miller, A. and Nadirshaw, Z. (2000) *Clinical Psychology, 'Race' and Culture: A Training Manual*. Leicester: BPS Books.
   Won first prize in the British Medical Association's 'Book of the Year' mental health category. This is a training manual in that it provides many resources for incorporating material on 'race' and culture into teaching, but it is also an excellent source of information on debates in these areas and their implications for practice.

Johnstone, L. (2000) *Users and Abusers of Psychiatry*. London: Routledge.
   A critical analysis of psychiatric services (mainly those for adults) which also provides a clear account of how a social and psychological analysis of mental health problems differs from a psychiatric account, and what might be the implications for practice. It therefore offers an analysis of what could be the distinctive contribution of clinical psychology in this area.

# 2 Educational Psychology

*Paul Curran, Irvine S. Gersch and Sheila Wolfendale*

## SUMMARY

*The first section of the chapter examines what the role of educational psychologist involves and emphasizes the encompassing nature of the work, ranging from individual work with children to a systems and organizational approach, working with institutions such as schools. The chapter then goes on to look at trends, issues and a number of recent and current developments and provides a number of key examples drawn directly from practice. The final part of the chapter explores a number of training issues and anticipates significant changes to the training and employment patterns of educational psychologists for the future.*

## What Does the Role Involve?

Reviewing the contents pages of professional journals that educational psychologists (EPs) in the UK tend to read and publish articles in over the last 25 years, particularly the journal from the British Psychological Society's Division of Educational and Child Psychology, or the Association of Educational Psychologists *Educational Psychology in Practice* journal; or, indeed, the many books (for example, Sigston et al., 1996), and a picture of lively discussion and debate about what psychologists do/should do is very evident. The most recent and thorough outline is provided in the well researched DfEE document (2000a) which aims to provide a reasonably current overview of the present role, good practice and future directions of local authority educational psychology services (EPSs) in England from a government perspective. This is discussed more fully later in this chapter. There are several useful 'official' sources of further information on what EPs do in the UK (BPS, 1995) and the USA (APA, 1995), but perhaps the fullest current summary of the types of professional activities EPs are involved with is provided, with examples, in Box 2.1. However, not all EPs or all EPSs provide all these services, and the time allocated to these various activities will often depend on the local context and priorities EPs are involved with (DfEE, 2000a). There are several good pointers as to where the profession may be going in the future (Wright, 1998; Maliphant, 2000; Stoker 2002), but perhaps the single most useful source of information on what EPs do for a reader of this chapter is to contact his or her local EPS and meet one or more of the EPs. The majority of EPs would agree that one of the main rewards of the job is the sheer variety of professional activities it is possible to get involved with during any given week, let alone during their career.

---

**Box 2.1 Specialist services offered by chartered EPs working within EPSs, with examples**

✦ *Assessment and intervention with individuals*, for example, evaluation of child's educational and social strengths and needs in a classroom setting.

✦ *Consultancy*, for example, on school systems functioning, evaluation of provision.

✦ *Preschool work*, for example, undertaking developmental assessment for a preschool child at home and in a nursery/playgroup setting to provide recommendations on future additional provision and mainstream school placement.

✦ *Organizational work*, for example, advising on recruitment and staff selection in schools.

✦ *Research and evaluation*, for example, quantitative and qualitative research evaluation of local authority provision for children on the autistic spectrum.

✦ *Inservice training*, for example, training other adults bereavement counselling skills.

✦ *Adolescent counselling*, for example, on eating disorders, school refusal.

✦ *Adults*, for example, assessment in further education or HE of students with specific learning difficulties.

✦ *Education Act*, for example, providing psychological advice for a formal assessment of a child's special educational needs under the Education Act 1996.

✦ *Counselling*, for example, parents' concerns about their children's behaviour.

✦ *Special Educational Needs and Disability*, for example, assessment of an individual child's physical/neurological needs and support required in the school setting.

✦ *Dyslexia/specific learning difficulties*, for example, providing inservice training for teachers.

✦ *Family-focused work*, for example, family therapy, usually clinic based in a child and family consultation service.

✦ *Group work*, for example, social skills training, stress management, mediation skills training.

✦ *Individual therapy*, for example, for emotional difficulties or family problems (usually clinic based).

✦ *Management of behaviour problems*, for example, advising teachers on writing home–school behaviour contracts involving pupils and parents.

*Source*: Adapted from BPS (2001)

---

Most EPs, despite the lively ongoing debate within the profession, would probably agree to the following general statements as to what the job actually involves:

✦ EPs are applied psychologists working both within the school system and in the community. They are primarily concerned with children's learning, behaviour and social and emotional development.

✦ Most EPs in the UK work within local authority psychological services, and all parents and children and all state-maintained schools are entitled to their services. EPs work at different levels within the system, applying different knowledge and skills as appropriate (see examples in Box 2.1).

✦ There is also an increasing number of educational psychologists in private practice who take referrals from parents, schools, doctors and others (BPS, 1995).

✦ A substantial amount of EPs' professional practice is with individual clients and families (DfEE, 2000a), but EPs also offer consultancy and research to a variety of organizations and institutions, particularly schools, including staff (or inservice) training, systems analysis and evaluation.

✦ The work of EPs is often conceived as being at three levels:

  – The *individual* (for example, assessment and intervention with an individual child).

  – The *organization* (for example, in a school providing inservice training of teachers).

  – The *system* (for example, in a local education authority, developing special or additional educational provision).

✦ EPs use their knowledge of the principles and techniques of psychology in applying them mainly, but not exclusively, in educational contexts. The professional activities or services provided by EPs are outlined in Box 2.1.

## Trends and Career Development for EPs

There are a number of common assumptions held about the professional practice of EPs. While many of these are true, some are not. Of the inaccuracies, some are based on confusion over professions with similar titles such as psychiatrist or psychotherapist. Others are to do with the precise nature of the work. It has often been assumed that EPs assess pupils who have been referred by teachers because of concerns about mental health problems, failure to learn, unacceptable behaviour or sensory and physical disabilities. In the recent past, children who might have attention deficit (hyperactivity) disorder or dyslexia have been added to this list. The received wisdom is that by utilizing the results of IQ and other tests, EPs can determine whether these children should attend a special school or at least attract special educational resources. In fact, none of the above is untrue. However, the context in which EPs work, the ages and range of concerns expressed about young people and the approaches and techniques that EPs utilize, are much broader than is usually assumed.

While it is evident that most EPs within the UK are employed by local education authorities (LEAs) and hence spend much of their time working in schools, there have been significant extensions to the age range of EP clients. EPs now routinely become involved with children at the preschool stage, virtually from birth in some cases. Advances in medical prenatal and neonatal care have resulted in many more babies surviving problematic early-life situations. There may, however, be consequences in terms of their development and educational provision, which need to be addressed at an early stage. EPs are often part of child development teams along with doctors, speech and language therapists and physiotherapists, who assess and monitor their development and consequent needs and advise on provision. Issues can include developmental delay, language development, physical and sensory development and autistic spectrum disorders (Wolfendale and Robinson, 2001).

At the upper end of the age range, there have been significant developments in the higher education (HE) sector in the UK, which have resulted in a new generation of students entering colleges and universities. This has led to a student population which is more diverse in terms of prior educational experience, ethnic and cultural background, age and family responsibilities than previously. In addition, moves towards the inclusion of students with disabilities and special educational needs (SEN) within the mainstream school sector have led to greater numbers of these students having the possibility of entering HE. Colleges and universities are responding to the fact that greater proportions of students require educational provision, both in terms of physical resources and delivery of curricula, which is different. EPs are now working with students and staff in these settings to identify needs and to provide support. Issues can include responding to physical and sensory disabilities, dyslexia and the development of study skills (Wolfendale and Corbett, 1996).

EPs employed by LEAs spend much of their time conducting assessments as part of the authority's responsibility to identify those pupils with educational needs that are special and making recommendations regarding appropriate educational provision. The methods employed by EPs range much further than IQ and other tests. Later in this chapter we address the important issue of seeking the views of children and young people as part of the assessment. When assessing a child's needs, it is possible not only to take these views into account but also to involve the child or young person directly in decision-making and taking some responsibility for his or her own future. Psychological approaches such as those based on personal construct psychology can enable young people to articulate their view of themselves and the world around them in a way that an adult questioning and a child responding cannot. This is paramount if subsequent intervention is to be based on an individual's awareness of him or herself and his or her circumstances as the individual sees them (Ravenette, 1999). Many of the issues in schools that EPs are asked to become involved with, such as learning difficulties, may result in the EP using psychometrics or other standardized procedures, at least as part of the assessment. Other concerns, such as instances of bullying or unacceptable and challenging behaviour, do not lend themselves to such approaches. In these situations approaches involving the use of personal construct psychology (Hardman, 2001) can prove useful in adding a new dimension to the resulting course of action.

A trend within educational psychology over a number of years has been the increasing emphasis on the teaching process, as opposed to perceived inherent shortcomings in the pupils. One approach has been to make a clear identification of the child's current skills in a given curriculum area and then to plan a detailed individual education programme based on clearly identified targets. Such an approach has been called curriculum-based assessment. Alternatively, there has been an increasing recognition that teaching is a two-way process. The influence of cognitive psychology on the practice of educational psychology has become more evident. There has been an increasing awareness that learning is a collaborative exercise between children and the adults working with them. Many young people have not acquired the necessary skills to become effective learners (such as rehearsing, reviewing and organizing information, and other techniques, which have been termed 'learning to learn'). EPs have begun to use approaches to assessment based on the work of Feuerstein (Feuerstein at al., 1980) termed 'dynamic assessment' which identify areas of need. A number of teaching programmes have been based on Feuerstein's theory in explicitly teaching individuals how to learn (Greenberg, 2001). Freeman and Miller (2001) provide an interesting comparison of three approaches to assessment and their subsequent usefulness to teachers.

Within the school system and beyond, EPs are increasingly becoming routinely involved when sudden or unexpected events occur which cause distress, known as critical incidents. Such events may include bereavement, accident, major vandalism, disappearance of a pupil or even major disasters. It is now recognized that post-traumatic stress disorder (PTSD) can occur at any age, including childhood, and can affect not only those directly involved but also eye witnesses, survivors or friends. Schools often provide a natural forum for children to express their feelings and teachers may feel overwhelmed or unskilled to deal with these. EPs who work in the schools are often called upon to advise and support staff and others during the immediate aftermath of an event (Houghton, 1996).

EPs, working as they do within an environment that is changing and developing rapidly, have a high regard for professional development. Updating skills and becoming involved in research to an increasing degree are now the norm. There are many opportunities for EPs to undertake further training, and an increasing number are now undertaking professional doctorates (cf clinical psychologists) to provide a structure and coherence to the development of their skills. Such professional doctorate courses are now available in a dozen or more universities throughout the UK (Wolfendale, 2001). EPs are generally undertaking these courses on a part-time basis while continuing to work as EPs. In this way a clear link between practice and research continues to be established.

## Key Issues and Developments

It can be seen from the earlier part of this chapter that the EP role and professional responsibilities are many and varied, with child-focused casework integral to these duties. The *raison d'être* of EP activity is to apply psychology within educational, family and community contexts (Sigston et al., 1996), and for the EP to be 'an applied social scientist' (BPS/DECP, undated, *c.* 1999: 2). Thus professional practice should not only be informed by research findings but should, cumulatively, also contribute to the canon of evidence-informed practice (Macdonald and Williamson, 2002).

This view is consistent with moves within a number of professions, such as medicine and social work, increasingly to relate research to practice, to improve provision and service delivery and to increase cost-effectiveness and accountability (Sinclair, 1998). It has been argued that the EP is uniquely placed to fulfil the role of action researcher and, indeed, research activity by EPs has been built into a set of performance indicators proposed for Scottish EPs (Mackay, 1999).

As applied social scientists, EPs are well placed to:

✦ undertake research into and evaluation of educational intervention and explore 'what works'; and

✦ apply a range of research approaches and paradigms consistent with the OECD definition of educational research (OECD, 1995).

Research training and application of research skills are a key strand running through the EP 'work cycle', from the initial undergraduate degree, to postgraduate EP training, to EP practice. Contemporary EP practice increasingly reflects the need to base intervention on an articulated theory base and to utilize methodologies that are 'fit for purpose' (Robson, 2002).

The first part of this chapter provided an introduction to the EP role; in this second section four areas of contemporary EP practice are selected as illustrative exemplars. What these four otherwise quite disparate areas have in common is that they are each based on articulated rationales, show EP involvement at 'micro' level and collectively epitomize the range of educational and social interventions with which EPs are associated.

## Four Areas of Contemporary EP Practice

### Example 1: EPs involvement in early years

EPs' early introduction to child development as part of the psychology degree, plus their subsequent teacher training, provides a sound grounding for later work with young children, from early years to beginning school. All EPs cover the early years to some extent – that is, assess and work with young children, their parents, carers and early years practitioners – but an increasing number of EPs choose to specialize in this age range. A flow chart in Wolfendale and Robinson (2001: 8) shows the range and scope of EP work within early years, encompassing 'macro' involvement (such as involvement in planning and reviewing local early years services) and training staff, to 'micro' involvement with individual children, families and staff in early years settings. The assessment 'menu' with young children EPs can select from includes interviews; observation; developmental checklists; play-based assessment and assessment linked to the early years 'curriculum'; and the early learning goals (further information from QCA: www.qca.org.uk).

Intervention approaches to develop young children's language, social and cognitive functioning, for example, have become increasingly based on an hypothesis-testing 'what works' approach. The booklet edited by Wolfendale and Robinson (2001) contains a dozen practice examples which show a wide range of EP involvement at 'macro' and 'micro' levels, and provides a comprehensive bibliography of relevant early years publications.

## Example 2: EPs in collaboration with parents

EPs' direct work with parents has remained a core part of the EP role. It incorporates undertaking home visits as part of a child-focused casework; planning and delivering home-based programmes in, for example, behaviour management, literacy and development; and running parent workshops and parenting programmes (Wolfendale and Einzig, 1999). According to a recent survey, referred to earlier, parents appear to value EPs' involvement, respect their expertise and perspectives and are clear as to what services they want and need from EPs (DfEE, 2000a). But in fact, during the last 20 or so years, EPs have had to reappraise their working relationship with parents in tandem with moves elsewhere in education to treat parents as partners (Wolfendale and Bastiani, 2000).

The traditional model of EP–parent involvement was characterized predominantly as the EP as expert, possessor of requisite skills, with the parent as client-recipient of EP services rather than as equal participant with equivalent but different expertise and skills forming a joint problem-solving venture (with the EP) on behalf of the children concerned (Wolfendale, 1995). This latter view is becoming a more prevalent casework model.

Although EPs accumulate, over years of practice, impressive repertoires of skills and competencies with working with parents, nevertheless it was only very recently that some EPSs have begun to consider the adoption of an overarching policy in this area which would set out core values and principles, clear parameters and guidelines for ethical service delivery. Wolfendale (1997) locates EPs' work with parents within broader societal contexts, arguing for a closer, reciprocal relationship between practice and research in this area, incorporating parental perspectives as a key part of planning, designing and delivering services (Wolfendale, 1999; Moorman et al., 2001).

## Example 3: EPs eliciting children's views

One major initiative with which educational psychologists have become involved is the development of projects to increase the involvement of children themselves in assessments and in their education, and in developing techniques to listen to children's views. These ideas have been emphasized as important in the latest SEN *Code of Practice* (DfES, 2001). It has been argued that it is important to increase the voice of the child for three reasons: legal (supported by the Education Act 1996 and the 1989 United Nations Convention on the Rights of the Child), moral and pragmatic (Gersch, 1992; 1996). On the latter point it is argued that if one wishes to alter the behaviour of children one is more likely to be effective if the child is fully engaged, consenting and clear about the goals agreed.

EPs have pioneered and evaluated student reports – for recording the views of children about their special educational needs (Gersch and Holgate, 1991; Gersch, 1995; 2000; Gersch et al., 1996) – and for pupils excluded from school to identify their views about what led up to the exclusion, how they saw events unfolding and what they wanted to happen next (Nolan and Sigston, 1993), and for young children specifically (Wolfendale, 1998). Other projects have included involving children in plans made about their education and about the school as a whole (Jelly et al., 2000). Informal evaluations point to children valuing being involved in such ways and there appear to be benefits for teachers and schools as a whole. There remains scope for major developments of techniques and projects in this area and, EPs are likely to be at the heart of such research.

## Example 4: EPs and systemic approaches

Although much of EPs' work is at the level of the individual child and family, given that they wish to make the maximum positive difference for children, many have become involved in projects to change the whole school system or parts of the system to improve behaviour or learning or the environment for all children. Burden (1981) has argued that to be effective, EPs need to be effective systems analysers and systems engineers. Typically, educational psychologists become aware of patterns of difficulties or issues which require an approach that needs a change of the organization rather than a focus upon a single child. Following a careful assessment of what is happening, and what changes are needed, sensitive negotiation takes place with the headteacher and school staff to implement certain changes in the whole school or indeed the whole LEA. These are usually implemented in stages and evaluated after an agreed period, with further changes being made if required. EPs will draw from their skills of scientific research, experimentation, organizational design, decision-making and group processes.

Such projects have included the following:

+ Improving the behaviour of secondary school students (Gersch, 1986).
+ Improving the behaviour of pupils in a primary school (Gersch, 1990).
+ Dealing with traumatic incidents, such as the death of a nursery child and a child who was murdered (Cameron et al., 1995).
+ Helping a school develop new procedures for dealing with and identifying children with special educational needs (Gersch et al., 2001).
+ Working with the whole teaching staff and students to reduce truancy (Gersch and Noble, 1991) and to increase school effectiveness (Gersch, 1996).

# Recent Developments and Trends in the Profession

The professional practice of educational psychology has developed, adapted and grown in line with major changes in educational legislation and continues to be influenced significantly by developments in education generally. All LEAs have educational psychology services, which offer a service to schools and the local community. Most services will undertake assessment, inservice training and intervention with children, organizational projects and, to a lesser extent, research. Senior members of the service will often play a key role in the policy development of the LEA as a whole. In recent years, much of the EP's role has been focused in the area of SEN, though many would argue that this has perhaps been restrictive (see Box 2.1).

EPs have a statutory duty under the Education Act 1996 and as outlined in the SEN *Code of Practice* (DfES, 2001). This has meant that their assessment role in respect of children with SEN, and particularly those with statements of SEN, has involved a major expenditure of their time. Many services have offered a regular visiting service to schools which, for many EPs, has resulted in them having responsibility for a group of schools and visiting them on a regular and planned basis. In 1998 the government set up an advisory group to examine the future role and training of educational psychologists. Two historic documents were published in 2000, namely, *Educational Psychology Services (England): Current Role, Good Practice and Future Directions: Report of the Working Group* (DfEE, 2000a) and *The Research Report* (Kelly and Gray, 2000).

The advisory group commissioned the largest survey of educational psychology practice since the Summerfield Report (DfE, 1968). Every LEA was surveyed, the views of parents, schools, chief education officers, EPs and other professionals were surveyed and a high response rate achieved. The key findings were that:

✦ EPs were highly valued by all the various groups;

✦ most wanted more time and more services from them;

✦ there was evidence of a lack of consistent quality of services across LEAs and between LEAs;

✦ there was not always a clarity of role;

✦ there was evidence of highly valued work in different areas (e.g. counselling service in schools, post-traumatic work, circle of friends, work with individual children, early years work, work with the child and family consultation service, portage, training, work with families); and

✦ psychologists themselves wanted to spend less time on statutory assessment work and more time on preventative projects.

The report itself set out a series of recommendations and a clear articulation of the aim of EP services, namely:

> Against the background of increasing multi-agency working . . . the published aim or purpose defining the contribution of educational psychologists [is] . . . to promote child development and learning through the application of psychology by working with individual and groups of children, teachers and other adults in schools, families, other LEA officers, health and social services and other agencies (DfEE, 2000a: 5).

It concluded that EPs' core role should be with a focus on *assessment* and *intervention*, early years work, work with schools and collaborative work with other professionals. It also stated that EPs should consider other roles (such as conciliation, parent partnership, crisis and responses) in negotiation with local stakeholders and LEAs. It invited every EPS to negotiate with their LEAs about the report and their role. The report will have served to provide some clarity but is only one factor in the development of the profession and, indeed, its impact will depend on its use since it was not given mandatory status but rather offered as a guide for local discussion.

Since the report, which appears to have been welcomed, educational developments have continued apace and have had an impact upon services, particularly the drive for best value for all services. Best Value is a mechanism whereby all services have to compare themselves with others and question whether they might be more effectively or economically provided by others, privately. Another noticeable trend has been the move to consultation models of psychological service delivery. This involves psychologists engaging in collaborative problem-solving with school staff colleagues on a wide range of school and pupil issues. The emphasis is on assisting with clarification and prioritization of key concerns and then identifying ways forward (see the articles in Watkins 2000, for a full discussion of this issue).

Speculating about the future always carries the risk of the most visible of errors, but Gersch (2001a, 2001b) has argued that, for the future, it is likely that:

✦ there will be strong demand for a range of educational psychology services;

✦ there will be a demand in particular for help with individual children who face problems with their learning and behaviour, through assessment, advice and direct intervention;

✦ there will be a need to work with whole families;

✦ there will be a continued growth in specialist and creative work – for example, project or organizational work with schools, specialist areas such as autism, crisis work, early years work, children who have been excluded from school or who are in public care (looked after by the local authority);

✦ there may be fewer EPs and their focus may be directed on complex cases and specialist work rather than undertaking routine work which may be undertaken by others – for example, guided and supported by EPs; and

✦ EPs might be employed by a variety of employers, LEAs, charities and, increasingly, working as self-employed.

## Training issues for EPs

The first school psychologist, Cyril Burt, was appointed in 1913 by the London County Council. The appointment was initially considered to be an experiment and was a three-year, half-time post. Burt (1969), commenting on the outcome of that 'experiment', reports that 'few practical branches of a new science have expanded so rapidly'. At the time he was writing, there were more than 300 full-time EPs and at least 100 unfilled vacancies. By 1982 this had grown to 1200 employed psychologists and the current figures for England and Wales are in excess of 2000 psychologists working either full or part time.

The founding of the first educational psychology post was linked to changes in both society and schooling in the latter part of the nineteenth century. The Education Act 1870 widened access to education for all children and meant that schools were admitting pupils with a range of abilities and difficulties. The Elementary Education Act 1899 introduced the notion of children who experienced difficulty in learning being educated in separate classes or schools. The issue of identifying these children was at first the remit of the medical profession but it soon became apparent that assessment from a psychological or educational perspective was required. This form of assessment came to be based upon the work of Galton, Binet and Burt who had been developing the new technology of psychometrics. The 1944 Education Act, with its focus on selection for secondary schooling at age 11, further expanded the need for EPs. Their work was split between schools and the child guidance clinics which had been established in many areas. The balance altered in favour of work with schools with the growing awareness of the individual needs of pupils and the Education Act 1981 with its requirement for statements of special educational needs to include psychological assessment and advice. The report of the working group (DfEE, 2000a), however, emphasized the need for EPs to broaden their field of work again and become involved more in work with communities and other agencies at both a systemic and individual level.

## Common routes into training

The current professional training course requires that entrants have a degree in psychology (sufficient to be accepted by the British Psychological Society as a graduate member) and a teaching qualification with at least two years' teaching experience. There are two common routes for achieving the required experience (see also Box 2.2):

1 After completing an undergraduate degree in psychology it is possible to train as a teacher via the one-year postgraduate certificate in education (PGCE). There is currently a shortage of teachers and finding a job anywhere in the UK, or abroad, is easy. While gathering two years' teaching experience, prospective candidates often seek out experience (in school or through voluntary work) directly relevant to the job of an EP. This might involve specializing in inclusive education practice, special needs or pastoral care. Frequently, this will involve liaison with other professionals who work with children and is often a good opportunity to liaise with the local EPS in order to find out more about the job.

2 Trained, experienced teachers can convert their teaching qualification into a psychology degree by taking a diploma in psychology (conversion for graduates) course. These courses are run in many universities. Some courses can be completed part time and during the evenings. The number of modules that need to be completed will depend upon the psychology content of the first degree. Achievement of the diploma will grant eligibility for graduate basis for registration with the British Psychological Society and, depending upon the relevance of teaching experience, the possibility of applying for an educational psychology course.

> **Box 2.2  One route into training**
>
> Jamal trained as a teacher after completing his psychology degree. He taught in a secondary school and, after two years, was offered the choice of becoming an assistant head of year or assistant special needs co-ordinator. After working for one year in the pastoral role he gained experience working with EPs, psychiatric nurses and social services. Jamal then successfully applied to become an EP. While training he undertook placements in both urban and county environments.

The DfEE green paper entitled *Excellence for all Children* (1997a) states: 'Changes in the balance of work of EPs will have implications for their training. New patterns of training will be needed to reflect their developing roles in areas such as strategic management, working with schools, curriculum issues and family therapy.' The green paper recognized that EPs were often spending too much time assessing children's needs and writing reports for children with SEN. This paper and subsequent *Programme of Action* (DfEE, 1998) proposed a number of changes to SEN processes so that educational psychology time would be used more creatively by schools, the local education authority and the community. An investigation into the inevitable change in role and the subsequent impact on training was carried out by a DfEE working party.

The DfEE issued a consultation paper about training in December 2000. The paper proposed extending the training to three years and dropping the requirement for a teaching qualification and prior teaching experience. The main argument for maintaining teaching experience has been that this would give EPs more credibility with teachers. Frederickson et al. (2001) explored this. They found that fewer than 30% of teachers were aware that EPs had been teachers. They also explored teacher perceptions of the credibility of EPs and whether this was related to awareness that EPs had previously been teachers. Overall the results indicated that teaching experience cannot be regarded as necessary to an EP's credibility with teachers. In 2001 the DfES circulated results of the consultation which showed considerable agreement with the proposed changes to a three-year course.

At the time of writing a working party set up by the DfES in conjunction with the British Psychological Society, the Association of Educational Psychologists, HE representatives and the employers organization is looking specifically at the future of training. It is working towards implementing new arrangements, perhaps a three year programme, in 2005.

## Views of EPs in Training

In a recent survey of EPs in training on a current training course, 45% indicated that they would have pursued training if a three-year course leading to a doctorate had been required, 45% would have considered a two-year but not a three-year course and 10% were unsure whether they would have applied for anything longer than a 12-month course. Some of the advantages of extended training identified by this group included the following:

✦ Changing the age profile of the profession since extended training is more attractive to younger people.

✦ Providing enhanced possibilities of EPs using different styles and approaches.

✦ Developing a more informed and skilled graduate with qualifications on a par with similar professions.

✦ Ensuring a more in-depth knowledge base and a more thorough grounding in research skills.

✦ Giving EPs in training greater opportunities to explore different approaches and to evaluate their effectiveness.

✦ Building the confidence of new entrants to the profession and advancing the knowledge of psychology.

Current EPs in training had few reservations about the notion of extending training although they were concerned that the limited funding available at present could not facilitate a three-year programme. They feared that the profile of the profession might become even less representative of the population than is currently the case. A number in the group expressed concerns that the change in expectation regarding teacher training would render the profession completely 'theoretical' and reduce their effectiveness in schools.

## Quality Assurance

All educational psychology training courses are accredited by the British Psychological Society at least once every 5 years. The accreditation is carried out by a team selected by the Division of Educational and Child Psychology Training Committee. The teams of four are made up of two 'field' EPs (generally those who work in LEAs) and two tutors on other courses. The report and recommendations are agreed by the training committee before being passed to the Membership and Qualifications Board for ratification on behalf of the British Psychological Society.

The aim of regular accreditation is to facilitate a high standard of education in the discipline of psychology and to ensure that those qualifying to practise as EPs are trained in ways that meet the criteria devised by the British Psychological Society training committee. These criteria are drawn up in compliance with the definition of quality produced by the British Standards Institution which defines quality as 'the totality of features or characteristics of a product or service that bear on its ability to satisfy a given need' (BS4778). The report produced by the accreditation team is public and may include a variety of recommendations. As well as making recommendations for improvements, the accreditation team can commend any aspect of the course they consider to be 'innovatory, exemplary or worthy of dissemination' (BPS/DECP, undated, c. 1999). Thus the accredition process has three main functions:

1 A registration or gatekeeping task.

2 The promotion of good practice.

3 The provision of assistance to programmes in obtaining resources necessary to maintain standards in training.

## Training Courses in the Future

Three-year training, may, if universities agree, lead to doctorate status for the profession. As indicated earlier, post-professional training part-time doctorate programmes for practising EPs are now established and popular with both EPs and their employers (Wolfendale, 2001), particularly where EPs are contributing to evidence-based practice and developments as research practitioners. Extending the initial training programme to three years has a number of implications which are likely to enhance the profile of educational psychology in general and further one of the objects of the British Psychological Society – that is, 'to promote the advancement and diffusion of a knowledge of psychology pure and applied' (The Royal Charter: 3ii). These benefits are likely to be reflected in the following:

✦ Closer links between training courses and employers, which may in turn lead to good employment opportunities.

✦ Within the universities, shared modules with clinical and occupational psychology courses leading to a wider knowledge base and more in-depth therapeutic skills.

✦ Bringing greater coherence to central government initiatives aimed at raising achievement and promoting social inclusion through a focus on research and evaluation.

✦ Extending work boundaries by providing opportunities and experiences that would allow graduates to work in other countries.

✦ Further distance-learning opportunities through multimedia and information communication technologies.

To conclude, the profession of educational psychology continues to change and develop in a dynamic and creative way. At the time of writing the profession is engaged in a period of further major transition, which many within the profession regard as both positive and suggestive of a bright future.

---

## QUESTIONS FOR REFLECTION AND DISCUSSION

1  In the future with reference to likely global, economic, technological and social trends, what will people want from applied child/educational psychologists?

2  Teachers in a school become concerned that a pupil appears unhappy and is making slow academic progress. The parents are worried that the child is increasingly reluctant to come to school. Teachers can find no obvious cause.

They claim to have tried everything and suggest a change of school. A referral is made to the school's educational psychologist. Whom should the educational psychologist regard as their client: the pupil, the teachers, the parents or the local education authority?

3 To what extent are educational psychologists agents of change in the lives of children?

4 What do you think are the key qualities needed for an educational psychologist to be effective in his or her work now? What particular skills, knowledge, understanding and personal qualities do you think will be needed in the future?

## Suggestions for further reading

BPS (undated; *c.* 1999) *The Professional Practice of Educational Psychologists.* Leicester: BPA. This A4 sized booklet describes core duties, responsibilities and activities of educational psychologists, encompassing assessment of and intervention with children, school-based work (including inservice training of teachers and other practitioners), and a comprehensive number of practice examples. It is a useful introduction to and description of professional EP practice.

DfES (2000) *Educational Psychology Services (England): Current Role. Good Practice and Future Directions: Report of the Working Group.* Nottingham: DfEE Publications. A good summary of the role and practice of educational psychology services.

Kelly, D. and Gray, C. (2000) *Educational Psychology Services (England): Current Role. Good Practice and Future Research: The Research Report.* Nottingham: DfEE Publications. The research report represents the largest survey of educational psychology practice in England that has ever been carried out and the views of nearly every local authority in England.

Sigston, A., Curran, P., Labram, A. and Wolfendale, S. (eds) (1996) *Psychology in Practice with Young People, Families and Schools.* London: David Fulton. The 16 chapters in this readable book give a very good flavour of the many areas in which educational psychologists continue to make a major contribution to professional practice.

# 3 Occupational and Organizational Psychology

*Christine Doyle*

## SUMMARY

*In this chapter I explain the nature of the discipline and profession of occupational psychology and the qualifications, training and experience needed to become a chartered occupational psychologist. I then go on to consider some issues relating to training and practice in this area. One question concerns the content of MSc courses – is the syllabus sufficiently business orientated and is it too overloaded? A case study of what would be needed when introducing new technology within an organization shows that knowledge and expertise of all areas of the discipline are needed. However, there is still fierce debate about whether graduates from MSc courses in occupational psychology are sufficiently prepared for work in the commercial world. A case study of one person's pursuit of chartership illustrates that this can be something of a 'stony road'. The second half of the chapter discusses the tensions of pursuing evidence-based practice in an environment where there are many conflicting pressures – commercial imperatives and the need for swift solutions among them. There is a need for 'pragmatic science' which addresses 'real world' issues but is also methodologically rigorous. However, academics may be led into research which is very rigorous but has no professional relevance, while practitioners may engage in 'untheorized and invalid practice'. Neither trend enhances or advances the discipline or the profession. I suggest that one solution may be for practitioners to undertake a professional doctorate as part of their continuing professional development.*

## Introduction

Occupational and organizational psychology attempts to understand and explain the behaviour and experience of people at work by applying theory and research methods from psychology. However, it is somewhat different from other branches of professional psychology such as clinical and educational psychology. For a start, even the name of the discipline and profession cannot be agreed on. In the UK it is called occupational psychology, in the USA it is called industrial/organizational psychology and in Europe it is work and organizational psychology. There was recent debate within the British Psychological Society's (BPS) Division of Occupational Psychology as to whether the name should be changed to come into line with the rest of Europe but little consensus was reached.

To complicate matters further, other disciplines also concern themselves with people at work (e.g. management science, human resource management, personnel management and a hybrid discipline known as organizational behaviour) which, according to Cherrington (1989), developed from psychology, sociology and anthropology with minor influences from economics, political science and history. The similarities, differences and definitions of all these disciplines have been explored in detail elsewhere (see, for example, Furnham, 1997; Brotherton, 1999). Suffice it to say that theory and research in occupational and organizational psychology contribute to all these related disciplines though not always at a very sophisticated level. For instance, Porteus (1997: 17) describes the role of a personnel manager as being largely concerned with administrative duties such as benefits, pensions, holiday rosters and so on. He continues: 'Many companies are totally unaware of the value of good occupational psychologists. Being qualified in occupational psychology is not the same as being qualified in personnel.' Others have argued the opposite – that human resource professionals frequently are more knowledgeable and skilled in their specialist areas than occupational psychologists are (Shaw, 1992; Ridgeway, 2000).

Some practitioners prefer to call themselves 'business psychologists' and they tend to argue that 'occupational psychology' is too inclined to inhabit academic 'ivory towers' with little concern for business imperatives (St Ather, 1999). This view was summed up for me by a delegate at a recent conference, who said: 'If I tell my clients that I *must* evaluate my interventions in their organizations, they'll just get out *Yellow Pages* and look up the nearest management consultant.'

From all this you might surmise that the discipline and profession of occupational and organizational psychology are currently in a considerable state of flux and you would be right. You might also conclude that the training of occupational psychologists should also be in a state of flux but there you would be only partially right. The BPS keeps firm control of training through its accreditation of MSc courses and has recently tightened up the rules for becoming a chartered occupational psychologist. It is worth looking at these rules briefly because, in the process, it explains much of what occupational psychologists actually do. There are currently three levels of training and practitioner experience which the would-be chartered occupational psychologist has to work through and provide evidence of. A first degree and suitable MSc are only the start and the process can be daunting – see the case study in Box 3.2.

## Level-1 training

All those who aspire to be chartered occupational psychologists should have the Graduate Basis for Registration (GBR) as a result of succeeding on a BPS-approved first degree in psychology. In addition they should have knowledge of the theory and research concerning eight areas of the discipline. This knowledge is acquired by taking an approved MSc in occupational psychology. The eight areas are summarized in Box 3.1.

**Box 3.1 Summary of the eight curriculum areas in occupational psychology**

1 *Human–machine interaction*
   The basic aim in this area is to design machines (for example, computers) or complex human–machine systems (such as power plants or passenger jets) so that human physical and psychological needs are met to promote maximum efficiency, productivity, safety and well-being. Specialists in this area increasingly deal with human–computer interaction since more and more processes are controlled by computer systems. They are also concerned with preventing accidents and disasters in hazardous industries so issues connected with risk perception and the promotion of a safety culture have come to the fore (see, for example, Reason, 1997: Cooper, 1998).

2 *Design of environments and of work*
   The basic concern of this area is to investigate how to design jobs and work spaces to maximize comfort, well-being, safety and efficiency with particular reference to the physical and psychological needs of people. Implicit in this is the notion of stress or rather how to create jobs and workplaces that do not create too much stress in workers. Sometimes one wonders how much influence specialists in this area have on organizations. For instance, we have known for 50 years and more that severely fatigued people are prone to errors and accidents. Despite this there has been a huge increase in night-shift work for reasons as trivial as allowing us to check our bank balances in the middle of the night, and many UK workers are pressured to ignore the EU directive on a maximum working week of 48 hours. Rice (2000) quotes UK managers as saying that 'sleep is the new luxury'. New ways of working (for example, telework and virtual teams) are current growth points in this area and are sometimes hailed as solutions to rising stress problems at work.

3 *Personnel selection and assessment*
   The aim of this area is to choose the best person for the job by means which are as reliable, valid and fair as possible, in order to maximize worker well-being and productivity. For instance, someone who has the skills, knowledge and ability to do a complex job is less likely to suffer undue pressure than someone lacking these attributes. Assessment might also concern analysing people's training needs or their potential for promotion. Computerized assessment and testing over the Internet are currently the focus of developments and of controversy in this area (see, for example, Bartram, 1997; 1999; 2000).

4 *Appraisal and career development*
   Performance appraisal involves measuring people's job performance so that they can be fairly rewarded or promoted. It also concerns helping people to develop their skills and improve their performance by, for instance, devising personal development and career management plans. With the demise of the notion of 'a job for life', specialists in this area are often engaged in

assessing strengths and weaknesses and offering careers guidance to people of all ages. Multi-rater feedback, whereby someone is rated by his or her boss, colleagues and staff to give a more accurate and rounded picture of work performance, is a growth point in this area.

5  *Counselling and individual development*

Counselling skills are needed in very many aspects of occupational psychology from the consulting process itself to specific tasks such as developmental forms of appraisal. There has also been a growth in employee assistance programmes (EAPs) which are designed to help workers deal with personal or work-related problems. In today's workplaces, helping people to cope with the impact of organizational change may be crucial in preventing stress-related ill-health. For these reasons all occupational psychologists need counselling skills and some become fully qualified counsellors. The role of executive coach and the process of coaching is a topic of current interest with some arguing that coaches should be qualified counsellors since theirs is essentially a counselling role.

6  *Training*

The aims of this area are to identify training and development needs, design and deliver training programmes and evaluate their effectiveness to increase people's work performance and well-being. Many organizations aspire to be 'learning organizations' where there is a climate of constant learning to promote improved performance and innovation. Such learning may be provided by on-the-job experience and computerized packages as well as by traditional classroom-based training courses. Specialists in this area are skilled in the design of training courses as well as their delivery. Given that much contemporary work is 'knowledge work', the subject of 'knowledge management' is a current focus of interest.

7  *Employee relations and motivation*

This area is most closely allied to 'people management' and aims to harness our knowledge of social processes at work to increase worker motivation, well-being and effectiveness. It also includes industrial relations and conflicts between groups such as managers and shopfloor workers. In recent years many people have experienced something of a revolution in the nature of their work. Jobs which were thought to be secure have been swept away (for example, traditional print workers), are no longer so numerous or no longer exist in the same form (for example, branch bank managers). Other workers have been forced to become self-employed and/or short-term contract workers. All this upheaval has caused distress to many and has reduced people's commitment to their organizations. Understanding how to motivate people and promote job satisfaction in this changed climate is a focus of interest. Many feel that developing leadership skills in managers holds the key (see for example, Alimo-Metcalfe and Alban-Metcalfe, 2000; Alban-Metcalfe and Alimo-Metcalfe, 2000).

▶

8 *Organizational development and change*
The aims of this area are to assist organizations and the individuals within them to adapt to change to cope with an increasingly turbulent business environment and so survive and flourish. For many organizations change is now 'the only constant' (Baruch and Hind, 1999: 297). Organizations have become more complex and effectively 'boundary-less', with partnerships, consortia, mergers and acquisitions and a focus on 'stakeholders' such as suppliers and customers. There is also more interest in international management and promoting organizational culture across national boundaries as well as a felt need to 'celebrate diversity'.

## Level-2 training

At this level people develop practical skills in five of the eight areas under the supervision of a chartered occupational psychologist. Some MSc courses (such as the one at the University of East London) – provide skills training in some areas – for example, interviewing, psychological assessment, designing and delivering a training programme, etc. Many of the requirements for Level 2 are met through supervised practice in the workplace but some may be obtained by attending training events such as those organized by the BPS's Division of Occupational Psychology Affiliates' Support Group.

## Level-3 training

To satisfy Level-3 requirements people have to demonstrate their competence to practise independently with members of the public but again under the supervision of a qualified practitioner. This will usually take the form of a work-based project in one area of occupational psychology, and the person is expected to take responsibility for the design and implementation of the project from inception to evaluation. For instance, a training intervention might begin with an analysis of the training needs of the workforce and proceed with an analysis of the knowledge and skills required, the design of the programme and its delivery, and, finally, a research project to discover whether the training was effective.

The three levels of training take a minimum of 3 years to complete and, during that time, people have to keep a log-book detailing their experience and reflecting on the lessons learnt. Obviously it helps if the person is employed in an occupation which allows the development of suitable skills. Becoming chartered can be a hard road (see Box 3.2) but those who are determined will always find a way and there are many benefits for enhanced employability and opportunities for varied and interesting work. However, many people are content to remain in their current jobs, say, as human resource managers or trainers and do not pursue chartership as occupational psychologists. They find that their careers have been

**Box 3.2  A case study of the process of becoming a chartered occupational psychologist**

I graduated in 1996 with a BPS-recognized degree in psychology, but without significant work experience or a job to go to. Suffering from study fatigue and hence with no desire (or funding) to go for a higher degree, I 'temped' for 6 months. Eventually, after many rejections from organizations offering assistant psychologist positions, major graduate recruiters and local employers alike, through the village grapevine I found an appallingly badly paid, short-term contract with a civil service department to do some applied research in hearing loss, for a specialist medical centre. I was hired purely because I could 'do' statistics, not for my knowledge of psychological principles!

This contract went well, the report being published in a peer-reviewed journal. A further contract in another part of the department was offered and accepted, this one being specifically for a graduate psychologist. In the 12 months spent there, I actually began to understand what occupational psychologists do, and had the opportunity to work alongside both occupational psychologists and ergonomists for the first time, doing a wide range of slightly off-the-wall work in human factors and the design of environments and work.

The end of this contract luckily coincided with an opportunity to interview for a position as an applied psychologist, in yet another part of the department, and thankfully I got a permanent contract in autumn 1998, two whole years after graduating. This was a chance to do a lot more human factors work and to stray to the edges of occupational psychology, into environmental issues and, rather unexpectedly, organizational development issues via quality management.

During this time I studied for my MSc, part time, from 1999 to 2001. Juggling a full-time job and MSc studies was challenging to say the least, but had two major advantages over a study-only route: my employer paid my fees as well as my salary, and I got to practise the skills I was learning in my everyday work. In 2001 I decided to diversify a little, taking an occupational psychology higher education lecturing post. And now, one academic year later, I find myself about to launch back into quality management, this time without the phrase 'occupational psychologist' appearing anywhere in my job description. So, 6 years after graduating, and despite having been supervised by a chartered occupational psychologist for 5½ years, I'm still not chartered. So, what's been going on?

My first 'top tip' is to keep that log-book up to date – I'm now writing mine retrospectively, which is a nightmare and is not recommended! I've been lucky enough to have the same supervisor since 1997, with whom I've been able to discuss any aspect of my work confidentially (very important!) and she is patiently waiting for the day I finally give her a complete draft of my log-book for her comment.

The level of support available from other affiliate members of the Division of Occupational Psychology is not to be dismissed. Having access to a network of other people in the same position can be a complete god-send, for information,

▶

advice, training, job offers or interesting bits of news, aside from good old-fashioned support during what can be a trying and bewildering process.

I never intended to become an occupational psychologist – that just happened along the way. Neither do I intend to pursue a career exclusively in occupational psychology consultancy. I wish to be chartered only because I think I've got just about enough practice days to get there (if I ever work out the BPS rules on evidence of practice, and if the log book ever gets written). Much more importantly, I'd like to be able to choose interesting jobs during my career, some of which may again be in mainstream occupational psychology. The attraction of the discipline for me is the range of work you're qualified to do – from ergonomics through human resources issues to organizational development – although, it must be said, most employers will not recognize this breadth of expertise unless your CV is crystal clear on that point!

sufficiently enhanced by undertaking the MSc since they can apply their new knowledge and skills to their specialisms at Level 3. This means that their specialist practice is still advanced but they skip Level 2 and can't become chartered occupational psychologists.

## Continuing Professional Development

All chartered occupational psychologists have to abide by a code of professional ethics, and part of that code requires them to engage in continuous professional development by keeping abreast of developments in their fields of expertise and by reflecting on their practice. One way of doing this is to embark on a professional doctorate in occupational psychology, of which more will be said later.

## Some Issues in Training and Practice

The huge Level-1 training syllabus represents only the basics. Many MSc courses also include a research methods and statistics unit and a requirement to conduct a research project in one of the eight areas, frequently by tackling a 'real world' problem within an organization. Furthermore, successful completion of such a course does not confer chartership: for that one needs two or more years of supervised practice in the field. Within occupational psychology itself, there is a recognition that the required knowledge base is becoming unmanageable and that gaining the necessary experience for chartered status is very difficult.

Human-machine interaction and the design of environments and of work together form the hybrid discipline of ergonomics and some argue that they should be split off from occupational psychology. It is true that few ergonomists also practise in the other six areas of occupational psychology or vice versa so such a split would seem to make sense. However, there are also sound reasons to keep ergonomics as a subdiscipline (albeit a large one) of occupational psychology. Consider, for instance, an organization which wishes to introduce new technology and consults an occupational psychologist for advice on how to manage this successfully. The ideal consultancy project would involve the following:

✦ An evaluation of how existing employees deal with the new technology (human–machine interaction).

✦ An evaluation of the impact the new technology has on their jobs and well-being (design of environments and of work).

✦ A training needs analysis and design of a training programme for existing and new employees (training and development).

✦ The design of an appraisal system to evaluate the employee's work performance to ensure fair reward systems (perhaps including the design of the new job which results from the introduction of the new technology to promote job satisfaction, work motivation and organizational commitment) (appraisal and career development; employee relations and motivation).

✦ The design and implementation of a selection procedure to recruit new workers (selection and assessment).

✦ A programme to manage the organizational change involved and to provide employee assistance (for example, much new technology involves the simultaneous introduction of autonomous work groups and it may demand significant changes to highly valued aspects of the person's current job which may provoke grief-like reactions) (organizational development and change; counselling and individual development).

The fact that all this rarely, if ever, happens when new technology is introduced may explain why organizations often experience serious problems and the expensive new hardware fails to deliver the expected gains in efficiency and effectiveness. (Witness the chaos a few years back in the UK Passport Office when a new computer system was brought in. But it is unfair to single out any one such failure. Other examples abound in the public and private sectors – most don't get widely reported!) However, the point of this example is that a knowledge of *all* eight areas of occupational psychology is necessary to avoid fiascos when new technology is introduced. Similar examples could be given of interventions in any of the eight areas. I believe that the best compromise would be for MScs in occupational psychology to incorporate separate 'specialization tracks' for ergonomics or individual/organizational psychology so that everyone gains an overview of all eight areas but concentrates knowledge in only one 'branch' of the profession. Thus an 'ergonomist' could advise an organization of the dangers of introducing new technology without heed to the wider system while concentrating on the usability of the hardware. An individual/organizational psychologist could design and help to implement the wider systems, such as designing selection procedures or training programmes, and advise on organizational change issues. Together with the engineers, human resource specialists and finance directors, both would contribute to a marvellous management team! MSc courses already tend to have strengths in one or the other area – ergonomics or individual/organizational psychology. The pity is that this means that people have to decide on their specialism as well as their course – it would be nice to choose the course first and then decide the specialism. Unfortunately, this implies more resources in personnel and equipment than many university departments can manage. However, the greater pity is that too many organizations seize on the hardware without thought for anything else or how a chartered occupational psychologist could help them to be more effective.

But this is not all. I have heard it said that new MSc occupational psychology graduates are generally 'unemployable' because of their lack of business accumen and experience. Most advertisements for jobs in occupational psychology consultancies confirm this sort of view in that they almost always ask for two or more years' work experience in a commercial organization. This encourages a 'chicken and egg' situation whereby people cannot get a job without experience and cannot get experience without a job. (This is a particular problem at training Levels 2 and 3.) At UEL we try to overcome this by various means – for example, we encourage people to gain work experience in a commercial setting before embarking on the course. Moreover, the course is part time so that most students have paid employment and can apply the theory they learn within their daily work. We also have plans to provide optional units like financial and project management and marketing in an attempt to instil 'business accumen'.

However, I think there are deeper issues here than merely the content of courses. One concerns the fact that, unlike in clinical and educational psychology, there is no one large-scale employer such as the NHS or local education authorities. Occupational psychologists can be found in a huge range of organizations such as psychometric test publishers, government agencies (for example, the Department of Employment and Pensions), private and public sector human resource and training departments, academic institutions, employee asistance programmes ('in-house' or external firms), as well as firms of occupational psychologists. Many become independent practitioners ('sole traders' in, for example, psychological assessment and career advice) or found their own general consultancies. How does any one course adequately prepare students for all these different contexts and specializations? The answer is, of course, that no one course can, which is why the BPS Division of Occupational Psychology is probably very wise in insisting, for chartership, on a period of supervised professional practice after completion of the MSc. One may also have to concede that the profession of occupational psychology calls for not one but several training courses. For instance, in many contexts an occupational psychologist would benefit from being also qualified in counselling or health psychology or in careers guidance. Those who choose the ergonomics branch would benefit from some background in engineering or computer programming. Those who teach occupational psychology in universities now need an additional qualification for teaching at this level. All need the additional BPS Level A and B (Intermediate) Certificates of Competence in Occupational Testing in order to administer and use psychometric instruments such as ability tests and personality inventories.

Do such considerations prove daunting for those who would embark on a career in occupational psychology? Undoubtedly! And this is a threat to the profession, especially if it is easier to enter related professions such as human resource management. The answer is for the profession to 'market' itself – to pursuade organizations of the benefits of employing a well qualified occupational psychologist. Thus there would be more employment and training opportunities for those beginning their careers. However, here we meet another obstacle – the 'quick fix' syndrome.

## Quick Fixes and Other Ethical Issues

At the 1998 BPS Occupational Psychology Conference, Briner called for our profession to ground its practice in systematic evidence and evaluation if we are to avoid the trap of the 'quick fix'. 'Quick fixes' involve the rapid implementation of policies or interventions with the aim of resolving a presenting problem. They are often driven by the need to be 'seen to be doing something' rather than careful analysis of the underlying causes, and can be strongly influenced by fads and fashions. They can be championed by an 'issue seller' who has much to gain but little to lose from the adoption of his or her recommendations and there is a focus on style of presentation rather than substance. The efficacy of 'quick fixes' is rarely evaluated. When they don't work, they may be followed by another 'quick fix' and so the process continues with failures rapidly subject to organizational amnesia.

'Quick fixes' have advantages which make their use a rational strategy for top management. They can be politically expedient and 'do-able' in a difficult situation; their speed commends itself to pressing problems; and the implementers can 'move on' before the full effects become apparent. For these reasons, commercially aware occupational psychologists may not be above using 'quick fixes'. Many related professionals certainly do.

However, 'quick fixes' are ethically dubious and often ineffective and wasteful of resources. They are also damaging to the profession of occupational psychology. No or limited feedback on effectiveness gives us little understanding of why interventions do or do not work or what steps must be taken to maximize the chances of success. 'Quick fixes' do not lead to better techniques and strategies so practice does not advance. Moreover, sometimes evaluation is itself a valuable part of the change process. One of my doctoral students evaluated an intervention designed to reduce waiting lists in the NHS and concluded that far from being a detached and impartial process, his research to evaluate its effectiveness had actually enhanced the impact of the intervention by giving workers 'a voice' and thereby increasing ownership of organizational change.

A denial of the value or practicality of evidence-based practice would not be tolerated in other professions such as medicine or engineering. Indeed, it is not tolerated in other branches of professional psychology. Why should occupational psychology be different? What else have occupational psychologists to offer which many related professionals do not, if it is not this careful approach to the accumulation of good evidence and evaluation of the success of our interventions? An evidence-based approach has also been shown to be very effective in ensuring continuing professional development.

However, there are very real obstacles for practitioners who want to use an evidence-based approach. Commercial pressures and realities mean that there may be limited opportunity to evaluate interventions, much less adhere to the traditional positivistic scientific paradigm. The rapidly changing nature of the work-place means that tried and tested techniques such as job analysis are being rejected as too cumbersome to meet business needs. Occupational psychology needs new methods which retain some rigour but also meet business imperatives. There is no room for academic purity in applied research but we do need to know what we would do in an ideal world so that we are alive to the limitations of what we do in this one and can draw cautious conclusions. That said, failure to evaluate can often stem more from lack of political will than from the extra time and costs associated with it. For instance, in implementing a training pro-gramme, the initial stages of a training needs analysis, task analysis and design of the programme can be far more expensive and time consuming than evaluation. One is tempted to conclude that the real reason is that managers do not wish to be told about costly failures.

We need to persuade and educate our clients to adopt good practice and an appeal to evidence can help. However, compared with other branches of psychol-ogy, there is a relative paucity of good evidence in occupational psychology. For instance, in a thorough literature review of the introduction of autonomous work groups, Day (2001) could find only *six* studies that enabled any causal inferences about their impact on outcome measures such as productivity and absenteeism. Yet autonomous work groups are often claimed as 'cure-alls' for organizational ills. Part of the problem may be that busy practitioners cannot find the time to publish their research or that some practitioners need to extend or develop their research skills. However, a more sinister reason may be that organizations (which do not want anything which might reflect badly on them in the public domain) suppress negative evidence. Understandable though this might be, if true, it has grave implications for the discipline and the profession. It would mean that the evidence on which we base our practice may be biased towards evaluations of interventions which produce favourable outcomes. (This is not necessarily a problem confined to occupational psychology. There is a bias towards publishing only 'significant' results in every area of the discipline.)

Judging by the debates which have been held at successive BPS occupational psychology conferences, there appears to be a split between the researcher and practitioner arms of the profession. Anderson et al. (2001) published a thought-provoking article in which they lament the fact that there has been a drift away from what they call 'pragmatic science' which addresses 'real world' issues but is also methodologically rigorous. This has happened because of the sorts of pressures already discussed but also because the scramble for funding has led academic researchers into ever more 'pedantic science' which may be very rigorous but has little professional relevance. The authors suggest that these trends have led to 'irrel-evant theory and . . . untheorised and invalid practice' or 'puerile science' and that the only way to halt this decline is to 'engage in political activity' to try to influ-ence major stakeholders such as governments and private sector companies (p. 407). There may also be another means of improving matters. At UEL we are concerned with the work of chartered practitioners which is being recognized in a doctoral degree and which aims to advance the profession as a whole. Thus some of the rifts between researchers and practitioners may be healed (see also Box 3.3).

> **Box 3.3  How might the professional doctorate help with continuing professional development and evidence-based practice?**
>
> 1  Once practitioners are reasonably established, there may come a point when they ask 'where next?' Taking time out to do a PhD is not usually feasible. The professional doctorate at UEL uses a 'work-based challenge framework' and is a research degree which involves the practitioner's ongoing work. Line managers or professional colleagues are encouraged to become honorary supervisors and mentors and to get involved in the programme. All this encourages a focus on real business issues.
> 2  There is a requirement to undertake two research projects, one mainly quantitative and the other one mainly a qualitative study which may broaden practitioners' research expertise and encourage development as a researcher practitioner. It may also foster the development of new research strategies and innovative practice.
> 3  Writing up the research fosters an evidence-based approach while the requirement for two publication-ready articles encourages publication of practitioner research in mainstream journals.
> 4  The doctorate can be completed within a minimum of two years and takes place within a mutually supportive climate. The model is one of a collaboration of equals in this endeavour. This, and monthly support seminars, helps to counteract the 'loneliness of the long-distance scholar'.
> 5  The main aim of the programme is to advance practice and the profession as a whole. Perhaps one way it can do this is by a doctorate raising the status of practitioners and making them distinctive from rival professionals. This collaboration between the researcher and practitioner arms of the profession may also help to heal rifts.

As part of our professional doctorate programmes at UEL we stage annual joint study days where students on all the postgraduate training programmes are invited to share their research and discuss issues of mutual concern. For example, Gale addressed us in 2000 with some thought-provoking ideas about the current boundaries between the various branches of professional psychology and questioned whether such divisions would be considered ideal if we were to start again. He posed questions concerning the need for occupational psychologists to be au fait with issues more in the province of clinical psychology, such as the need for employees to 'work through' the anxiety – grief even – of losing one's job or losing valued aspects of it in organizational change (Vansina (1998) also laments the split between occupational and clinical psychology). Gale also argued convincingly that an understanding of occupational psychology was of inestimable benefit for those psychologists working in educational or clinical settings. After all, most of us work in organizations, and this includes schools and hospitals. The treatment of a child's learning difficulties, for instance, is set within a context of people, resources, policies, practices, communication networks, relationships, hierarchies, roles, organizational climate and culture and so on, which all exert an influence on outcomes. Many of those present who were training in educational psychology expressed the wish for occupational training too – or for occupational psychologists within their teams. Indeed, given the huge amount of organizational change in UK schools in recent decades many educational psychologists are taking MSc courses in occupational psychology. Likewise, occupational psychology consultancies are employing clinical and counselling psychologists. If no one person can encompass all the knowledge and skills required, at least there is a growing awareness that there should be a team that does.

At the 2001 joint seminar Hayes reflected on 'the researcher in the organization'. She pointed out that undergraduates in psychology are inducted into a traditional research paradigm based on an idealized version of research in the natural sciences. Even though most undergraduate courses in psychology (including UEL's) now also teach qualitative methods which do not involve the reduction of all the evidence to numbers and statistical analysis, she argued that this induction still tended to instil the feeling that anything 'less' than the full 'scientific method' must be inferior. Yet, as she pointed out, many aspects of the 'full scientific method' are totally unsuitable for research in organizations – or indeed for any research with human beings. For instance, the traditional scientific method assumes that the researcher is an impartial and objective observer who does not influence outcomes. When an organizational intervention such as a change or training programme is involved, this assumption cannot hold. What is needed is a careful, rigorous and honest evaluation of the influence of the researcher practioner in the overall process. Further, the traditional research paradigm has the goal of defining immutable laws of human behaviour yet, as everyone's own experience shows, the one constant is change. Our feelings, judgements, behaviour and so on change constantly, especially in the context of organizational change or a personal development programme. Hayes further argued that a 'snapshot', single variable approach is encouraged by the ethos and methods of the traditional paradigm, yet within organizations effects have multiple causes and change over time. She was not dismissing the traditional approach; rather she advocated a range of methodologies which can complement each other. Her real message was that 'scientific rigour' does not necessarily equal a traditional laboratory experiment and that the different ways in which this can be achieved should not be considered as 'second best'.

So here perhaps we reach some sort of conclusion regarding the training of occupational psychologists. They need to be reflexive practitioners and researcher practitioners firmly grounding their practice in good, rigorous theory and evidence – otherwise they may be no better than 'quack doctors'. At the same time, the theory and evidence need to be grounded in the realities of what happens in organizations – the timescales, financial constraints, politics and a hundred other pressures against the 'pure' scientific model. What counts as 'rigour' perhaps needs to be redefined and new techniques developed to cope with a rapidly changing world of work. The recognition awarded by the professional doctorate for practitioners' daily evidence-based practice may also confer a valuable cachet in the competitive world of work professionals eager to promote their particular version of 'the truth'.

In a 'search conference' organized for the BPS Occupational Psychology Conference in January 2000, a large group of academics and practitioners were encouraged to consider the future of the discipline and the profession (see *The*

*Occupational Psychologist* special issues nos 39 and 40 – April and August 2000 – for details). Beech (2000: 23) writes: 'our first priority is not to advance the interests of the employer and in the process advance the interests of employees; it is to apply objective truth and advance human well-being.' Indeed so! Occupational psychologists should expose 'quick fixes' whenever possible, especially when they lead to negative outcomes. But at the same time nothing will be advanced if their training does not equip them to deal with the 'real world'.

*Note*: For full details of how to become a chartered occupational psychologist and of available MSc courses, apply to the British Psychological Society, St Andrews House, 48 Princess Road East, Leicester LE1 7DR; tel.: 0116 254 9568, email: enquiry@bps.org.uk, society website: www.bps.org.uk.

## QUESTIONS FOR REFLECTION AND DISCUSSION

1  Are occupational psychologists 'shooting themselves in the foot' by making it so difficult to get chartered? What might be the consequences for the profession, and what could we do about it?

2  What should be the main purposes of occupational psychology?

3  Why do managers sometimes ignore the lessons from occupational psychology?

4  Imagine you are asked to advise top management in a company where the workers are frequently absent and tend to leave after a short time. What methods of inquiry would you use to get at the root of the problem?

5  If you wanted to become a chartered occupational psychologist, what strategies could you use to get the necessary breadth of experience both before and after your degrees?

## Suggestions for further reading

There are many excellent general introductions to occupational psychology. A small selection follow.

Arnold, J., Cooper, C.L. and Robertson, I.T. (1998) *Work Psychology: Understanding Human Behaviour in the Workplace* (3rd edn). Harlow: Financial Times/Prentice Hall.
A well established and respected textbook which is also very readable.

Chmiel, N. (ed.) (2000) *Introduction to Work and Organizational Psychology: A European Perspective*. Oxford: Blackwell.
An excellent collection of chapters each written by people with an international reputation within their chosen specialisms. The European focus is valuable in a discipline which can be too much dominated by work emanating from the USA. Ergonomics is often neglected or missing from introductory textbooks but here it is given good coverage.

Doyle, C.E. (2002) *Work and Organizational Psychology: An Introduction with Attitude*. Hove: Psychology Press.
A new kid on the block! An unconventional, opinionated, provoking book which breaks most of the rules governing sober academic tomes. You will either love it or hate it.

Noyes, J.M. (2001) *Designing for Humans*. Hove: Psychology Press.
A good starting point for those interested in ergonomics.

Mabey, C., Skinner, D. and Clark, T. (eds) (1998) *Experiencing Human Resource Management*. London: Sage.

Thompson, P. and Warhurst, C. (1998) *Workplaces of the Future*. Basingstoke: Macmillan Business.
Two books which contain thought-provoking sets of articles about the changing nature of work and its effects on the workforce. Good for those interested in the 'people management' aspects of occupational psychology.

# 4 Counselling Psychology

*Jill Mytton*

## SUMMARY

*This chapter opens by very briefly setting the developing profession of counselling psychology in its historical context. The next section describes the nature and philosophy of counselling psychology from a number of different perspectives: official (British Psychological Society), operational, historical, philosophical, and comparisons with other professions. After reading the relevant chapters in this book, the reader may be feeling somewhat confused by the similarities among counselling psychology, clinical psychology, counselling and psychotherapy. I argue that it is the underlying philosophy that often differentiates one profession from another. The next section seeks to give the reader an impression of what it is like to work as a counselling psychologist. A description of the current routes to training and a discussion of a number of issues and tensions faced by the trainee counselling psychologist along with possible future changes to the syllabus follow. The final section returns to the future of counselling psychology, especially its evolving identity, using debates about diagnosis and the medicalization of distress for illustration.*

## The Historical Context

Human beings have always been fascinated by the search for the causes and treatment of emotional problems and behaviour regarded as abnormal by the society in which an individual lives (Ellenberger, 1994). Early theories often focused on supernatural causes, including possession by the devil or evil spirits. The cures ranged from wearing of charms, drugs, massage and diet to exorcism and confession. In some tribal societies 'abnormal behaviour' was seen as evidence of supernatural gifts and the person would become the tribal shaman. The notion of 'talking cures' probably began with Freud in the nineteenth century (Ellenberger, 1994) and since his time a variety of psychotherapeutic professions has emerged, some of which are described elsewhere in this book.

The recent context of counselling psychology begins during the 1970s when counselling (not counselling psychology) was expanding rapidly in Britain, focusing largely on providing counselling for problems of living rather than for the mentally ill. Psychologists played a role in this development and wrote much of the growing literature on counselling, and yet they had no 'home' in the British Psychological Society (BPS); none of the existing divisions were appropriate (Nelson-Jones, 1999).

In 1979 a working party was set up to consider the practice of counselling and its relationship to the professional interests of the society. They concluded that there was a need to provide a structure to enable the society to broaden its interests. A new Section of Counselling Psychology was therefore set up in 1982 and, by the end of that year, it already had 225 members. Ten years later, in 1992, the society set up a Diploma in Counselling Psychology to provide a route to chartered status for psychologists whose interest lay in counselling. Two years after this, in 1994, the BPS established the Division of Counselling Psychology. In June 2002 there were 1322 members of this division of whom 414 are chartered counselling psychologists. Chartered counselling psychologists are still relatively few in number. However, the profession is now growing fast with over 500 students currently on university courses and about 100 currently enrolled on the BPS Diploma in Counselling Psychology via the independent route.

## The Nature and Philosophy of Counselling Psychology

Since its early beginnings, counselling psychology has struggled with its identity. In order for the profession to exist as a distinctive and separate entity there need to be clear statements about its nature and philosophy and how it relates to other areas of psychology. Can we encapsulate in words what counselling psychology is? What makes it particularly difficult to do so is the evolving nature of the profession. Attempts to define and describe its activities have been made from a number of different perspectives: the official BPS definition; the operational; the historical; the philosophical; and by comparison with other similar professions.

In a recent BPS publication (Division of Counselling Psychology, 2001: 1), the following statement is made:

> Counselling psychology is distinctive in its competence in the psychological therapies, being firmly rooted in the discipline of psychology whilst emphasising the importance of the therapeutic relationship and process. The practice of Counselling Psychology requires a high level of self-awareness and competence in relating the skills and knowledge of personal and interpersonal dynamics to the therapeutic context.
>
> Counselling Psychology competencies are grounded in values that aim to empower those who use their services, and places high priority on anti-discriminatory practice, social and cultural context and ethical decision-making.

Although this statement emphasizes our psychological roots and hints at our underlying humanistic philosophy with its emphasis on the therapeutic relationship, it leaves out many aspects of the profession, some of which are mentioned below.

An operational definition is that counselling psychologists are graduate psychologists who have undergone three years of full-time (or part-time equivalent) training in the theory and practice of counselling psychology to a standard recognized by the BPS. In common with clinical psychology, training emphasizes the application of psychology to the therapeutic endeavour, and the integration of theory, practice and research. It is the emphasis on psychological principles, on research and the acquisition of a working knowledge of at least three theoretical models (though this is likely to change, discussed later in this chapter) that differentiates us from most counselling and psychotherapy training courses. With its focus on the trainees' competencies and knowledge acquisition this definition gives a rather limited impression of the nature of counselling psychology: it says little about what actually happens between counselling psychologist and client.

Historically, counselling psychology has been described as a move away from the medical model, from diagnostic categories and from the language of pathology and sickness. At one time, this was used to distinguish counselling psychology very clearly from clinical psychology, but now counselling psychologists are found working in mental health centres, seeing clients with quite severe mental illness, while, conversely, clinical psychologists work in primary care with the 'walking wounded'. Nevertheless the difference of emphasis remains and this derives from the respective historical and philosophical origins of counselling and clinical psychology (Woolfe, 1996).

In common with clinical psychology, counselling psychology adopts the scientist-practitioner model (discussed in Chapter 1). However, unlike clinical psychology, the philosophical roots of counselling psychology lie in the phenomenological (humanistic) tradition. Briefly, the phenomenological model, as applied to therapy, takes the view that valid knowledge and understanding of what clients bring to the session are best gained by exploring and describing the way they, the clients, are experiencing their world. To achieve this therapists have to suspend their own assumptions and values. Phenomenologists often call this a 'bracketing off' of their own theoretical assumptions about the clients' experiences.

Is there, then, a conflation of paradigms here? Traditionally psychologists try to make sense of the workings of the human 'mind' from the outside: we play the role of the scientist who attempts to measure objectively what is and tries to predict what will be. (This is not so true these days with the emergence of so-called 'critical psychology' and the increasing use of qualitative methods of research.) However, when working phenomenologically with clients we are working from an internal not an external perspective.

Comparisons with similar professions do not enable us to set up distinct boundaries between us, as there are clear overlaps. I have already mentioned the links with clinical psychology in our common use of the scientist-practitioner model with its ideas about evidence-based approaches and outcome research. The phenomenological tradition of valuing the person and his or her subjective experience and the wider context of the person's cultural and social life provides the links to counselling and psychotherapy.

Hammersley (2003) believes that a counselling psychologist, in addition to being practitioner, researcher, scientist and philosopher, also needs to be ' "creative" and innovative to produce the particular "moments of change" or internal shift which should result from the deep engagement with the client in a therapeutic relationship'. It is this emphasis on the 'deep engagement with client' and the therapeutic relationship that is distinctive to this particular branch of applied psychology although, again, it is an obvious area of overlap with counsellors and psychotherapists.

In Chapter 1 Boyle et al. discuss the emergence of the concept of the 'reflective practitioner' (Schön, 1983) and suggest that clinical psychology training is moving towards this model (as has teacher training, nursing and social work training). Schön (1983: 49) suggested the need for recognizing 'the artistic, intuitive processes which some practitioners do bring to situations of uncertainty, instability, uniqueness, and value conflict'. Counselling psychology has been using the reflective-practitioner model for some time in its move away from the more mechanistic approach towards one in which personal reflection and development play essential roles.

After reading this section, the reader may feel confused and ask: 'but what do counselling psychologists actually do?' To describe what a good counselling psychologist does when engaged in the 'inner world' of a troubled client is very difficult. So much of a good counselling psychologist's activity (when to remain silent, when to paraphrase, when to mirror back the client's words, when to ask questions, when to challenge, etc.) is based on intuition and instinct and thus the process is difficult to describe. Theory and techniques can be taught but something more is needed above and beyond the knowledge and practice.

I find the following analogy helpful here. Stott (pers. comm.) describes the 'good counsellor' as someone who is like a well trained and experienced yachtsman or yachtswoman:

> all the theory and knowledge is there as a guide but in the immediate turbulence of wind and water something more is needed – a capacity to work on instincts, to improvise, to be able to turn in one's own length, to fail and then immediately to find another way, to maintain steady objectivity even when chaos is threatening . . . each counselling psychologist has to find her or his own way through the wind and water and has to do it freshly with each new client.

## Working as a Counselling Psychologist

In this section I want to give a taste of what the work of a typical counselling psychologist is like, the problem being that there is probably no 'typical' counselling psychologist! We work in a wide variety of settings, work from many different theoretical frameworks and with a very broad range of client issues and problems.

Counselling psychologists can be found working in many different settings, including the following:

✦ The National Health Service:
 – primary care
 – community mental health teams
 – specialist services such as eating disorder clinics, services for older adults, child and family services, services for learning disabilities.
✦ Prison and probationary services.
✦ Voluntary organizations.
✦ Employee assistance programmes (EAPs).
✦ Student counselling services (schools, colleges and universities).
✦ Private practice.

Counselling psychologists initially train to work with individuals but many go on to work with couples, families and groups. They practise in all the mainstream theoretical orientations including psychodynamic, person-centred, cognitive-behaviour therapy, narrative therapy and family systems therapy. Counselling psychologists work therapeutically with clients of all ages presenting with a wide variety of problems and difficulties. These might include life issues and crises (such as relationship breakdowns, bereavement and domestic violence), mental health problems (for example, depression, anxiety, eating disorders, drug and alcohol addictions, dementias and psychoses) and medical problems (following strokes, HIV and AIDS counselling, cancer). In Box 4.1 an experienced counselling psychologist describes her work.

---

**Box 4.1  The Central Stress Management Unit (Kasia Szymanska)**

The Central Stress Management Unit (CSMU), based in central London, employs psychiatrists, counsellors and counselling/clinical psychologists and provides psychiatric assessments and counselling to a variety of clients. Clients are usually referred by doctors (workplace doctors or GPs) or refer themselves. The majority of clients are initially assessed by a psychiatrist and then allocated to a member of the counselling team.

The therapeutic approach I use to work with clients is known as cognitive-behaviour therapy (CBT). CBT is an evidence-based approach which suggests that an individual's emotional response to a negative situation is largely determined by his or her views about the specific situation (Palmer and Szymanska, 1996). The approach is generally short term, collaborative and, on the basis of a shared case conceptualization, aims to help clients to manage their problems by utilizing a number of techniques which they are taught during the sessions. CBT is applicable to a number of problems, including stress, phobias, anxiety (for example, panic disorder), depression, obsessive compulsive disorder, substance misuse, and post-traumatic stress disorder.

My day starts when my first client arrives, which is usually at 9 am. I see clients for 50 minutes, usually once a week, and at the most I see six different clients per day. If I'm seeing a client for the first time I usually read the referral letter from the psychiatrist and then see the client for an assessment session. This involves taking a case history and making an assessment of the client's needs. Based on this I draw up a case formulation, which is essentially a plan for the therapy and is shared with the client. After seeing a client I write up my notes – that is, a short summary of the client's progress, and what we focused on in the session. At the end of the day I may have a team meeting or spend time writing letters to the doctors who initially referred the clients to the service. Administration is a key component of my work in addition to the face-to-face counselling. On a regular basis, I receive external counselling supervision from an experienced psychologist, with whom I discuss my client caseload.

**A recent case study**

Hugh is 27, single and works in the City. He came to see me because he was experiencing panic attacks on the tube. Consequently he was avoiding the tube

▶

and instead was travelling to work by bus which took a long time. He was often late into work. He wanted to get back to travelling on the tube without panicking.

**The therapy (sessions 1–6)**

*Session 1*

An important aspect of my work with Hugh (and with all my clients) is the establishment and maintenance of a sound therapeutic alliance. During the first session I carried out an assessment of Hugh's problems. Hugh had no prior history of panic attacks; he first experienced panic when he was stuck on tube in the rush hour between stations. He felt breathless, noticed his heart racing, his palms were sweating, he felt dizzy and he thought he was going to die. The next time he experienced a panic attack on the tube he got off at the next station and, from then on, he travelled into work on the bus.

In this session I explained to Hugh the rationale behind CBT, agreed on a set number of sessions and together with Hugh identified his goal. Also, I developed a tentative case conceptualization, shared it with Hugh and then went on to talk about the evidence-based techniques Hugh could adopt to help him deal with his problem.

The treatment package Hugh and I decided to follow included:

✦ psycho-education about panic attacks

✦ breathing retraining

✦ cognitive restructuring

✦ *in vivo* exposure.

*Sessions 2–6*

These sessions involved the application of the above techniques starting with psycho-education. Secondly, I went on to explain the role of hyperventilation in panic attacks and taught Hugh breathing exercises which he went on to practise as part of his homework assignments (breathing retraining). Thirdly, Hugh and I focused on his unhelpful thoughts such as 'I'm going to die' and 'I cannot stand this', which contributed to his level of panic. We worked on examining his unhelpful thoughts and modifying them with more helpful thoughts (cognitive restructuring).

Throughout the sessions, Hugh wrote down some of the techniques discussed on an index card, which he read regularly. Fourthly, I recommended that Hugh should start to travel into work on the tube again and, while on the tube, carry his index card so he can practise his techniques to reduce his level of panic (*in vivo* exposure).

After several journeys Hugh found that his panic had greatly reduced. While he still felt a little uneasy on the tube, he was no longer experiencing panic attacks.

# Training Issues for Counselling Psychologists

Counselling psychology training is rigorous and not for the faint hearted. There are six elements: psychological knowledge, theoretical models, personal development, professional development including ethical issues, supervised client work and research. All these components are compulsory and trainees need to find a way of integrating them in order to become competent professional practitioners – no easy task when also having to run their personal lives, raise their families and earn money. Currently, counselling psychology (and counsellor/psychotherapy) trainees, unlike their cousins, the clinical psychology trainees, do not receive any funding for their fees, clinical supervision or personal therapy. Thus personal and financial pressures are combined with the difficulties of finding placements, beginning work with clients, the tensions experienced when embracing both the scientist-practitioner and phenomenological philosophical perspectives, carrying out research and meeting the requirements of the BPS (and, for course-route trainees, also those of their university).

As with all other applied psychology training leading to chartered status, the first step is to acquire the Graduate Basis for Registration with the BPS, which is usually gained by having a first degree in psychology. This provides the future counselling psychologist with fundamental knowledge of the various branches of psychology of particular relevance to counselling psychology, such as human development, the biological basis of behaviour, personality theory, cognitive and social psychology, along with quantitative and qualitative research methods and skills.

When the Diploma in Counselling Psychology was originally set up, a syllabus was created, divided into two parts. By the end of their training, students are expected to be competent in at least three theoretical models (although this is currently under review; see later in this chapter). The first part of the syllabus builds on the knowledge of psychology acquired at undergraduate level and begins to apply it to the theory and practice of counselling psychology. During this first half of their training, trainees are introduced to at least two empirically supported therapeutic approaches, which they then apply to their work with clients (at this stage only on an individual basis) on their clinical placements. Professional, ethical and legal issues, clinical supervision, counselling skills and techniques, overview of research methods, critical perspectives on literature and personal development all form part of this stage. Personal therapy of 40 hours is a compulsory component and regarded as essential to trainees development as reflective-practitioners.

The second part of the training builds on the knowledge acquired in part one and takes the trainee through to eligibility for chartered status. The syllabus includes additional therapeutic models; more advanced counselling psychology theory and practice; research methods culminating in a dissertation; working with clients in a wider variety of placements; working with families, couples and groups; psychological knowledge underpinning practice; and understanding of difference (e.g. individual, socio-cultural, spiritual and physical).

Chartered status can be achieved by one of two routes or even a combination of the two. Trainees can either undertake a BPS-accredited counselling psychology course at a university or can enrol with the BPS to study the Diploma of Counselling Psychology independently under the guidance of a co-ordinator of training. Sometimes trainees will use a combination of the two routes, so they might for example complete part one via the university course route and complete part two via the independent route. The syllabus described above was devised for the independent route and was not produced with university courses in mind. Universities running counselling psychology courses have had to adapt it to suit university regulations.

The University of East London (UEL) offers both parts of the training with stepping-off points. After completion of part one a postgraduate Diploma in Counselling Psychology is offered. Students who also complete a research dissertation are awarded the MSc in counselling psychology. Students continuing on to and completing part two are awarded the MSc in Advanced Counselling Psychology and are then eligible to apply to the BPS for chartered counselling psychology status. Currently the course is undergoing development in light of changes to the syllabus being brought in by the Division of Counselling Psychology (see below) and it is intended in the near future to add a practitioner doctorate. In part one the course focuses on the person-centred and cognitive-behavioural theoretical frameworks and, in part two the focus shifts to the psychodynamic perspective but also includes more advanced work with the person-centred approach and cognitive-behaviour therapy.

By the end of their training the counselling psychology trainee is expected to be able to respond appropriately and flexibly to the needs of his or her clients and contexts. Some will have chosen to work with only one approach such as the psychodynamic, others will be happy working in more than one approach depending on the needs of their client, and yet others will have developed their own integrative approach. They will have achieved a number of competencies in addition to the therapeutic work with clients; many of these are very similar to those of the clinical psychologist, counsellor and psychotherapist. These competencies include the following (Division of Counselling Psychology, 2001):

✦ Assessment, including assessment of mental health needs, risk assessment and psychometric testing (depending on the context).

✦ Formulation – that is, a psychological explanation of the genesis and maintenance of the psychological problems.

✦ Report writing and record-keeping.

✦ Evaluation of the outcome of therapy.

✦ Supervision and training of other counselling psychologists, applied psychologists, assistant psychologists and related professionals.

✦ Mutlidisciplinary teamwork and team facilitation.

+ Service and organizational development.
+ Audit and evaluation.
+ Research and development.
+ Management of services.

A current (2002) challenge for the Division of Counselling Psychology is the revision of the syllabus for training chartered counselling psychologists. This revision is long overdue given the changes in the profession since 1994 when the division was first set up. The syllabus for any profession encapsulates its identifying philosophy and defines the knowledge base that underlies the competencies of its practitioners. It influences the identity of the profession but is itself also influenced by an evolutionary process. Discussions currently revolve around a number of fundamental questions: should we keep the two parts of the diploma intact? How many therapeutic models should counselling psychologists be competent in (perhaps three are too many)? Should we move towards alternative research methodologies, such as the qualitative, so that we can use more meaningful modes of inquiry in line with our phenemenological philosophy? How will the trainees compentencies be assessed? The new syllabus is being devised to suit both the independent and course-route training and eventually will be linked to the National Occupational Standards. The National Occupational Standards (first published in 1998) outline generic standards applicable to all branches of applied psychology. Currently standards specific to each division are being developed and are likely to become the benchmarks for judging the competencies of practising applied psychologists. The standards describe working practices in the form of statements of competence accompanied by details of the underlying knowledge and understanding required.

## Challenges for Trainees

The challenges facing counselling psychology trainees depend to some extent on the route they have chosen: the independent or the course route. One challenge that all trainees have to face regardless of their chosen route is a financial one. Currently there is no structure providing funding, and the bill for training can run into thousands of pounds. For course-route trainees there are the university fees to pay while the independent-route trainees have to pay their co-ordinators of training as well as for any short courses they attend. All trainees have to fund their clinical supervision (unless they are fortunate enough to find placements where supervision is provided) as well as personal therapy. Some trainees fund themselves at least partially via career development loans; others manage to persuade organizations they are working for, such as the NHS, to pay their fees but the majority of trainees obtain part-time employment to cover the expense.

The issue of obtaining funding for counselling psychology trainees, so that they have parity with clinical psychology trainees, is currently being investigated by the Division of Counselling Psychology. It is likely that, in the future at least some trainees will be funded by an NHS scheme although there are some concerns about how this could affect the syllabus. Will the funding body want to have some say in what the trainees are taught?

Trainees choosing to follow the independent route (sometimes known as the 'portfolio' route) face particular challenges. Their first task it to find a co-ordinator of training, normally a chartered counselling psychologist. Gaskins (1997) reported that many trainees she contacted experienced difficulty in finding a co-ordinator, especially in the north of England and Scotland. Many of the 414 chartered counselling psychologists have not followed the independent route themselves and the need for training them to be co-ordinators of training is being addressed by the division. Training workshops have been held at regular intervals and these are likely to become compulsory in the near future for all co-ordinators. Independent-route trainees also reported that finding suitable workshops was a problem, especially in more rural areas, although this is now improving as co-ordinators are beginning to arrange regional workshops themselves (Gaskins, 1997). The biggest challenge reported is isolation. Independent-route trainees lack the support and opportunity to discuss and debate issues and concerns with other trainees. Some efforts are being made by the division through the setting up of induction meetings, workshops and email discussion groups to facilitate networking.

Course-route trainees face a different set of challenges though some of these may also be shared by independent-route trainees. Szymanska (2002) identified a number of expectations that trainees bring that can lead to disillusionment with the experience of training. Trainees often have the expectation that the course route will provide them with all they need to know and that once they have finished the course their knowledge base will be complete. The reality is somewhat different: attendance on a course is simply the first step along the pathway of professionalization. Learning for all trainees, whatever route they choose, is a continuous process that does not end when chartered status is achieved. Linked to this expectation is the one that trainers will have all the answers, that they are all-knowing. In reality trainers on the course route have a number of roles: to provide information, to give guidance and support and to encourage individualization, thus enhancing the trainees' professional and personal growth (Szymanzka, 2002). While the trainers may be experts in their chosen specialization(s) and/or area(s) of research, trainers cannot be 'masters of all they purvey'.

The expectation that somehow the course will fit into their current lifestyle and not be disruptive is another fallacy (Szymanska, 2002). As stated earlier, training via either route is arduous and demanding. It is time consuming but more particularly it is energy draining. Applicants for course-route training often minimize the impact that a course will have on their life so it comes as quite a shock, roughly 6 months into the course, when they realize just how disrupting the course can be. Time pressures as deadlines loom, relationship difficulties as family and friends feel threatened by the trainee's new insights and by the demands of the course and, of course, financial pressures can all impact seriously on the trainee's lifestyle. It is not uncommon for serious life events (partnership break-ups/divorce, accidents, serious illness, pregnancy) to occur during the first two years of training!

# Counselling Psychology's Identity

The future for counselling psychology surely lies in its innovative, imaginative and creative ways of working with clients while remaining grounded in empiricism. A quick glance through the book of abstracts for the Division of Counselling Psychology's annual conference 2002 gives a snap-shot of the diversity and variety of research and practice interests. Nestled among papers on occupational stress, counselling psychology in the NHS, depression, obsessive compulsive disorder, post-traumatic stress disorder and evidence-based practice can be found papers on the use of metaphor, living with nature, hypnosis, evolutionary psychology, men's talk about body weight, coronary heart disease, McDonaldization (fast-food therapy) and Sartre's lessons for counselling psychology.

However, counselling psychology is still a relatively young discipline in the UK and it is difficult to forecast its future precisely. All evolving professions seek to define their core features and identify the characteristics that distinguish them from other allied professions. This process of professionalization is still in its early stages in the UK as the diversity found within its ranks poses quite a challenge to the integrity of counselling psychology. According to Niemeyer and Diamond (2001), this challenge still faces counselling psychology in the USA where the profession can no longer be described as 'young'. They describe calls for counselling psychology to align itself more closely to neuropsychology and clinical psychology, and some authors have even predicted that counselling and clinical psychology will merge in some way. As we view clinical and counselling psychology in the same way in the UK, similar predictions may be made as both professions evolve over time. Concern over this led Brammer et al. (1988: 411) to state: 'It is important that counselling psychology be able to define its uniqueness if it is to avoid efforts by some to merge the current applied specialities.'

In a recent letter to *The Psychologist*, Ray Woolfe (2002) wrote that the answer to questions about the differences between counselling and clinical psychology may lie in the lyrics of the song 'It aint what you do, it's the way that you do it'. He wrote:

> [counselling psychology] argues that the most crucial factor in healing is not what we do with clients but how we are with them. In this formulation the emphasis is placed on the power of the therapeutic relationship (being) rather than the application of specific skills or techniques (doing) (p. 168).

In the same journal, Jill Wilkinson, the current Chair of the Division of Counselling Psychology, notes the development of the National Occupational Standards for applied psychology and expresses the hope that this initiative will highlight some of the differences and similarities among all the existing divisions.

# Diagnosis, the Medicalization of Distress and Other Debates

Working alongside clinical psychologists and psychiatrists poses a number of challenges for the counselling psychologist. It is easy to be drawn into the framework of the medical model when working within the NHS or within employee assistance programmes (which sometimes use diagnostic categories to market themselves). Pilgrim (2000: 302) suggested that psychiatric diagnosis raises more questions than answers and that it creates 'a simple dichotomy between the sick and the well'.

For the counselling psychologist this raises a number of questions and concerns. We are more interested in producing psychological formulations about a person's difficulties than in giving him or her diagnostic labels. We ask: how can we account for this person's actions and experience in a particular biographical and social context? We search for an understanding of the person's psychological difficulties, so how can we also be interested in reducing those difficulties to diagnostic constructs?

Many reasons are put forward to support the use of these labels: they are said to facilitate communication between professions, to enable research to be carried out on the specific groupings created, to be essential in the law courts and for insurance and compensation claims. But how do they really help the person who is being diagnosed? The counter-arguments are much more about individual needs. How does the diagnosis of schizophrenia enable the practitioner to help the client? Such a label can unfairly render the communications of individuals invalid, pathological and therefore meaningless.

By using diagnostic categories are we guilty of pathologizing normal human experiences? Common human experiences, such as bereavement, childbirth, work stress and difficult living situations, can be very distressing but is it appropriate to call this distress depression or even post-traumatic stress disorder? Such labels locate the difficulty inside the person involved when in fact it might be more appropriate to regard the problem as a social or cultural one. A young mother living alone with three children in a high-rise flat surrounded by noisy neighbours may well go to her doctor with classic signs of stress. But is this a personal problem, a mental illness or a social problem?

There is little evidence that diagnostic categories have any validity and as yet almost no progress has been made through research into the actual causes of these so-called disorders. The labels used are based on symptom clusters. Psychiatrists have yet to discover any signs linked to them: there are no blood tests or neurological tests that can verify or validate these constructs. It is possible for two people to have the same diagnosis yet have very few or no symptoms in common. Psychiatrists themselves are now beginning to question the use of pathologizing labels. In a recent debate at the Institute of Psychiatry the following motion was highly supported: 'This house believes that the trauma industry inappropriately medicalizes normal suffering.'

Another current debate revolves around the use of psychometric testing. Employers (including the NHS), expect applied psychologists to be trained in their use although, up to now, this has not been part of the counselling psychology training. Some universities, including UEL, nevertheless provide some workshops in the use of psychometric tests and it is possible that such training will become a compulsory part of the new syllabus. Psychometric tests are typically used to evaluate therapy and to aid the planning of therapeutic interventions. This traditional use of tests ignores the potential for a more direct therapeutic usage. Finn (1996) convincingly describes how the Minnesota Multiphasic Personality Inventory-2 (MMPI-2) can be used therapeutically to help clients understand themselves through the use of feedback sessions. Clients become engaged as collaborators, whose ideas are essential to the assessment. Testing is then no longer something being 'done to' the client but 'done with' the client and for his or her benefit.

## Conclusion

Counselling psychology can be a very rewarding profession. When asked why they want to train in counselling psychology, many applicants to the UEL course reply that they get personal satisfaction out of helping others overcome difficulties in their lives. During their training, students often comment on how they appreciate the variety offered to them and the choice that they have in deciding their own specializations and interests. They feel empowered to develop their own pathways to professional status. The fact that students emerge at the end of their training as different from each other in terms of knowledge areas of expertise as 'chalk is from cheese' is seen as one of the strengths of this profession.

In addition to the therapeutic work, there are many other interesting roles open to counselling psychologists. These include providing clinical supervision, carrying out research, developing workshops for chartered counselling psychologists as part of their continuing professional development or for trainees on the independent route, becoming a training co-ordinator or a university lecturer teaching on counselling psychology courses. Some people even manage to fulfil a number of these roles, thus experiencing the richness and variety of tasks that this profession offers.

### QUESTIONS FOR REFLECTION AND DISCUSSION

1  Are there any real differences between clinical and counselling psychology?

2  By engaging (even though peripherally) in the medical model, are counselling psychologists supporting the pathologizing of normal human misery and distress?

3  Should we be thinking about merging the two professions of counselling and clinical psychology?

4  In what ways are counselling psychologists helping/hindering with problems of daily living?

5  Should we perhaps instead be leaving our consulting rooms behind and joining the campaign trail for social and political change?

## Suggestions for further reading

Bor, R. and Watts, M. (eds) (1999) *The Trainee Handbook*. London: Sage.

Anyone thinking of becoming a counselling psychologist wanting to know what the training involves or a student currently in training will find this book useful. It covers a wide range of 'how to' chapters on process reports, case studies, essays, and research and a useful chapter on training routes for counsellors, psychotherapists and counselling psychologists.

Dryden, W. and Mytton, J. (1999) *Four Approaches to Counselling and Psychotherapy*. London: Routledge.

Many students at UEL both on the undergraduate psychology degree and on the counselling psychology masters degree have said that they found this book to be an excellent jargon-free introduction to four of the mainstream approaches to counselling and psychotherapy: psychodynamic, person-centred, rational emotive behaviour therapy and multi-modal. Each approach is clearly examined in terms of its historical context and development, its main theoretical concepts, aims and practice. In the final chapter these four approaches are compared.

Wilkinson, J. and Campbell, E. (1997) *Psychology in Counselling and Therapeutic Practice*. Chichester: Wiley.

This book explores how psychological knowledge and research can inform counselling psychology practice. Areas of psychology addressed include personality theory, emotion, memory processes, thinking, states of consciousness, lifespan development and the social psychology of self and relationships. Throughout, case material, examples and discussion illustrate the text in a very useful way.

Woolfe, R., Dryden, W. and Strawbridge, S. (eds) (2003) *Handbook of Counselling Psychology* (2nd edn). London: Sage.

For those interested in counselling psychology, this would be a useful textbook to dip into to obtain a good overview of what this profession is about. It has six sections covering the nature of counselling psychology, research methodology, perspectives on practice, developmental issues, themes and contexts and social, professional and ethical issues.

# 5 Forensic Psychology

*Brian R. Clifford*

## SUMMARY

*This chapter documents in broad terms the evolution of forensic psychology and its current growth and future trends. It then indicates how forensic psychologists work in all phases of the criminal justice system: investigation, trial, post-trial and release phases, as well as in the logically prior phase of the aetiology of criminal behaviour. It then discusses the education and training of forensic psychologists, pointing out that the British Psychological Society is progressively tightening its rules for charter-ship. Pay, prospects and conditions are next presented. Then, professional issues, stresses and strains, and ongoing areas of disputation or professional unease are discussed at some length. Forensic psychology is argued to be a broad church with ample scope for subspecialisms. The chapter ends by stating clearly what professional expertise is expected if the obligations and responsibilities of forensic psychology are to be fully discharged.*

## Introduction

Arguments rage about the *precise* meaning of the term forensic psychology. The *Oxford English Dictionary* defines 'forensic' as 'pertaining to, connected with, or used in courts of law'. Others are accused of using the terms 'crimino-logical psychology' and 'forensic psychology' interchangeably (Coolican et al., 1996; Brown, 1998). The definition employed here is that offered by the British Psychological Society (BPS). In its view forensic psychology is the appli-cation of psychological theories, research and techniques to the criminological and law areas. This definition obviously serves to increase the scope of the forensic psychologist well beyond the confines of the court and the matter of judicial evidence.

## Evolution of Forensic Psychology

It is always interesting to trace the evolution of a new discipline, forged by the melding of two or more disciplines. Often the beginning of the merging process can be quite inconsequential or trivial. In the case of forensic psychol-ogy, however, psychologists have been aware of the possible importance of their knowledge, skills and expertise, and its application, since the turn of the twentieth century. In 1908 Hugo Munsterberg (see Clifford, 1997a) called upon the legal profession to appreciate the relevance, and apply the findings, of psychology to their profession in his book *On the Witness Stand*. In the 1920s Burt (1925) produced his book, *The Young Delinquent*, while in the 1940s and 1950s Bowlby's (1944; 1951) work on attachment argued that a lack of attachment to a maternal figure 'caused', or at least was a critical factor in, criminal behaviour. These early works served to keep the relation between psychology and law in the forefront of the interested layperson's mind. In 1964 Eysenck produced his well publicized theory of criminality whereby neurotic extraverts were argued to be more likely to become criminals as they were less conditionable and therefore less likely to learn and adopt the social norms and rules of society. A more specific reference point is that of Haward's (1981) book, *Forensic Psychology*, which sought to detail how a psychologist should behave in his or her role as a forensic psychologist. This book addresses forensic psychology in its narrower, courtroom, etymological sense.

Of more recent origin, Brown (1998) suggests that critical incidents in society served to 'throw' psychologists and criminal justice system personnel together, especially in the case of the police. In the USA, Reese (1995) highlights the instances of the kidnap and killing of a police patrolman in Los Angeles; the shooting of a gunman by police in Texas; and the beating of a black suspect by Californian Highway Patrol officers and the subsequent public disorder that ensued, as cases that highlight the 'unplanned' evolution of a discipline. In Britain, Brown (1998) instances the Home Office circular which required chief constables to make better use of civilian staff to free up police officers for operational duties.

## Current Context and the Future Trends

Clearly, then, psychology has always felt that it had something to offer the legal and criminal justice system. Of late, however, this perception has become an imperative. Crime rates have soared and recidivism is endemic in all industrialized societies. Something has to be done. Pure punishment – incarceration and 'throwing away the key' – is seen as neither a practical, logical nor a moral option. Rather, a stress on prevention and rehabilitation has to be wedded to the immediately satisfying but ultimately demoralizing socially acceptable incarceration response. It is now realized that simple protection of the populace by incarceration is not a long-term solution that is sustainable. From this proposition, the current growth in forensic psychology can be traced.

Forensic psychology looks set to become one of the most popular areas of applied psychology. There is both a supply and a demand side to this prediction. In terms of the supply of recruits, there can be little doubt that the explosion of interest in forensic psychology demonstrated by undergraduates has been fuelled by the increasingly ubiquitous presence of crime both on the small and big screens. In addition to books, films and dramas, such as *Red Dragon*, *Silence of the Lambs*, *Cracker*, *Silent Witness*, *SCI* (scene of crime investigation) and many other dramatic portrayals of 'forensic success' over 'evil', numerous fact-based television programmes have focused upon offender profilers as they either interact with the police to produce profiles of current perpetrators, or engage in retrospective profiling ('psychological autopsy') of deceased persons, or discuss sensational real-life murders – whether they be serial, mass or sexual sadistic killers. These media portrayals serve to increase the demand for undergraduate units, modules, options or even full degrees variously named forensic psychology, criminological psychology or investigative psychology.

The demand side is the present government's espoused aim of being 'tough on crime and on the causes of crime'. The implications of this assertion are that the prison population will continue to increase (as it is doing); that sentences other than custodial will continue to proliferate (as they are doing); and that prevention will be seen as the most economically and humanely viable strategy. Thus there will be an increasing demand for forensic psychologists to research the precursors of crime and criminal behaviour and to produce policy-orientated and best practice guidance in the prevention of crime. There will be a concomitant demand for forensic psychologists to organize, monitor and manage non-custodial sentenced offenders, and an ever-increasing demand to service the increasing prison population by innovations and evaluations of existing and potential rehabilitation treatments that ensure earlier release dates and decreased levels of recidivism. At the court phase, increasingly pressure will be brought to bear upon forensic psychologists to offer advice and guidance on how best to handle defendants that come before the courts, and to prioritize categories of criminals in terms of the various and myriad options confronting judges, or more likely magistrates, who have to pass sentence against the backdrop of sentencing policies and frameworks, government dictats and ever-changing societal patterns.

As an example of this increased expansion of the forensic psychologist's role it is likely that the 54 autonomous probation services in England and Wales who amalgamated into the new National Probation Service in April 2001, at the same time as amalgamating with the Prisons Psychology Service, will create a much higher profile for forensic psychology. A key driver in this joint venture is the delivery of an offender behaviour programme in both prisons and the probation service, and the development of the Offender Assessment System as a joint risk-assessment tool. It is clear that forensic psychologists will become central players in the multidisciplinary delivery and management of these programmes. As a result of these developments while, historically, probationary services used forensic psychologists sparingly, and usually on a consultancy basis, currently some 26 probationary areas are in the process of recruiting forensic psychologists. This development promises to enlarge the working roles of forensic psychologists and to introduce different routes for career progression.

## Spheres of Influence and Growth Points

Increasingly, then, psychologists have become involved in all stages of the criminal justice system: the investigatory phases of the criminal justice system, where police are the main beneficiaries of psychology; at the trial phase; at the post-trial (penal) phase; and, eventually, at the release phase. A major area of activity of academic forensic psychologists is at a still earlier phase – the investigation of the causes, contexts and risk factors associated with crime and criminal behaviour. That is, a significant number of forensic psychologists located within universities facilitate, at least potentially, the criminal justice system by trying to document and understand criminological behaviour and evolve policy recommendations that will progressively decrease the need for pretrial, trial and post-trial phases. These multiple areas of operation mean that the concept of a forensic psychologist is multifarious and his or her sphere of influence is varied and diverse.

Academic forensic psychologists are found in academe where their main focus is empirical research into precursors of crime (genetic, biological, psychological, sociological). They are also found working with police in terms of selection procedures, organizational change, stress management and improvements in operational efficiency. They also engage with training and education.

In the field they can be found offering guidance on interviewing suspects, victims, and witnesses and critiquing line-up (identification parade) procedures that maximize the likelihood of achieving a valid identification while minimizing the possibility of obtaining a wrongful identification. Perhaps the best known but, in reality, infrequently utilized role is offering an 'offender profile' which aids police in reducing their search space, increasing their awareness of what (and whom) to look for and providing additional insights into the case and how to question the perpetrator once apprehended.

Another area of possible involvement, predating the trial process but crucially involved with evidence, is interviewing of children under the Memorandum of Good Practice (1992). Research has indicated that this crucial evidential interview is poorly constructed in the sense of being incompletely executed and poorly staged. At the moment it is conducted primarily by the investigating police officer, supported by a social worker. A forensic psychologist, with a deep knowledge of child development, linguistic and cognitive development, and an appreciation of how the law requires questions to be put, would seem ideally suited to unburden the police with this task and ensure the best quality of evidence is produced in court.

A role that forensic psychologists may come to play increasingly in the future is as court or evidence facilitator. Children who come before the courts either as witnesses, victims or defendants have been shown to benefit greatly from receiving prior information about, and visits to, the court. Guidelines have been produced by the NSPCC but what research clearly indicates is that such pretrial preparation is piecemeal and in need of professionalization. This would be a natural role for a forensic psychologist to fulfil, given his or her background in psychology.

At the trial phase, forensic psychologists are normally involved in providing reports on a variety of questions that are central to the trial being conducted. Much less frequently they can appear as expert witnesses. Now this is a highly contentious issue (see Ebbsen and Konecni, 1996; Clifford, 1997b; Yarmey, 1997). First, courts have little problem with experts who testify on physical as opposed to human matters (e.g. a ballistics expert), because bullet markings and properties are beyond the knowledge of the jury. Secondly, courts have little problem with physical trauma or illnesses as opposed to mental illnesses as a topic for expert opinion (e.g. the potential or actual damage caused by a blow to the head). Thirdly, courts have little problem with expert testimony on mental abnormality as opposed to mental normalcy (e.g. paranoid schizophrenia as a condition causing atypical behavioural dispositions).

What the courts have a real problem with is experts who testify (offer opinions) on what are regarded by the court as normal mental processes such as memory, perception, thinking and attention. These normal mental processes are assumed to be within the knowledge and experience of the jury, and thus the introduction of an expert offering an opinion on their operation is held to be more prejudicial than probative – that is, acts against the offering of evidential proof which helps the jury to reach a reasoned and reasonable decision. As such, this type of evidence is much more likely to be rejected or disallowed than accepted.

Now what has been discussed above is experimental forensic psychologists giving opinions as experts on matters of, for example, disputed identification evidence. To date the court has baulked at admitting such evidence. Other areas of forensic psychology have a much easier passage when it comes to having their professional input admitted. Forensic reports will be readily accepted on educational, clinical or occupational issues that are currently before the court. This differential ease of access to the courts by different types of expert speaks volumes for how the law views psychology and its 'proper role' (but more on this below).

In the post-trial phase, once a defendant has been 'sent down', forensic psychologists will be found in the prison system, special secure hospitals, remand homes or youth offender institutions, assessing offenders' needs, their likelihood of reoffending (risk assessment) and devising, executing and evaluating various treatment regimes and programmes.

The majority of forensic psychologists are found in the prison service. Here their chief role is as treatment officers. The range of therapeutic offerings is wide, stretching from one-to-one psychoanalytical therapy to group discussions, and involving behavioural, cognitive-behavioural and/or cognitive techniques. Cognitive restructuring, anger management and social skills are key objectives of all treatment and rehabilitation regimes. While it used to be believed that 'nothing works' (Martinson, 1974) it is now firmly believed that some treatments work for some inmates, some of the time (e.g. Hollin, 2001; Redondo et al., 2002). Forensic psychologists are prime movers in organizing, monitoring, delivering and evaluating this treatment philosophy.

## Education and Training

While there are numerous undergraduate course that either offer joint or major and minor honours (of psychology and law or other cognate disciplines) or at least modules or units in forensic psychology, to date there are very few masters courses that provide BPS-accredited courses. At the time of writing, masters courses are offered at Birmingham, Glasgow Caledonian, Kent at Canterbury, Leicester, Liverpool, Manchester Metropolitan and Surrey. Several of these run part-time as well as distance-learning courses in addition to their full-time, one-year courses. More specialized courses also exist. For example, Portsmouth and Leeds (as a consortium) run a child forensic studies masters course by distance learning.

As with educational psychology and clinical psychology before it, forensic psychology currently suffers from this 'bottleneck' problem. Many hundreds of undergraduates leave with the intention of pursuing a masters in forensic psychology but find places extremely restricted. How can you best maximize your chances of getting on a masters course in forensic – increasingly a sine qua non of becoming a chartered forensic psychologist?

The BPS has clearly documented the route that must be taken to obtain chartered forensic psychology status. You must have attained an accredited first degree in psychology (or a joint or major-minor equivalent), an accredited masters in forensic psychology (or an equivalent, however named) and undergone a two-year period of appropriate practice as a forensic psychologist under the supervision of a chartered forensic psychologist. This is a noticeable tightening of the rules designed increasingly to professionalize the field of forensic psychology.

As has been said, the bottleneck appears between undergraduate and postgraduate masters. A sifting device that has been used in both educational and clinical psychology is to ask for a specific number of years of relevant experience. This is the infamous catch 22 problem – you cannot get work because you don't have the qualifications: you can't get the qualifications because you haven't got relevant experience. This will not cease to apply, but current study patterns in higher education make it possible – and acceptable – to mix full-time undergraduate study with part-time (or even flexible-time) employment. If you are set on forensic psychology as a career then you must choose work that relates to forensic concerns. In this way you can accumulate work experience that can go someway to overcoming the sieve that is applied by masters courses to keep numbers of applicants within manageable bounds.

You must select courses from among options/units that relate clearly to forensic concerns (research methods, cognitive psychology, social psychology, child development, personality and individual differences, etc., etc.). Obviously you must select any and all options that contain forensic material. Your undergraduate project (individually determined research) should be forensically related as you are likely to present this at interview for a masters place.

An important consideration is the possibility that an employer may pay for your masters degree as part of continuing professional development (CPD). This is the case with many government agencies or statutory bodies. To go to an interview able to say that you will be funded by your employer puts you well ahead of any equally good but unfunded opposition!

The new requirement that you be mentored/guided/supervised by a chartered forensic psychologist, on balance, is a desirable innovation. As long as the mentoring aspect is played up, and the line-management control aspect is played down, the availability of an experienced person who 'has seen it all before' can be a great help as you struggle to find your feet in what could be an alien environment.

## Pay, Prospects and Conditions

Forensic psychologists who work in the Prison Service have the same conditions of employment as other civil servants. Those working in special hospitals and regional secure units are employed under NHS conditions. Both these bodies pay higher rates than university lecturer scales. All systems have ladders of promotion with clear guidelines as to principles and procedures for advancement up the promotional scales.

Increasingly, forensic psychologists are becoming self-employed consultants. Consultants charge fees and these are commensurate with training, expertise and reputation. Consultancies will employ novice (trainee) or newly qualified chartered forensic psychologists and salaries will be paid in line with negotiated schemes. Clearly, consultancy is a 'middle' or 'late' career consideration, but it is an option that should be countenanced at the earliest opportunity. Consequently, any and all generic and/or transferable skills curricula offerings should be grasped whenever and wherever possible. CPD is now an integral part of any profession and professional advancement.

## Professional issues in Forensic Psychology as a Profession

There is no doubt that forensic psychology, like all other professions, contains hidden stresses and strains. Some are overt – such as caseload, oppressive environments, nature of clients who have to be dealt with, and frustration with the lack of perceived best practice evidence-based or at least evidence-guided policy implementation.

There are, however, latent, more philosophical issues that need to be considered before entering the forensic psychology arena. As I and others have argued elsewhere (Carson, 1995; Clifford, 1995; 2002), while psychology's premises, methods and values are not necessarily antithetical to those of the law, none the less they are different from them. At particular times and in particular situations within the psychology–law interface that is forensic psychology these differences can surface and be a source of contention, dispute and contestation. So what are these differences?

While both law and psychology have human behaviour and its control as a central focus, the law's control tends to be immediate, direct and explicit. Psychology's control, on the other hand, is indirect, long term and implicit. Thus the courts control a defendant's behaviour, once found guilty, by directly imposing an immediate sentence that is explicitly extracted or enacted (fines, community sentence or imprisonment). Psychology attempts to control unwelcome or undesirable behaviour by indirectly changing that behaviour over an extended period of time by changing thought processes or perceptions, or by empowerment via social skills training and anger management. In this way, it is hoped that implicit cognitive restructuring, training or treatment will eventuate in explicit behavioural change.

Law individuates: psychology generalizes. This is a fundamental difference between the two disciplines. While the law has to make decisions about a particular individual – at trial and at release – psychology's knowledge which informs that debate emanates from experimental or empirical findings. However, these findings almost always refer to *group* means, not *individual* scores. Thus it is frequently the case that when we talk of group A being better than group B, or treatment X being better than treatment Y, none the less, some group-B members will be better than some group-A members, or some people receiving treatment Y will react better than some people receiving treatment X. This immediately raises issues in courts of law where specific decisions have to be arrived at about the specific defendant in the case. It also becomes an issue when risk or dangerousness has to be decided upon, or allocation of a specific treatment or rehabilitation programme has to be made to a specific prisoner.

Another running battle forensic psychologists frequently have with legal personnel is the issue of reasons versus causes of behaviour. The law operates on the principle of free will and thus talks of humans having reasons for behaviour. Psychology, on the other hand, talks of causes of behaviour in the sense of multiple causes eventuating in the behaviour at issue. Psychology endorses the concept of determinism. Free will and determinism are uncomfortable bedfellows. Yet this issue frequently has to be resolved in courts of law where defences involving premenstrual tension, postnatal depression, post-traumatic stress disorder and battered wife syndrome are advanced as explanations and thus mitigating circumstances in cases of infanticide, manslaughter and even murder.

Related to, but distinct from, reason vs. determinism is law's emphasis on common sense and psychology's emphasis on empirical fact. The 'person on the Clapham omnibus' is often the touchstone of law's reasoning – i.e. common sense. Psychology's emphasis on intersubjective verifiability of object fact frequently does not agree with common sense (Furnham, 1992). When it does agree with common sense law tends to scoff at the redundancy of the discipline: when it doesn't, psychology is usually ignored. One of the frequently espoused reasons given by appeal court judges for refusing the entry of psychological findings into the proceedings is that psychology is a pseudo-science. This was the explicit statement made in a case I was involved in with the Scottish Criminal Cases Review Commission. Now while it may be that judges are simply confusing the subject-matter of science (if its physics, then it is science: if it is human behaviour, then it is pseudo-science) with the *approach* and *method* of science (where both animate and inanimate entities can be investigated by the same methods of science), none the less, that people in high positions of authority can still make these pronouncements, and presumably believe them, should worry any would-be forensic psychologist.

Another area of potential disputation is where the law requires dichotomies (guilty or not; culpable or not; suggestible or not; treatable or not) but psychologists suggest dimensions (of, for example, intelligence, suggestibility, capacity, competence). Many issues that forensic psychologists become involved in are underpinned by this conflicting conceptualization. A good example is in the assessment of risk and dangerousness. There are simply no universal predictors of future behaviour and the factors associated with predicting different types of behaviour are different. Hodgins (1997) also draws out the important distinction between predictors and causes. Predictors of dangerousness are often simple – age and previous criminal history. The causes of dangerous behaviour are complex and multi-causal. At present there are two fundamental approaches to risk and dangerousness assessment: clinical judgement, and statistical or actuarial assessment. Neither of these assessment methods eventuates in categorical dichotomies of certainty; at best they are probabilistic 'guesses'.

The last area to be discussed where law and psychology can conflict is in policy-making and policy implementation. The law argues that litigation is a matter purely for the law, psychology has no place. Where psychology does have a place is in legislation – that is, the formulation of law that is then litigated. If the primary motivation for entering forensic psychology is to make a difference (in what, and to whom, being left unspecified) then this acceptance by law of psychology's role is gratifying. And certainly there are areas of law and legislation where psychologists have made a difference.

To take just one example let us look at how academic forensic psychologists have been instrumental in bringing about massive changes in one particular aspect of law and litigation. Until a few decades ago child witnesses were not welcomed by the courts. If they did appear they had to pass competency tests and their evidence had to be corroborated by other witnesses. For a variety of reasons, chief among which was the increased number of cases of sexual abuse coming before the courts, the law was faced with a problem. They distrusted the reliability and validity of children's testimony, yet cases involving such evidence were increasingly being presented for adjudication.

Coterminously with this social movement, experimental psychologists were producing empirical data that showed that children could give reliable testimony especially if supported by the court, its setting and its procedures. By making representation to royal commissions, by 'giving psychology away' (Miller, 1969), by writing in popular journals, newspapers and appearing on radio and television and by engaging with the legal profession at conferences, symposia and meetings, successive acts of legislation have both increasingly allowed children to be heard and progressively eased their passage and facilitated their delivery (e.g. live-link, pre-exposure to the court and its procedures, removal of wigs and gowns, videoed evidence-in-chief etc.). At the time of writing, allowing children to give their evidence-in-chief *and* to be cross-examined outside the court setting is a battle still to be universally won, but which is none the less being fought tenaciously by psychologists. This case study, and many others like it across the law–psychology interface, bodes well for the future of forensic psychology and its practitioners.

## A Broad Church

Forensic psychology is a very interesting profession to be in, and promises to be even more so in the future. Some of the most exciting topics in undergraduate psychology are actually real-life, everyday topics or issues in forensic psychology. Almost any recognized area of psychological expertise can be 'transported' to forensic psychology. Thus an educational psychologist could expect to research and inform the legal profession on such matters as, *inter alia*, educational subnormality, language and fitness to stand trial or recovered memories. A clinical psychologist would be interested in such matters as the psychopathology of crime, mental disorders and states of mind, dangerousness, violence and sexual disorders. Occupational psychologists can be involved in training and civil suits involving damages, liability and compensation.

Academic psychologists with a background in developmental psychology would have expertise in juvenile delinquency, attention deficit disorders, moral development, hyperactivity, knowledge of right and wrong. Experimental psychologists are already heavily involved in investigation of suggestibility, false memory syndrome, identification evidence, witness/victim questioning, lie-detection techniques and false confessions.

From the above it can be seen that many of the issues that engage psychologists are issues that the law struggles with daily. The melding of law and psychology in the production of forensic psychology is a development that promises to be a win-win-win situation. Psychology wins by being confronted by real-life situations and issues which can be resolved by the knowledge that psychology has accumulated. Law wins by gaining insights and new perspectives on what appear as intractable issues, and the defendants and appellants win by making legal procedures more of a process predicated upon reason, fact and justice rather than blind precedent, rhetoric and persuasion, and appeals to common sense.

## Increasing Rigour in Professionalism

However as a profession the gatekeepers have to be vigilant. Until a few years ago anyone could set him or herself up as a forensic psychologist and sell his or her wares. The BPS has begun to close the door on this danger. As we saw above, to become a chartered forensic psychologist requires an extensive education and training. They (the BPS) believe that chartered status, with all that that entails, should only be conferred on members who are able to demonstrate the following:

1  A sound conceptual basis of the context within which they practise, involving both criminal behaviour and the law and criminal justice system.

2  A sound understanding of the contribution of applied psychology to the criminal justice system as it involves investigative, trial, custodial and treatment processes.

3  A detailed understanding of key individuals in the criminal justice system, including offenders, victims, witnesses and investigators.

4  A sound understanding of forensic psychology in practice including assessment, processes of investigation, prosecution and defence, decision-making in terms of innocence, guilt, sentencing, custody, treatment and rehabilitation, professional criteria for report production and giving of testimony, and extensive practical experience in engaging in at least one area of forensic psychology.

Broadly 1–3 above are covered by your first and second degree. The last is covered by the two-year supervised practice. While it may seem a somewhat protracted process, this duration is necessitated by the nature of the job and the sensitivity of issues that a forensic psychologist would be expected to meet. The nature and duration of training are also mandated by the critical consideration that only the highest level of professional expertise should be brought to bear on issues of life-changing importance to the clients you will be dealing with.

Forensic psychology can be an exciting topic at undergraduate level: it is a very serious business as an occupation. It can be frustrating, exasperating and dis-heartening but also rewarding, engaging and enlightening. But then again isn't this true of all professions!

---

## QUESTIONS FOR REFLECTION AND DISCUSSION

1  What is the debate between free will and determinism? How have both law and psychology relaxed their fundamental beliefs in these matters?

2  Which of the various work locations of forensic psychologists would you find most and least convivial? Give your reasons for both choices.

3  The prediction of risk of reoffending is easy: the prediction of actually reoffending is complex. What do you understand by this assertion?

4  How realistic do you feel the various dramatic representations are of psychology's interaction with the police and crime solution? Consider such portrayals as *Cracker* and Jodie Foster in *Silence of the Lambs*.

5  Why do people commit murder?

6  'Once a criminal always a criminal.' What do you think?

---

## Suggestions for further reading

Howitt, D. (2002) *Forensic and Criminal Psychology*. London: Prentice Hall.
  A recent volume on forensic psychology which serves to illustrate the range and scope of the discipline. It covers all phases of the criminal justice system and spheres of influence of the forensic psychologist in good depth.

Coolican, H., Cassidy, A., Cherchar, A., Harrower, J., Penny, G., Sharp, R., Walley, M. and Westbury, A. (1996) *Applied Psychology*. London: Hodder & Stoughton.
  Only one chapter of this book is devoted to forensic psychology but, once again, it exposes the scope of work within the criminal justice system covered by forensic psychologists.

Colman, A.M. (1995) *Applications of Psychology*. London: Longman.
  The chapter by Clive Hollin, now Professor of Forensic Psychology at Leicester, is a useful chapter which sketches out the scope of forensic/criminological psychology and then goes into depth in three areas – psychology in the courtroom, advances in theories of criminal behaviour and the impact of these theories on crime prevention strategies.

# 6 Health Psychology

*James J. Walsh and Mark R. McDermott*

## SUMMARY

*Health psychology is the most recently evolved branch of applied psychology. It was granted divisional status by the British Psychological Society in 1997. While its origins date back to the 1970s in the USA, it is really only in the last few years that health psychology has sought to establish its own identity by differentiating itself from more established professional groups such as clinical and counselling psychology. As might be expected with any new profession, its development has sometimes been erratic. Indeed, even defining what actually constitutes health psychology has proved problematic. This latter issue is discussed here wherein the rationale of McDermott's (2001a; 2001b) recommendation to refocus health psychology around Matarazzo's (1980) conception of 'behavioural health' rather than 'behavioural medicine' is considered. The next section of the chapter examines job content and career prospects, with a mixture of survey results and personal accounts. Next, we outline training in health psychology and provide a guide through the new regulations designed by the UK Health Psychology Training Committee, as ratified by the British Psychological Society in 2002. In overview, this chapter illustrates that health psychology remains an emerging subdiscipline. Even though now 30 years on from its inception, health psychology is still rewriting its frontiers in terms of theory, practice and application.*

## What is Health Psychology?

To appreciate the identity of health psychology we need to consider its brief and recent history. In 1973 the American Psychological Association (APA) appointed a task force to examine the role of psychology in relation to physical health. Its report in 1976 concluded that insufficient work had been done by psychologists on health and illness, particularly with reference to the maintenance of health, the prevention of illness and the delivery of health care. Shortly after this in 1977 George Engel published a key paper in *Science* in which he argued that the prevalent biomedical approach to health and illness needed to be replaced with a new organizing framework that recognized the intimate and reciprocal relationship among psychological, social and biological variables – the 'biopsychosocial' approach was born. Such an approach, eschewing as it does the false dichotomy of the Cartesian split between 'mind' and 'body', quickly became a key feature and cornerstone of health psychology. In 1980 further focus for health psychology in the form of an influential paper was published by Joe Matarazzo in the

*American Psychologist*: 'Behavioral health and behavioral medicine: frontiers for a new health psychology'. He followed up with another paper in 1982 in the same journal in which he outlined behavioural health's challenge to academic, scientific and professional psychology. In both these papers, he articulated a broad and inclusive definition of health psychology which has been adopted widely by many ever since, including both the British Psychological Society (BPS) and APA Divisions of Health Psychology:

> the aggregate of the specific educational, scientific and professional contributions of the discipline of psychology to the promotion and maintenance of health, the prevention and treatment of illness, the identification of etiologic and diagnostic correlates of health and illness and related dysfunctions, and the analysis and improvement of the health care system and health policy (Matarazzo, 1980: 815).

Very little discussion as to whether this definition is still appropriate has taken place until recently, despite health psychology now entering its fourth decade. So, health psychology's genesis has been swift, with relatively little opportunity as a fledgling discipline to reflect critically upon its own identity.

McDermott (2001a; 2001b), however, has argued that Matarazzo's (1980) definition of health psychology is over-inclusive, it not being possible for its exponents to inhabit all the domains of health care delivery, whether it be primary, secondary or tertiary care. He points out that secondary interventions and rehabilitative ones have been delivered for many years by clinical psychologists who have involved themselves in the practice of behavioural medicine, as well as with the remediation of mental health difficulties. Behavioural medicine can be defined as integrating behavioural and biomedical science and applying this to the treatment of and rehabilitation from illness and related dysfunction. In the UK some clinical psychologists who practise behavioural medicine have rebranded themselves as *clinical health psychologists*. Thus there is potential for confusion and duplication of professional roles if Matarazzo's (1980) definition is to be accepted in its totality.

McDermott (2001a) proposes a solution to this problem. Turning again to Matarazzo (1980) for guidance, he notes that, alongside consideration of health psychology as 'behavioural medicine', Matarazzo articulated another equally important frontier for the discipline, namely, *behavioural health*, which he defined as a 'new interdisciplinary subspecialty . . . specifically concerned with the maintenance of health and the prevention of illness and dysfunction in currently health persons' (McDermott, 2001a: 807). McDermott (2001b) argues that this focus for health psychology has been relatively neglected but yet should be at the core of the subject since the emphasis herein appropriately is upon health, upon the psychology of health promotion, the maintenance of health, upon psychological processes involved in risk reduction and the primary prevention of illness, rather than upon the treatment of or recovery from illness. In this way, secondary and tertiary care would remain the domains of clinical psychology while health psychology could focus upon territory which as yet is not inhabited by other applied psychologists. Such a proposition is also consistent with Marks (1996) who likewise has been critical of the 'clinical' and 'illness' foci of health psychology. Such a proposal also agrees well with the emergence in recent years of *positive psychology* (Seligman, 1997) which seeks to move psychology away from its preoccupation with pathology, repairing damage and other 'down-sides' of human existence, to explicating those processes that support what is prosocial, productive and fulfilling. Such a move towards health psychology as behavioural health would be apposite since Matarazzo (2001, pers. comm.) has made clear since his 1980 paper that he was as interested in sustaining the healthy person as he was in advocating a health psychology which sought to remediate illness.

This more focused view of health psychology as 'behavioural health' is not shared by all but, given that prevention is considered better than cure, it is a direction in which health psychology should ensure it is moving as it enters its fourth decade. Notably the seven members of the European Federation of Professional Psychologists' Associations (EFPPA) Task Force on Health Psychology in their final report about the development of health psychology beyond the year 2000 agree with such a view, stating that 'health psychology is concerned with the psychological aspects of the promotion, improvement and maintenance of health' (Marks et al., 1999: 8). Some psychologists are already working energetically on health promotion, in particular those trying to influence population-level factors that affect health and who work in departments of epidemiology, public health and population sciences. In recognition of this, Wardle (2000) has suggested that an additional appellation is needed to describe this role, namely, that of *public health psychology*. This conception is similar to Matarazzo's (1980) notion of behavioural health with its focus on health promotion and illness prevention, and so is evidence of growing interest in this form of health psychology.

The apposite defining of health psychology is an important issue for this emerging discipline since, if it is unable to define itself clearly and distinctly, its development as an applied field will encounter difficulties in future. For example, professionalizing the activities of health psychologists will be problematic if their collective identity cannot be agreed upon. As McDermott (2001b: 61) writes: 'Academic health psychology may have provided an evidence base, but applied health psychologists need to know what part of this resource they have license to use. Agreeing upon an apposite definition of health psychology is the key to solving this problem.'

No doubt the debate about what health psychology is and what it is not will continue with, hopefully, a meaningful resolution as the eventual outcome. Until that point arrives it is important for health psychologists to recognize that for the time being the frontiers of their discipline are twofold, in the form of 'behavioural medicine' and of 'behavioural health', though a strong preference for the latter as its exclusive focus has been argued for here.

## Working as a Health Psychologist

So far, there has been only one empirically based report on the career trajectories of post-MSc health psychology students (Wallace, 2000). In order to build up a more complete picture of the range of opportunities available, individual anecdotal reports from practitioners also need to be considered. An examination of the research evidence, together with individual experience, will be made and potential areas of work in which health psychologists can reasonably engage will be assessed.

## Survey research

First, what can survey research tell us? Wallace (2000) was commissioned by the BPS Division of Health Psychology (DHP) to examine factors relevant to the employability of masters graduates in health psychology. Three hundred respondents (253 women and 47 men) from 15 courses returned completed questionnaires. The majority (77%) had completed their course after 1994, and many had self-funded their fees (69%) and subsistence (53%). Notably, over one third of the sample (38%) had previous qualifications (mainly in nursing and social care). In terms of pay, the first positive finding was that median earnings increased significantly after completing the course. Higher earnings fell to students with previous qualifications, particularly if they were older and male. However, pay levels were lower than those of other postgraduate practitioners such as clinical psychologists.

In terms of destination, the largest employer was the NHS. However, many respondents indicated that their previous qualifications were decisive in procuring their current job, though most of these regarded themselves as better equipped to perform it. Only three respondents indicated their job title as health psychologist, and all three worked in the NHS. The second major outlet was education where 82 respondents worked mainly in research contract posts or further training (PhD). A significant number of students returned to non-health-related work (sales, hotel management, HGV driver) after obtaining their degrees, citing low pay and difficulties in obtaining a suitable job as determining factors, especially when substantial loans also had to be repaid. Smaller numbers (between 5 and 20) ended up working in local authorities, prisons, GP services, the voluntary and charity sectors, private health care and self-employment. Of concern is that just over one quarter of the sample was assumed to be unemployed as either they reported no job or left blank the relevant section of the questionnaire. The comments of some of these students clearly conveyed their sense of frustration as the anticipated rewards from taking their MSc course did not materialize. While the majority of students expected to enhance their career and improve their pay, this did not happen for up to half the sample. The main reason cited was an inability to obtain patient care jobs for which they (but not their employers) felt they were qualified.

Wallace's (2000) report made three clear recommendations to the DHP: 1) the role of the health psychologist required greater clarification; 2) hands-on training in patient-related skills and knowledge must be enhanced; and 3) the skills and knowledge of health psychologists must be marketed much more vigourously to potential employers. Indeed, earlier research by Wallace (1998) had indicated a lack of awareness among chief executive officers and medical directors about the potential contribution of health psychologists overall.

While it is difficult to be upbeat about these findings, any pessimism must be tempered for a number of reasons. First, the sample represents the first wave of trained postgraduate health psychologists to appear in the job market; there was no trail already blazed for them to follow. Secondly, it is clear that employers were slow to distinguish health psychologists from other practitioners such as clinical and counselling psychologists, and were inclined to favour those professions already established. Thirdly, while enormous effort and resources have gone into designing suitable academic programmes for trainees to follow, much less effort has been devoted to considering eventual job and employment prospects. Because of the absence of a career structure, this cohort of health psychologists was left to its own devices to obtain suitable outlets for their skills. Therefore, factors such as individual differences (personality, initiative, energy, etc.) and variable opportunities may have exerted a greater influence on employment outcome than might be expected in more established areas such as clinical or educational psychology. Illustrative of this are the contrasting experiences of Barlow (1999) and Allen (1999). In response to three speculative letters submitted by Barlow to jobs which had been advertised as clinical posts, two offers of employment were obtained. On the other hand, Allen submitted 156 unsuccessful job applications before being offered a job. There were important differences between the two applicants. Barlow had obtained postgraduate experience as a health research fellow, whereas Allen had obtained a lower second-class degree at undergraduate level. Differences in experience and training over and above the successful completion of stage-1 (MSc) training, then, are predictive of employment prospects.

Many have found the MSc a useful springboard to further academic training (PhD) and a career in academia. For example, Munafo (1999) found that his grounding in research and the breadth of topics covered in the MSc enabled him subsequently to provide teaching input not only to psychology students but also to those in medical and nursing schools.

Whereas the survey by Wallace provided an overview of the jobs and destinations of postgraduates in health psychology, a more detailed insight into the varied activities in which they engage can be obtained by adopting a case-by-case approach. The next section reports on the activities of a number of health psychologists currently working at the vanguard of the profession. While some engage in research and others in practice, they have all published their experiences in *Health Psychology Update* (the BPS Division of Health Psychology journal) over the past few years, partly as a way of alerting others to possible career paths and work opportunities, partly as a way of highlighting some of the difficulties they have encountered, and partly as a way of keeping the employment debate alive.

## Case studies

As a chartered health psychologist working at the Royal Brompton and Harefield NHS Trust, Claire Hallas (2001) describes her multifaceted role in adult cardiology in terms of: 1) conducting psychological assessments with a view to designing preoperative interventions to maximize the benefits of transplantation for potential transplant recipients; 2) providing education and support for ward, intensive care and out-patients; and 3) educating health professionals (for example, social workers, GPs, rehabilitation nurses) regarding psychological outcomes of transplantation. While the job clearly offers autonomy and great variety, the downside takes the form of a lack of supervision and continuing professional development.

In the related field of paediatric cardiology, Jo Wray (2001) describes her work with children with congenital heart disease from the perspective of normal children (and families) coping with abnormal circumstances. In the course of her 'chats' she covers areas such as the meaning of illness, how patients can influence their health positively, how they see themselves and how others see them, social and academic progress at school, and on to how they are frightened to sleep at night in case they don't wake up for fear of the donor wanting to reclaim the transplanted heart. She calls for much greater input from health psychologists into paediatric cardiology in particular, and into more chronic conditions in general.

Implementing some of the many changes in health policy emanating from the present government provides considerable work opportunities. An example is reported by Joanne Locker (2001). In 1999, the Department of Health launched a white paper entitled *Smoking Kills*, and initiated a smoking-cessation programme backed up by £100 million over a three-year period. Specialist smoking-cessation clinics were set up in health authorities across the country offering a mixture of behavioural and pharmacological support for those wishing to quit the habit. The model employed was Hajek's (1989) 'withdrawal orientation therapy' which offers motivational and behavioural support to individuals and groups, particularly during the first few weeks of withdrawal. Being well trained in the methods of research, health psychologists are suitably placed to undertake evaluation of these interventions and, possibly with some additional professional development, undertake the interventions themselves. Locker concludes that the promotion of smoking cessation provides opportunities to practise many of the competences required for chartership (for example, teaching and training, research, professional development).

Another important white paper which provides impetus for potential areas of work for health psychologists was published by the government in 1999. *Saving Lives: Our Healthier Nation* (Department of Health, 1996) set out a public health strategy for England designed to prevent up to 300 000 unnecessary deaths per annum. Four areas were identified and targets laid down for achievement. Among those under 75 years, deaths from cancer are to be reduced by 20%, from chronic heart disease and stroke by 40%, from suicide and accidents by 20% each and from injuries by 10%. Health improvement, in the form of better diet, increased exercise and physical activity, and reduced consumption of alcohol and tobacco, was incorporated into the plan. Sexual health, food safety and drug abuse were also targeted. Local authorities, in partnership with the NHS, set up Health Action Zones and Healthy Living Centres aimed at breaking down the barriers in the provision and uptake of health services.

With this context in mind, a typical example of such emerging opportunities for health psychologists is to be found in Catherine Swann's (2001) work for the Health Development Agency (HDA), which was set up to raise the standards and quality of public health provision and to reduce health inequality. Her work is mainly in the area of putting together and maintaining evidence-based databases which inform and guide public health provision. Recent priorities include teenage parenthood, coronary heart disease and obesity. She is also engaged in a project investigating 'social capital' – a hypothetical construct relating to community engagement and cohesion which has been found to discriminate healthy from less healthy communities (Putnam, 1993). Swann (2001) describes herself as a public health psychologist: 'a new cross-breed of practitioner working at the interface of public health, health policy and [aspects of] health psychology' (p.24). She sees health psychologists as having much to contribute to public health policy and practice in improving health and reducing inequalities. In particular, their extensive training in research methods coupled with their analytical and evaluative skills equip them to deal with the research and intervention initiatives required by public health providers.

Swann (2001) and Meyrick (2001) (who also works at the HDA) appear to be using their research knowledge and expertise in a slightly more flexible and applied way than either might have anticipated. They find themselves inhabiting the occupational space between basic health research, public health policy and evaluation of interventions – a more 'rounded role', according to Meyrick (2001: 27). What they share in particular is an appreciation of the factors beyond the individual (social, political, structural) that determine health behaviour and a desire to use government frameworks to change these factors. Such involvement in public health is very much part of the future of health psychology according to the last chair of the DHP, Professor Jane Wardle (2001). As well as addressing inequalities and disparities, Wardle suggests that as much (or more) emphasis should be placed on changing health behaviour as is dedicated currently to understanding it.

The National Service Frameworks have also been initiated by the government as part of its strategy to improve the effectiveness of its health care delivery. Such frameworks for cardiovascular disease and mental health are already in place. The National Institute for Clinical Effectiveness (NICE) was also created to improve treatment. It set up six collaborating centres dealing with mental health, primary care, acute care, chronic care, women, and children's health, and nursing and allied professions. Each aims to produce guidelines for best practice and to oversee their implementation. The BPS has set up its own clinical effectiveness unit called CORE (Centre for Outcomes Research and Effectiveness) which is based at University College London. Stephen Pilling (2001) believes there are opportunities for health psychologists in developments such as these. Indeed, recently Earll and Holmes (2001) reported an example of health psychologists engaged in the production of guidelines on the management and support of patients with motor neurone disease and of their carers. Additional opportunities in clinical neuropsychology were identified by Beaumont (2001), with a specific example in the case of multiple sclerosis described by Rigby (2001) involving health promotion, coping training, stress management, self-esteem and confidence building, as well as fatigue and pain management.

## Supervision and continuing professional development (CPD)

A frequent issue in the literature relates to mentorship, supervision and continuing professional development (CPD). This is hardly surprising given that the profession of health psychology is still in its infancy. For example, Hallas (2001) acknowledges the limitations of her own experience in her field and craves supervision both clinically as well as in more general areas such as managerial and financial responsibilities. Working as a health psychologist at the Royal Hospital in Gloucester, Bath (2001) also raises the issue of supervision and suggests a possible way forward. He refers to a draft paper entitled *Policy and Guidelines on Supervision in the Practice of Clinical Psychology* (BPS/DCP, 2000a) which suggests that supervision should continue throughout a clinical psychologist's career, that it should be needs led, appropriate to the level of experience, and as frequent and regular as possible. The document outlines four areas for consideration during supervision – reflection, conceptualization, planning and experiencing. Bath (2001) endorses the non-prescriptive nature of the supervision implied in the draft document, but suggests that the supervision needs of trainee health psychologists might be better organized around the competences set out in the stage-2 training document, namely, research, teaching and training, consultancy and generic professional skills.

The general lack of mentorship experienced by postgraduate students was also discussed by Braithwaite and Meloni (2001). While academic skills were emphasized and courses on statistics and research methods were widely available, few if any short courses specific to health psychology seemed to be on offer. In response, the DHP drew up proposals for annual training workshops to be delivered by leading health psychologists to be made available just prior to its annual conference. Professional development typically emerges as a key topic in these workshops.

Given the present state of development in health psychology it is not surprising that the amount of supervision available stands in stark contrast to the amount required. The suggestion by Bath (2001) to use stage-2 competences as a framework for supervision while simultaneously incorporating the four areas suggested (by clinical psychology) looks like a useful way of proceeding for the time being. Like the evolution of any profession, much will have to be learnt by experience along the way. However, adopting good practice from related fields is a sensible strategy in the first instance.

## Health Psychology Work in Overview

The aims of the DHP, as agreed at the AGM of 2000, are essentially twofold: first, to study scientifically the psychological processes of health, illness and health care; and secondly, to apply psychology to 1) the promotion and maintenance of health, 2) the analysis and improvement of the health care system and health policy formation, and 3) the prevention of illness and disability and the enhancement of outcomes of those who are ill and disabled. The various white papers that have been published by the government over the past few years, designed to bring about improvement in the nation's health and to reduce economically driven health disparities, all require, either implicitly or explicitly, some form of behavioural change, be it at the individual, group or community level, or on the part of health providers. Health psychologists, given their expertise in behaviour change, are ideally placed to secure not only suitable employment opportunities to match their interests and qualifications but also to develop individually and collectively as a profession.

With an eye to the future, Michie (2001) suggests that applied psychology ultimately may be defined in terms of competences (skills) rather than disciplines (for example, clinical, educational, counselling). If so, the development of certain competences will enable individuals to apply for a broader range of jobs – that is, across disciplines. She argues that the primary aim is to persuade employers that many tasks on their agendas require attitude and behaviour change and that health psychologists are appropriately qualified to meet such tasks. Representatives from the DHP have met with the Department of Health to discuss ways in which psychologists can contribute to the targets set out in key policy documents such as *Saving Lives: Our Healthier Nation* (Department of Health, 1999: 6) and *The NHS Plan* (Department of Health, 2000). In addition, a new single pay scale has been agreed for all psychologists working in the NHS.

Overall, it seems that, while the first wave of health psychologists to descend upon the job market met with mixed degrees of success, the employment opportunities for trained health psychologists are beginning to expand and, with appropriate marketing and awareness building, should continue to grow. The reports from practising health psychologists employed in a wide variety of settings reflect diverse, exciting and engaging work.

## Training as a Health Psychologist

Members of the DHPs training committee have devoted enormous amounts of time and energy to designing a suitable training programme which, if followed, would ensure that anyone describing themselves as a chartered health psychologist would have a broad knowledge base, and a core set of professional competences, each of which had been rigorously examined during their training. By guaranteeing the presence of such knowledge and competences it is hoped that health psychology will attract the sort of professional recognition that it deserves and that is enjoyed by other branches of applied psychology. This section provides a brief overview of the existing and novel routes to becoming a chartered health psychologist.

Before September 2001 it was possible for practising health psychologists with five years' supervised practice from a chartered health psychologist to become eligible for registration as a chartered psychologist. This route was closed in 2002 and replaced by the more comprehensive stage-1 and stage-2 routes.

Those who completed a postgraduate training course in health psychology between 1997 and 30 September 2001 can apply individually to have their training approved by the Committee of the Division of Health Psychology. If approved, and they can show additional evidence of practice supervised by a chartered health psychologist, they become eligible for registration. The postgraduate training and subsequent experience (developing research, consultancy and teaching skills) must total at least three years.

Those who began their postgraduate training in health psychology before 1 September 2001, but who had not completed it by 30 September 2001, will need to complete their qualification and have it accredited (if necessary) by the BPS. In addition, they will need to develop research, consultancy and teaching skills in health psychology under the supervision of a chartered health psychologist. Confirmation of competency will be required from two appropriate referees. Again, the total period of training and practice will be not less than three years.

Those who wish to train in health psychology beginning on or after 1 September 2001 will do so under the training committee's new regulations. To begin with, they will be required to undertake either an accredited postgraduate masters course or the (BP) society's stage-1 Qualification in Health Psychology. Thereafter, candidates will then have to complete the society's stage-2 Qualification in Health Psychology, or an equivalent course accredited by the society, in order to be eligible for chartered status.

## Stage-1 Qualification in Health Psychology

One of the key remits of the BPS is to set examinations and to issue certificates to persons qualified to practise and teach psychology. A new Board of Examiners in Health Psychology was established in 2000 in order to carry out such tasks. The BPS's Qualification in Health Psychology (stage 1), under the auspices of the board of examiners, is awarded on successfully passing an examination which is designed for those who have not taken an accredited postgraduate qualification in health psychology. Applicants must hold the Graduate Basis for Registration and either 1) hold, or be enrolled on, a postgraduate *research* degree relevant to health psychology, or 2) be a chartered psychologist seeking a lateral transfer from another area of psychology. Applications must be made by 1 November in the year preceding the examination which itself takes place annually in February. Exemption from certain components may be negotiated, depending on experience.

The examination consists of four written papers of three hours each and a research project. All parts of the examination must be attempted on the first occasion; only one resit of failed parts may be undertaken. There is an oral exam of the research project and candidates may be called for additional oral examination following the written papers.

The first two papers assess the main content areas of health psychology. Paper 1 examines cognitions and individual differences in health-related behaviour. These include self-efficacy, control and health beliefs, as well as personality traits such as dispositional optimism and negative affectivity. Paper 2 examines knowledge of psychological processes in illness and health care delivery. Included here are factors such as stress, coping and social support; the management of chronic illness and disability; communication in health care settings; and lifespan, gender and cross-cultural issues (such as children's perceptions of illness, death and dying). Paper 3 deals with research-based practice. Knowledge of different research methods is examined, as well as insight into health-related educational interventions (for example, media campaigns, worksite interventions). Paper 4 examines knowledge of broader areas such as the epidemiology (for example, factors associated with morbidity and mortality) and biology (for example, genetics, psychoneuroimmunology) of health and illness. The position of health psychology vis-à-vis related disciplines (for example, medical sociology, health economics) is also examined. Finally, an original empirical research project must be designed and conducted under the guidance of a supervisor approved by the board of examiners. It must not exceed 15 000 words and must conform to the requirements of the BPS *Style Guide* (1989). As well as the traditional format for reporting psychological research (introduction, methods, results, discussion), a plan demonstrating how the findings would be disseminated must be included.

The purpose of the stage-1 qualification is to ensure that intending practitioners possess an adequate knowledge base regarding health psychology. While the examination may be taken via the BPS, it is far more likely that most potential health psychologists will acquire their knowledge base by undertaking a taught masters degree in health psychology. A growing number of universities are offering such courses, usually over one year full time and two years part time. Most courses have already been accredited by the BPS, with newer courses in the process of obtaining accreditation. Obtaining an MSc in health psychology is equivalent to passing the BPS's stage-1 qualification. Anyone wishing to find details of masters courses is advised to contact the BPS or examine their website.

## Stage-2 Qualification in Health Psychology

In recent years, one of the most pressing questions regarding training was what exactly post-MSc students should do in order to qualify for chartered status. The training committee has recently answered this question in the form of the stage-2 Qualification in Health Psychology. To be eligible to enrol, an applicant must be a member of the BPS and hold the Graduate Basis for Registration (usually obtained by possessing a degree in psychology from an accredited institution). In addition, they must hold (or be about to hold) the society's stage-1 qualification (as described earlier) or an accredited postgraduate masters degree in health psychology. Furthermore, if they are not already chartered psychologists they must obtain conditional registration for the duration of their training.

The stage-2 qualification is based around supervised practice – a well established system for training new members of a professional body. By obtaining hands-on experience in a variety of health psychology tasks, trainees acquire the skills necessary to develop ultimately into independent practitioners. Four areas of competence have been identified as central to the work of a health psychologist.

First, generic professional skills include activities such as providing advice and feedback to clients and others, as well as instituting and maintaining systems for legal, ethical and professional standards. Secondly, research skills involve the design, conduct and analysis of psychological research. Thirdly, consultancy skills relate to the planning and conduct of consultancy projects, assessing their impact and maintaining harmonious relations with clients throughout the process. Finally, teaching and training skills involve the planning and design of training programmes, as well as their delivery and evaluation. In total, 19 specific competences have been delineated in relation to these four general areas, and trainees must be able to demonstrate expertise in each. In addition, competence in two optional units must be obtained – for example, implementing interventions to change health-related behaviour, or providing expert opinion and advice in formal settings. The stage-2 qualification is dependent upon the acquisition and demonstration of these skills or competences.

The process begins by identifying a supervisor who must be a chartered health psychologist approved by the board of examiners. A formal supervision plan then must be drawn up and submitted to the board for approval. The plan must specify the areas of work in which the skills will be obtained, the type of evidence that will demonstrate skill competence and target dates for achievement of each specific skill (later changes to the plan are permissible if necessary). Normally, skill competence in two separate areas (for example, client groups, target populations) must be achieved. It is recommended that the trainee reports to the supervisor on a monthly basis, and at least six face-to-face meetings should take place annually.

Once the plan is approved, the candidate may enrol for the qualification. The minimum period of enrolment is two years (though this may be back-dated, at the discretion of the board, to when the supervision plan was submitted initially) and the maximum is five years (though extensions may be granted in certain cases). The sort of activity through which competences may be achieved includes health psychology related work within 1) the health system, 2) the community or private sector, 3) an academic setting or 4) the voluntary sector. The deciding factor is that opportunities must be available for the trainee to exercise the full range of key competences. Normally, the trainees' place of work would afford all or most of these opportunities. Job descriptions should be submitted to the board when sending the supervision plan. Benchmarking suggests that a trainee would need to work five days each week, 46 weeks per year, over two years to obtain the full complement of skills. Extensions may be required for trainees who work part-time.

At the end of the supervised period the candidate submits a portfolio of work to the board for assessment; an oral examination must also be undertaken. The portfolio will contain a practice and supervision log; records of completion; supporting evidence; and a supervisor's report.

A practice and supervision log must be kept by the trainee and sent to the supervisor on a monthly basis. It should contain details of tasks engaged in, work completed and work-related activity. It should specify the trainee's role together with the outcome and further action to be taken. It should indicate, and reference, any core or optional units addressed by the activity in question. Also recorded in the log should be supervision details, in particular frequency and duration, and units and competences addressed. An additional purpose of the log is to encourage reflection on experience acquired and implications for practice.

As each area of work specified in the supervision plan is accomplished, a record of completion form is filled in. It invites candidates to specify the area of work in question, the unit or competences involved and the main learning points. Both a supervisor's report, and a workplace contact's report are required in each case. Supporting evidence (in the form of reports, research papers, notes of meetings and video/audio tapes) of having finished the work must be included with each completion form. Care must be taken to ensure that all supporting evidence, which must be counter-signed by the supervisor, should be prepared confidentially (for example, by disguising clients' names). The supervisor also submits a report relating to the trainee's practice as undertaken, difficulties encountered and how they were treated, and the strengths and weaknesses of the candidate in question.

Once the examiners are satisfied that the portfolio potentially meets the stage-2 requirements, a viva voce is arranged, the aim of which is to ensure that the trainee has achieved the requisite competences during his or her period of supervision. Questions can relate to any aspect of the submitted portfolio, as well as any omissions, errors or deficiencies. Successful completion of the qualification confers eligibility for full membership of the DHP and chartered status. A maximum of two resubmissions is permitted. If major deficiencies still persist, the trainee will be deemed to have failed the Qualification in Health Psychology (stage 2) and no further applications will be permitted.

An alternative means to the same end (stage-2 qualification) is currently under discussion at a variety of academic institutions which are being encouraged to provide supervision in the form of accredited programmes (Yardley, 2001). As well as attaining the stage-2 qualification, candidates choosing this route may also be eligible for an additional postgraduate qualification (for example, an MPhil).

## Issues in Training

Given that the new stage 1 and 2 qualifications have just been published and no students as yet have completed either programme, any evaluation of the new system inevitably must be speculative. However, a number of issues do stand out for initial consideration. First, on the credit side, the training committee's aim for flexibility seems to have been realized. There are a number of ways of obtaining chartered status – for example, obtaining an MSc in health psychology followed by the stage-2 qualification; obtaining stage-1 and stage-2 qualifications while doing a PhD; completing a taught doctorate or MPhil in health psychology; plus other combinations (Yardley, 2001). Secondly, when students begin to qualify via the new training scheme there will be little doubt about their levels of competence. By acquiring and demonstrating such overall competency, health psychologists will be suitably equipped to meet the demands likely to be placed upon them as word of their existence spreads across the health sector. Indeed, at the time of writing the training committee is busily publicizing the competences of health psychologists to government bodies and clinical institutions. Thirdly, in the event of applied psychology ultimately becoming competency based (as advocated by Michie, 2001), health psychologists may find themselves well equipped to tackle psychological problems beyond the health sector.

Other aspects of the new system, however, give cause for concern. First, there is the issue of duration. It is likely that the most common method of qualifying as a chartered health psychologist will be to obtain a first (undergraduate) degree, then a taught masters and finally the stage-2 qualification. Undertaking each step in a full-time capacity will mean that the total duration will be 6 years (assuming all exams are passed). If, however, a candidate decides on a part-time first degree (4 years, at least), a part-time MSc (2 years) and a part-time stage-2 qualification (say, 4 years), the duration of training spirals up to 10 years. In these times of diminishing financial support for higher education (removal of grants, introduction of fees, taking out loans), it is likely that some students will be deeply in debt by the time they eventually attain chartership. This might be endurable if eventually one could be guaranteed a well paid job but such guarantees currently cannot be offered. A second concern arises when health psychology training is compared with the increasing number of doctoral training programmes – for example, in occupational or educational psychology. Despite similar periods of training, those in the latter groups emerge with the letters 'Dr' in front of their name, a title that can only be acquired in health psychology by continuing on to a PhD training. Indeed, some health psychologists will qualify via the PhD route in the first instance, thus opening up the possibility of a two-tier health psychology profession in the eyes of those holding the purse strings. A final concern relates to the amount of work that will have to be engaged in by supervisors both during supervision and examination. Although a cohort of committed and enthusiastic members of the DHP is willing to provide such supervision for the only reward of seeing the profession develop, it is possible that there will not be enough supervisors to meet the anticipated growth in demand and that some form of training bottleneck will occur.

## Summing up

Inevitably, the emergence of any new professional body is likely to have teething problems, some of which might be anticipated and others not. While it is likely to take some time to digest the training requirements laid down in the new qualifications and to discover the most efficient ways of demonstrating the various competences, in time they will be accommodated. Also, undoubtedly further new and as yet unanticipated frontiers for health psychology will emerge in the future which will present exciting challenges in terms of theory, research and practice for successive generations of health psychologists to come. It will be interesting to see how health psychology unfolds.

## QUESTIONS FOR REFLECTION AND DISCUSSION

1   Is health psychology better conceived of as 'behavioural medicine' or 'behavioural health'?

2   What distinguishes health psychology from clinical psychology?

**3** Has the development of training and the professionalizing of health psychology ensued prematurely, given debates over its identity?

**4** Who might employ a health psychologist who has just completed phase-2 training?

**5** What do you see as the new frontiers and the main tasks for health psychology over the next 30 years of its existence?

## Suggestions for further reading

Engel, G. (1977) 'The need for a new medical model: a challenge for biomedicine', *Science*, 196: 129–36.

In this article, Engel highlights the limitations of the traditional medical model of illness and provides an eloquent rationale for a 'biopsychosocial' alternative which, in addition to biological factors, takes into account social, cultural, behavioural and psychological aspects.

Marks, D. (1996) 'Health psychology in context', *Journal of Health Psychology*, 1: 7–21.

In a self-confessed polemical introductory article by the editor to the first volume of a new academic journal, Marks identified a number of problems with health psychology which, he argued, if left untouched would limit its development. As a partial solution he advocated the need for interdisciplinary working, a community-wide focus instead of the more traditional individualistic approach and a tackling of inequalities at a socio-political level.

Matarazzo, J. (1980) 'Behavioural health and behavioural medicine: frontiers for a new health psychology', *American Psychologist*, 35: 807–17.

The origins and emergence of health psychology in the USA were set out in this landmark article which sought to distinguish between behavioural medicine with its emphasis on treatment and remediation and behavioural health with its emphasis on prevention and health promotion. Interestingly, Matarazzo also highlighted the need for interdisciplinary working.

# Careers Guidance

Jenny Bimrose, M. Rachel Mulvey and Nelica La Gro

## SUMMARY

*This chapter presents careers guidance as a professional pathway open not only to psychology graduates but also to those from other disciplines who are interested in helping people manage their careers. Careers guidance is a relatively young profession, and the underpinning theory for professional practice derives primarily from psychology and sociology, with education and human resource management also offering significant contributions to the knowledge base. This chapter considers some of the current issues within careers guidance. These include debate about what exactly careers guidance is and what constitutes best practice. It considers the philosophical origins of some of the major schools of career theory and poses a challenge to develop theory relevant to the client. It introduces the training pathways which include postgraduate courses and work-based learning. Along the way, case studies, derived from lived experience, give a flavour of this nascent profession.*

## The Big Picture

Careers guidance is a rapidly expanding labour market and current demand for qualified practitioners is greater than supply. This offers a wealth of opportunity for practitioners who can find employment in a range of organizations, including public service and private sector careers companies; colleges of further education and universities; and community-based and voluntary organizations. People completing their training in careers guidance at the University of East London (UEL) in recent years have secured employment as varied as the Bank of England and the Big Issue. In addition, many initiatives delivering lifelong learning or economic regeneration subsume careers guidance within their programmes. Whether you are called a careers adviser or a careers consultant, a personal adviser (careers) or an outreach worker, it should be possible to locate a space in which to practise careers guidance congruent with your own value system.

Careers guidance is a relatively new profession. It originated in North America at the turn of the last century (Sharf, 1997) and has gradually become integrated into employment and educational practice in the UK. Most recently, the strategic importance of careers guidance in the UK has been acknowledged in an unprecedented manner. Various government reports and papers published during the 1980s and early 1990s positioned guidance as crucial in the imperative to increase the country's international competitiveness (Department for Trade and Industry, 1994; Department for Employment, 1995). In the early 1990s, the provision of careers guidance (to young people) was privatized and, in the late 1990s, careers guidance in England was 'refocused' on the socially excluded. This led to the creation of the Connexions service which offers 'the best start in life for every young person' (DfEE, 2000b). The policy imperative here is to reintegrate the 'disadvantaged' and 'disaffected' into society (Social Exclusion Unit, 1999; DfEE, 2000b) by means of personal advisers working within Connexions partnerships.

Despite the shifting ideological emphases of governments of the day regarding the primary purpose of careers guidance, the policy focus has consistently assumed that if individuals who are in transition (having completed a stage in their education), who are not in employment or who wish to change jobs, are matched with the 'right' jobs, training or education courses as quickly and effectively as possible, everyone gains. This begs a number of questions. Two important ones are: who defines 'right' in this particular context, and what exactly are the forces operating which prevent the matching of individuals to these opportunities without the intervention of guidance?

The answer to the first of these questions (who defines 'right'?) immediately highlights a potential tension between those who practise guidance and those who decide the funding of guidance services. On the one hand, fund-holders demand measurable outcomes from guidance, usually in the form of placement into employment, education or training. On the other hand, guidance practitioners will try to establish with their clients what their particular needs are. For some clients, placement (into employment, education or training) may not be what they want.

The answer to the second question (what prevents clients matching to jobs without the intervention of a practitioner?) highlights a professional practice issue. Do the forces preventing harmonious transition of all individuals from education into employment lie within the individual, or within society? Practitioners subscribing to the first option will prefer to work exclusively with individual clients, enhancing self-esteem and empowering them to take the decisions and action required to ensure a positive result – a measurable outcome. Practitioners, however, who believe that individual action is largely constrained by social structures beyond their control (for example, racism and sexism) will be more inclined to work within such systems, in addition to working at the individual level. Hodkinson et al. (1996) drew attention to the policy focus on the individual in the UK, arguing that focusing on the individual distracts attention from the need to change structures (p. 137). This is a fundamental issue for careers guidance practice – should its focus rest with the individual client or, rather, on the systems and structures in which clients, and indeed practitioners, are perforce located?

## The Nature of Careers Guidance

So exactly what is careers guidance? A clear-cut definition remains elusive. One of the major conclusions of a review of careers literature by Collin and Young (1986: 839) was that the area 'lacks rigorous definition and clarification of its basic concepts'. Miller et al. (1983) offer one way of making sense of the relationship between careers guidance practitioners and their clients by proposing that guidance consists of five activities: informing, advising, teaching, counselling and feeding back. In recent years (Oakeshott, 1990; Standing Conference of Associations for Guidance in Educational Settings, 1991) 'guidance' has been conceived as consisting of a number of related activities. European research findings (Watts et al., 1994; Watt, 1996) also proffer similar definitions of guidance as a collection of activities, with no clear consensus. No one definition is generally accepted (Hawthorn and Butcher, 1992: 11; Killeen and White, 1992: 1) so the ambiguity continues, exacerbated by the changing nature of 'career' as a construct.

In the North American context, Osipow and Fitzgerald (1996: 50) postulate that the concept of career has recently undergone a transformation, and they distinguish between career choice as a point-in-time 'event' in contrast to career choice as a developmental 'process' over a longer period of time (p. 54). While acknowledging that broader definitions which include life roles and lifespan have emerged, they suggest a more 'parsimonious' definition (p. 51), limited to vocational behaviour and vocational development. This is one offered by Arthur et al. (1989: 8) who proposed that career is 'the evolving sequence of a person's work experiences over time'. Young and Collin (2000) consider career to have been a key notion in twentieth-century western societies, and identify a range of meanings. These include career as an abstract concept (referring to the 'individual's movement through time and space'); as a construct used in academic, professional and lay discourse; as a construct used in organizational and social rhetoric (to motivate and persuade employees); as a construct embracing attitudes and behaviours associated with work-related experiences over a lifespan; and finally, as a construct involving self-identity, hopes, dreams, fears and frustrations (p. 3). 'Overall, career can be seen as an overarching construct that gives meaning to the individual's life' (Young and Collin, 2000: 5).

Because of the ongoing debate about the nature of careers guidance, a number of terms that variously combine 'guidance', 'counselling' and 'careers' are currently used to imply subtle, but important, distinctions in practice: guidance; careers guidance; vocational guidance; vocational counselling; adult guidance; educational guidance; careers counselling; and careers education and guidance (Bimrose, 1996: 54). An examination of practice in the area reflects this rich if confusing nomenclature. Watts (1991: 232) identifies no less than four professional guidance associations: the Institute of Careers Officers (now the Institute of Career Guidance), the National Association of Careers and Guidance Teachers, the Association of Graduate Careers Advisory Services and the National Association for Educational Guidance for Adults. Recently, an attempt has been made to establish a Federation of Professional Associations in Guidance (FedPAG) and thus reduce the fragmentation within the sector and harness areas of common interest. The extent to which this will succeed is uncertain. (www.fedpig.com).

This overview of careers guidance has identified a relatively new occupational area which is emerging with a knowledge base in its own right and establishing its own identify as a profession. Just as there is a plethora of names for practitioners, and a wealth of contexts within which to practise, so there is variation within what constitutes typical practice. So what could careers guidance practitioners find themselves doing? What do they actually do? (See Box 7.1.)

**Box 7.1 Careers guidance work**

*As a careers guidance practitioner you would:*

✦ Help clients to understand themselves and move on in career decision-making through individual interviewing and some group activity.

✦ Help clients make sense of opportunities in education, employment or training, evaluate their options and implement a plan of action.

✦ If necessary, use referral and advocacy to meet particular client needs.

✦ Use software and databases as part of your toolkit with clients.

✦ Liaise with employers, training providers and other organizations.

*As a personal adviser (careers) in a Connexions partnership you would:*

✦ Work intensively with clients aged 13–19 to win trust so as to address their needs in relation to effective choices in education or employment.

✦ Work with their parents, carers and families.

✦ Work in a multidisciplinary team to meet the needs of clients with multiple difficulties (e.g housing or drug abuse).

✦ Mediate between young people and other agencies.

✦ Network with agencies to remove barriers to learning and employment for young people.

*As a careers adviser in further or higher education you would:*

✦ Offer services which help students to develop career management skills.

✦ Work with individual students either through drop-in sessions or booked interviews to devise and implement career plans.

✦ Run career development programmes or workshops.

✦ Devise innovative approaches to job search strategies.

✦ Manage career resources, including ICT or web based.

*As a careers adviser working with adults you would:*

✦ Help individual clients navigate the labour market by making informed choices about work and employment.

✦ Administer psychometric testing where called for.

✦ Support adults currently in employment who want career change or development.

✦ Devise and deliver group-based programmes for career decisions.

✦ Work with community groups (for example, refugees).

## Does Current Theory Serve Current Practice?

This is an important time for the development of career guidance: the policy spotlight is on current practice and the profession has to clarify who they are and what they do. Emergent issues question the adequacy of existing, static theory to sustain developing, dynamic practice. Savickas (1995) traces current problems with theory to the fundamental issue of differing philosophical origins. He identifies inherent tensions which arise from the academic traditions of different theories: 'sharp lines have been drawn on which philosophy of science to choose' (p. 15). Arguing for theoretical convergence, he concludes that: 'vocational psychology could benefit simultaneously from refinements forged within the distinct career theories, from advances produced by convergence among career macrotheories and from breakthroughs induced by divergence in work-role microtheory' (p. 29).

As a result of comparing theories, Osipow and Fitzgerald (1996: 323) conclude that they differ not only because of the different philosophical orientations of authors but also because they are trying to achieve different objectives. They distinguish those that focus on explanations of the choice *process*; those that focus on career development over *time*; and those that focus more on providing *practical techniques*. A common weakness of these theories is their tendency to claim universality for their concepts (Osipow and Fitzgerald, 1996: 323) – a claim which seems not to be justified in practice.

This in turn gives rise to two distinct trends in the development of theory, trends which are sometimes overlapping. One is towards developing theories that attempt to meet the needs of specific client groups, such as minority ethnic groups or girls and women. Traditional theories tend to assume choice and autonomy for the individual, whereas some critics question this as a reasonable assumption for some client groups within their cultural context. For example, Osipow and Littlejohn (1995) discuss serious weaknesses in applying theory to minority ethnic groups. A major problem is the manner in which all theories use concepts which 'assume cultures that are relatively affluent and have good opportunities for education, upward mobility and family support and encouragement' (p. 255), because, in practice, many members of minority ethnic groups do not always have access to these privileges. Attempts are being made to develop approaches that address the particular issues related to these client groups. Leong (1995), for example, presents theory and research on particular ethnic groups such as Asian Americans, Hispanics and African Americans, and discusses progress towards developing a multicultural theory of career development. In addition to minority ethnic groups, another client group for which the relevance of traditional theories is being questioned is girls and women.

The second trend within the development of career theory is a move towards a postmodern approach (Savickas, 1993; Collin and Watts, 1996). Savickas (1993) discusses this move away from 'logical positivism, objectivist science, and industrialism' towards 'a multiple perspective discourse' (p. 205), and summarizes key differences between the modern and postmodern era (p. 209). Career counselling, he suggests, has produced six notable innovations to mark its entry to the postmodern era. These are, first, a rejection of the notion that careers practitioners are experts: 'instead of portraying themselves as masters of truth, counselors are creating a space where those involved can speak and act for themselves' (Savickas, 1993: 211); secondly, the replacement of the concept of 'fit' with 'enablement' and the affirmation of diversity; thirdly, recognition of the importance of context and culture, together with the broadening of focus beyond a preoccupation with work role (together these signal a move towards life-design counselling and grand narratives) (p. 212); fourthly, there is a questioning of the legitimacy of separating the career from the personal, with a move towards the greater integration of these two domains; and, fifthly, the realization that career theory has provided objective guidance techniques which practitioners have increasingly had to combine with subjective techniques derived from counselling theory for their practice. Embryonic career theories are thus being developed which focus more on meaning, invention and construction, and move towards 'co-construction or social construction of meaning' (p. 213). Finally, there is a shift away from objectifying clients by measurement to a preference for autobiography and 'meaning-making'.

Savickas (1993) suggests that changes in career counselling redefine the practitioner as a co-author and editor of career narratives. Instead of diagnosing abilities and achievements, assessing potential and matching clients to the most suitable education, training or employment opportunities, practitioners would authorize careers by narrating coherent stories; invest career with meaning by identifying themes and tensions in the storyline; and help clients learn the skills necessary for the next episode in the story (Savickas, 1993). So an exploration of significant events, turning points or positive role models in a client's life history confirms for the clients that these events or people may, legitimately, be important and influential to their future personal development. Indeed, by sifting through life history, patterns might very well emerge. For example, a client might identify two or three significant people who have had a positive influence on him or her during a particular event or period in his or her life. The careers practitioner would then tease out patterns or similarities among these people with their client and discuss possible meanings to identify lessons to be learnt, thus indicating pointers or preferences for his or her future career development.

The changing policy context for careers guidance and the developments in theory are inevitably influencing trends in practice. In addition, the introduction of Connexions partnerships in England demands a different way of working with clients in the publicly funded sector. These partnerships require an interagency approach to helping and supporting young people over a period of up to two years, particularly those regarded as 'at risk'. A more holistic, developmental, approach is increasingly required in contrast to the traditional 'one-off' interview so common in the past. Additionally, the increased need for interagency working creates a new set of demands about the nature of the relationship with the client and the question of ethical standards (Mulvey, 2002). Different guidance sectors have also developed different preferences for how they work with clients. For example, practitioners working with adults (for example, in 'information, advice and guidance' organizations and in careers services in higher education) often express a preference for offering a client-centred, counselling approach aimed at empowering individuals. In another example, those working privately as career management consultants typically work more with personality, psychometric tests and other objective forms of measurement. This requires a more 'expert' approach whereby the client is dependent on the special expertise of the counsellor both to test and assess his or her abilities and potential and to interpret the information for future career development.

In summary, there are a number of key trends and issues facing careers guidance practitioners:

+ A series of policy initiatives has resulted in a continuous process of change which can at times seem relentless.

+ Careers guidance is firmly on the agenda in the context of economic regeneration and lifelong learning.

+ Challenges to established ways of working in guidance can be perceived as threatening.

+ Or can offer new opportunities for both practitioners and their clients.

## Training for the Profession

Over the past decade, government policy has paid attention both to the organization of careers guidance delivery and to the appropriate training for careers practitioners and their managers. Policy-makers for careers guidance uncritically accepted the ideology underpinning narrow forms of work-based assessment in the early 1990s. National Vocational Qualifications (NVQs) for guidance (levels 3 and 4) were introduced in the mid-1990s with apparently no account taken of published critiques which discussed problems with (NVQ) competence-based assessment in practice in other occupational areas (for example, Hyland, 1994; Hodkinson and Issit, 1995; Wolf, 1995). A new 'Qualification in Careers Guidance' (QCG) for practitioners, with a heavy bias towards workplace assessment and competency, was implemented nationally from the academic year 2001/2002. It seems likely that those successfully completing the QCG off the job in higher education will then be required to complete (at least part of) the NVQ4 in Guidance in the workplace, before being deemed occupationally competent. There are, therefore, currently two distinct routes into the profession: either education based or work based. The education-based route involves either a one-year full or two-year part-time course in higher education. The workplace route sees practitioners working towards occupational competence over a period of at least 18 months, and typically 2 years.

## Becoming Qualified: Individual Journeys to Professional Practice

There are 14 centres offering the training: 3 in Scotland, 1 in Wales, 1 in Northern Ireland (from September 2002) and 9 in England. Details of course centres can be obtained from the Institute for Career Guidance (http://www.icg-uk.org; tel.: 01384 376464). Twelve courses have been validated as postgraduate courses and two as undergraduate. Progression from the initial professional qualification can take the form of a masters degree in careers guidance. At UEL, this is a two-year part-time course. The work-based route involves assessment on the job towards a National Vocational Qualification at level four (NVQ4 in Guidance). For those wishing to qualify as a personal adviser within a Connexions partnership, a Diploma for Personal Advisers is available if you have a relevant initial qualification (like the Qualification in Careers Guidance) and are employed by a Connexions partnership.

The case studies in Box 7.2 are compiled from the experiences of people who have undertaken their professional training at UEL, but do not relate to a specific individual. They offer an illustration of the kind of journey taken to professional careers guidance practice.

---

**Box 7.2  Experiences of people undertaking their professional training at UEL**

**Saima**

Having completed a degree in business studies, Saima found employment in a local authority housing department, working directly with members of the public. She most enjoyed the aspects of the work in which she felt she was developing positive relations with people and 'making a difference'. After several years, however, Saima felt her role was limited and the scope of her work predictable. She undertook the Qualification in Careers Guidance (QCG) at UEL and, once qualified, secured employment in a local school as a learning mentor, working to boost achievement and raise aspirations.

**Andy**

Some years after leaving school, Andy started a part-time degree course in modern languages. Unsure what he wanted to do once he graduated, he took a job in a national bookstore chain. Once he and his partner started a family, Andy went part time to combine employment and childcare. He also became involved in a local community group, working with refugees, which allowed him to develop effective interpersonal and communication skills. Realizing that this was an area of work he found fulfilling, he wanted to undertake formal training and came on the QCG course. On completion, he went to work for a local careers company, working with young people in inner-city schools.

**Wendy**

Wendy left school at 16 and went to her local further education college where she gained a Distinction in GNVQ Level 3 Business Studies. She found work in a local employment agency, and enjoyed helping local people get local jobs. From there she moved to the economic development team of her local council, and undertook an HND in public management. She found herself managing a local project to regenerate a neglected housing estate. As part of her own training needs she is undertaking the NVQ4 in Guidance, developing competence in the workplace and gathering evidence for her portfolio.

---

Of course, where there are students, there are also teachers. The recent changes in training routes have made demands on those delivering professional training to adapt to a rapidly moving external environment. From our work both within the Centre for Training in Careers Guidance at UEL and from our contacts with other trainers at other centres, we have identified the kind of issues which currently exercise the trainer:

◆ Safeguard standards and embrace change.

◆ Embed careers guidance in wider provision.

◆ Straddle professional and academic agenda.

◆ Maintain a professional presence within the spectrum of practice.

◆ Contribute to the knowledge base underpinning practice.

## Conclusion

Careers guidance is a fast-developing professional area which requires postgraduate training. It offers excellent, varied employment opportunities in a range of contexts. Indeed, as the practice of careers guidance has become more established, policy requirements in the UK have increased its range of clients and tasks. The new professional contexts and roles for guidance practitioners are being accompanied by the development of new theories for practice which signal a rejection of scientific, positivist approaches to career and their replacement with paradigms embracing more holistic, fluid models of human behaviour. The process of working out (and working through) the implications of new approaches for practice is underway, with a key challenge for this community of practice likely to be in reconciling new approaches and thinking to policy directives embedded in traditional theory.

---

### QUESTIONS FOR REFLECTION AND DISCUSSION

1  In terms of policy, is careers guidance part of the welfare provision, there to look after people, or is it part of a national economic strategy to get everyone who can be engaged in work or training?

2  Thinking about your own career path up to this point, do you see psychological or sociological factors playing the greater part?

3  Thinking about your career planning for the future (either immediate or long term), would a rational-positivist or a postmodern approach be more helpful to you?

4  Where do you think *real* learning as a professional takes place: more in the classroom or in practice?

5  If you are considering training for careers guidance, what kind of client group or work context appeals most to you?

---

## Suggestions for further reading

Hodkinson, P., Sparkes, A.C. and Hodkinson, H. (1996) *Triumphs and Tears: Young People, Markets and the Transition from School to Work*. London: David Fulton.
This is a good text for getting the sociological perspective on careers guidance and a close understanding of what careers mean for the individuals involved.

Institute of Career Guidance (ICG) (2002) *Constructing the Future, Social Inclusion: Policy and Practice*. Stourbridge: ICG.
This is the second in a series of papers published by the largest professional body in careers guidance, the Institute of Career Guidance. Far from being the official voice of the guidance profession, this is a collection of very individual voices each presenting a particular take on the social inclusion agenda which is the policy currently shaping the provision of careers guidance.

Savickas, M.L. (1995) 'Current theoretical issues in vocational psychology: convergence, divergence, and schism', in W.B. Walsh and S.H. Osipow (eds) *Handbook of Vocational Psychology: Theory, Research and Practice* (2nd edn). Mahwah, NJ: Lawrence Erlbaum Associates, pp. 1–34.
While the Savickas chapter in particular is good for the postmodern perspective, the handbook overall gives a good insight into the issues currently engaging the careers guidance community of practice.

Young, R.A. and Collin, A. (2000) 'Introduction: framing the future of career', in A. Collin, and R.A. Young (eds) *The Future of Career*. Cambridge: Cambridge University Press, pp. 1–17.
A useful and timely publication which presents the debates which are taking place throughout the field of career guidance and which inform career thinking.

# 8 Counselling

Rowan Bayne, Tony Merry and Gladeana McMahon

## SUMMARY

*After touching on whether or not there are differences among counselling, psychotherapy and the energetic (and very successful) newcomer, coaching, this chapter is in three main sections. First, we try, in various ways, to give a 'flavour' of what it is like to work as a counsellor. Secondly, we discuss some current trends in counselling – those towards brevity (six sessions is almost becoming standard in some settings), evaluation, specialisms, professionalism and statutory regulation. These trends are also issues. For example, is brief counselling ethical? How valid is evaluation? Are specialisms specious? What are professionalism and statutory regulation really for? What role should the British Association for Counselling and Psychotherapy (BACP, formerly BAC) play in moves towards statutory regulation? Thirdly, we say a little about counsellor training and education and, in particular, about whether or not personal therapy is necessary for students on counselling courses.*

## Counselling and Psychotherapy

A simple and useful definition of counselling is 'helping people explore problems so that they can decide what to do about them'. Part of the British Association for Counselling (BAC) (1996: 1) more spelt-out attempt is:

> Counselling may be concerned with developmental issues, addressing and resolving specific problems, making decisions, coping with crisis, developing personal insight and knowledge, working through feelings of inner conflict or improving relationships with others. The counsellor's role is to facilitate the client's work in ways that respect the client's values, personal resources and capacity for choice within his or her cultural context.

Psychotherapists, clinical and counselling psychologists, psychiatrists, social workers, priests and friends, among others, might well agree with these aims as part of *their* roles too. To take just counselling and psychotherapy, there have been many attempts over a long period to distinguish between them (Feltham, 1995; McLeod, 1998). Some writers and practitioners believe there are fundamental differences, others that there are none and that searching for them is a 'dismal quest' (Thorne, 1992).

In contrast, there are clear differences between the various theories or orientations common to both counselling and psychotherapy (McLeod, 1998; Feltham, 1997; Prochaska and Norcross, 1999) – for example, psychodynamic, humanistic, cognitive and existential. Here though the trend is more towards attempted integration than possibly spurious differentiation.

However, trying to formulate a harmonious and coherent grand theory from two or more theories which make radically different assumptions about human nature and how, and to what extent, people can change may be impossible. For example, the concept of a 'dynamic unconscious' is central to psychoanalytic theories of counselling but absent from many other theories. To them, the evidence for a dynamic unconscious is open to alternative and simpler interpretations. Thus, slips of the tongue may reflect conscious feelings or feelings which are just below the surface, rather than hypothetical 'deeply submerged' ones, or they may simply be speech errors (Reason, 2000). When a speaker was congratulated on giving a 'millstone' lecture, the host was probably aware of his boredom!

Similarly, dreams may be the result of trying to make sense of random brain activity rather than unconscious wishes struggling for expression. Dreams can still be helpful in clarifying our real emotions, feelings and intentions, but not because they are anything to do with the 'unconscious'. Contemporary psychology recognizes that we process a lot of information outside awareness but this is a much more gentle conception of 'unconscious' than the dynamic one, more like a robot or a computer than a set of forces or energies. On this view, the dynamic unconscious in its Freudian sense is a myth, though a slippery one (Spinelli, 2001), and thus cannot be part of a useful integration with other theories. However, to leave it out or substantially dilute it isn't a real integration either.

The list of types of goal for counselling and psychotherapy in Box 8.1 illustrates further the issues raised so far. Some of the goals are clearly more in harmony with some orientations than others but what proportions of counsel-

---

**Box 8.1  A provocative list of possible goals in counselling**

✦ Support.

✦ Psycho-educational guidance.

✦ Adjustment and resource provision.

✦ Crisis intervention and management.

✦ Problem-solving and decision-making.

✦ Symptom amelioration.

✦ Insight and understanding.

✦ Cure.

✦ Self-actualization.

✦ Personality change.

✦ Discovery of meaning and transcendental experience.

✦ Systemic, organizational or social change.

Source: Summarized from Feltham (2000a)

lors versus psychotherapists would claim or reject each of them? And does what each group actually do and feel with their clients vary accordingly, or are other factors more important?

## Counselling and Coaching

Recently another player has entered the helping field and is likely to cause much discussion in the future: coaching. There are basically two types of coaching. The first is business or executive coaching which focuses on improving performance at work by helping individuals get the best out of those they work with as well as helping them identify personal strengths, weaknesses, opportunities and threats (Fleming and Taylor, 1998).

The second type is life coaching, which is more general. For example, a life coach could help a person become more assertive with friends, enabling the individual to tackle people and situations he or she may have avoided for fear of looking silly or being rejected. Life coaching also helps people overcome personal blocks, such as taking up a healthier lifestyle, and encourages the individual to make the most of his or her most precious resource – him or herself (Harold, 2000). Although business and life coaching are seen as separate activities, many find they are linked. Sometimes what seems like a business problem may have its origins in the past and be related to other life factors.

There are coaches and coaching programmes for many individual areas such as stress, confidence, happiness and success. However, whatever the programme and presenting problem, coaching tends to be of a practical, skills-based nature, individually tailored to each person's requirements and fitted around his or her life and needs. It also tends to be outcome driven, usually short term and is not a substitute for personal motivation – the person still has to take responsibility for the problem, the changes he or she makes and the amount of work he or she chooses to do (Martin, 2001).

Coaching obviously closely resembles (at least) counselling as defined at the beginning of this chapter. However, its 'image' is different and it may be more suitable than counselling for some clients because they are likely to feel less of a stigma in visiting a coach than a therapeutic practitioner. It would be interesting to discover in which circumstances people would prefer to see a coach, counsellor or psychotherapist.

A political criticism of coaching is that it is a means of helping people to 'fit in' with dominant and controlling ideas of what it means to be a 'successful' person, rather than enabling people to challenge existing ideas and helping them to make changes in their own lives that may not be approved of by others but are more personally satisfying to the individual concerned. However, many coaches too are concerned with the personal development of their clients and some of those clients do not feel that they have a 'problem' as such but would rather explore how they operate and who they are in a bid to improve the way they function in the world. As in counselling, the agenda is then based around the client's own wishes and goals (Neenan and Dryden, 2002). Moreover, in both coaching and counselling there are practitioners who think they know better than their clients and try to influence them accordingly, often in a well meaning way. (A central ethic of counsellor training is to challenge this motive and behaviour and thus respect client autonomy.) Many counsellors also work as coaches.

## Working as a Counsellor

In this section we approach the question of what counsellors do, in three ways: snapshots of typical days from two experienced counsellors chosen for their contrasting settings and personalities; an indication of the stresses and rewards of counselling; and a discussion of some aspects of private practice. The work settings of counsellors and psychotherapists are:

◆ Voluntary agencies;

◆ Residential care;

◆ Education;

◆ The workplace;

◆ Primary health care; and

◆ Private practice (Feltham, 2000b).

Numbers of counsellors are increasing quite dramatically in at least some of these settings. For example, 51% of a representative sample of general practices in England and Wales were found in a 1998 survey to employ an on-site counsellor compared with 31% in 1992 (Mellor-Clark, 2000). This raises another issue: the emphasis in counsellors' work on what might be called problems with living or 'psycho-education' (Dryden, 1994, who hoped this aspect would remain central) or on more clinical problems, like those common in primary care (Mellor-Clark, 2000).

In Box 8.2 we include notes on two counsellors' days. There is no implication in these two accounts that either style fits either setting more comfortably and effectively. Indeed, many counsellors have a portfolio approach to work. Their activities may include supervision of others, training, research, their own supervision, their own personal counselling or therapy, writing and professional body activities.

---

**Box 8.2  Two counsellors' days**

**A day in the life of a student counsellor (Niru Williams)**
Getting to work is always a bit of a rush as I drop my son off to school first. Then I brave the traffic to get to work by 9.30 a.m. I work at the University of East London (UEL) as a student counsellor, within the Counselling and Advisory Service.

I believe it's very important not to be late for my student clients. I also don't like to rush straight into a counselling session so I usually start my first appointment at 10 a.m. This also gives me time to check any messages, catch up on emails and get myself a drink. I normally see between four to five clients

▶

per day and I work across three different campuses. It can be quite challenging trying to manage three diaries simultaneously. I have to confess that I wouldn't be able to do this without our administrator. The support I receive from my colleagues too is invaluable, especially as we often work alone at each campus. It's reassuring to know that I can pick up the telephone and know there will be someone to offer a listening ear to me!

I usually see three clients in the morning and two in the afternoon – four on-going clients and one assessment. The sessions last for 50 minutes. This gives me 10 minutes in between to get a drink and prepare for my next client. I like to leave the last hour at work to write up my case notes, check emails and deal with any matters that may have arisen during the day. A normal day can be quite hectic, challenging, frustrating but rarely dull or boring!

A typical day varies according to when it is in the academic year. For example, in September I am busy giving inductions to new students about the Counselling and Advisory Service. At this time I usually offer more assessment appointments but, by mid-October, I usually have a full client load. There are points during the academic year when I try to keep a few appointments available for crisis work, for example, Christmas and examination times. During the summer vacation, I continue to see some regular clients although it is generally quieter as most students are away. This period is used to collate evaluations and statistics, write our annual report, update information leaflets, prepare for the next induction period and to take my summer holidays.

I am also involved in other activities such as offering workshops – for example, stress and relaxation, staff development, team meetings, supervision, teaching on the Postgraduate Diploma in Counselling and keeping up to date with my own professional development.

I work with a very diverse student group and they bring a variety of problems – academic, relationship, depression, cultural, self-harm, sexuality, etc. There are many different ethnic groups from the local community and we also have many international students from around the world. The age range can be 18 to 50 plus, with students from different social groups. Traditional learners, who come via the A-level route, mingle alongside mature students, who may have few or no formal qualifications. This latter group of students often lack confidence, have high expectations and are trying to juggle caring for young children alongside their studies.

It is a joy to see how education can change a student's life and the important role that counselling can play in this process. A student I finished working with last year, whom I saw on and off during her degree, told me in her first session, 'I'm a single mum from Dagenham with a criminal record. What am I doing here?' She graduated with a 2:2 and is now working with vulnerable adolescents. Education gave her an opportunity to transform her life and through the process of counselling she gained self-respect and self-confidence. She is typical of the inspirational students we see at UEL.

**A day in the life of a self-employed practitioner (Glade and McMahon)**

| Time | Activity |
|------|----------|
| 7.45 a.m. | Open office and prepare for first client. |
| 8.00 a.m. | First client session. |
| 9.00 a.m. | Enter payment details in cash book, write account details on back of cheque and enter in paying-in book for banking later in the week (repeated for every client). Complete client notes and make a note to write to the client's GP later in the day. |
| 9.15 a.m. | Second and third client sessions. |
| 11.30 a.m. | Payment details etc. Make note to speak to supervisor about one of my clients at next supervision session. I have concerns regarding therapeutic alliance and my own part in this. Have a hot drink and listen to messages on answerphone Check emails and letters and respond. Reminder letter from accountant regarding books, receipts, invoices, bank statements and all relevant financial materials for annual auditing and submission to tax office. Make a note to ensure all cash book entries are up to date, basic book-keeping completed and materials ready to be taken to accountant in 4 days' time. |
| 12.30 p.m. | Fourth client session. |
| 1.45 p.m. | Lunch. |
| 2.45 p.m. | Write letter to GP about first client. Prepare entry for the BACP resources directory. Complete application for one day training towards continuing professional development (CPD), also complete relevant forms to demonstrate what is hoped will be achieved by attending. Complete entry for last CPD activity undertaken stating what benefits were gained from the seminar. Start to read article in *The Psychologist* on changes in chartership criteria. |
| 3.45 p.m. | Fifth and last client session for the day. |
| 5.00–6.00 p.m. | Prepare brief letter to be sent to all complementary health practitioners in the area as part of a marketing exercise for client referrals. Complete application form to become an associate for an EAP (Employee Assistance Programme) scheme. Prepare items for discussion in supervision session for 9 a.m. the following morning. Check voicemail, return calls to two possible new clients. One wishes to attend for an assessment interview, prepare information sheet and covering letter. Second client not available, make a note to ring later in the evening. Ensure all client files and notes safely locked away. Take letters to catch post first thing the following day. |

## Some Stresses of Counselling

Stress is difficult to define well (Jones and Bright, 2001). However, a useful working definition is 'the experience of unpleasant over or under stimulation, as defined by the individual in question, that actually or potentially leads to ill health' (Bond, 1986: 2). This definition emphasizes individual experience, hints at feeling threatened and strained to the extent of being overwhelmed, and includes too much stimulation as well as too little, as in 'bored out of my mind'.

Boredom can be used therapeutically by counsellors through the skill of immediacy (Bayne et al., 1999). However, counsellors are more likely to feel overwhelmed than bored by their work. Working with clients who were abused as children or in later life, who are seriously ill or emotionally disturbed, or who may be felt as threatening or potentially violent, demands a lot from counsellors who are expected to remain calm, understanding and relatively non-judgemental. Many challenging experiences of these types in a short space of time, or even routinely for some counsellors, can accumulate and become very stressful. They may also become stressed by becoming unhelpfully over-involved with the distressing details of a client's life story, or overanxious about a client's safety or threat of suicide, for example. In such circumstances, inadequate or infrequent supervision, or a lack of emotional support in the workplace or at home, can exacerbate the stresses involved.

Feelings of inadequacy or lack of skill, knowledge or experience in dealing with some very challenging or complex issues can also be very stressful. Good supervisory and other support is essential at these times. Counsellors also need to develop the self-awareness and professional judgement that are required to refer clients who they find too difficult to other counsellors or forms of help, without accompanying feelings of personal failure or inadequacy.

Stress can also be experienced when the demands of the working environment are felt to be excessive (large amounts of bureaucracy or inadequate resources, for example), or when they conflict with a counsellor's personal values or ethics. Excessive workload is another source of stress. We know of some counsellors who are expected to work with more than 20 clients each week. Together with the required paperwork and finding time for supervision, these counsellors find little time or opportunity for quiet reflection on their work, or for relaxation between sessions.

Working in private practice brings its own stresses. Finding enough clients willing or able to pay an appropriate fee can be a problem, especially when starting out and more so in some geographical areas than others. The need to keep proper accounts for tax purposes, to pay for consulting rooms and insurance, for example, can cause anxiety and a feeling of insecurity. Clients who are in employment may need appointments in the evenings or at weekends, and this can disrupt family life and erode opportunities for recreation and relaxation. Difficult counselling sessions can leave counsellors unable or unwilling to attend to the needs of their children, and there are many other problematic aspects of working from home (Syme, 1994).

There is quite extensive research on stress in counsellors. For example, Brady et al. (1995) distinguished seven 'burdens':

1 Patient (client) behaviours such as suicide, dependence, not turning up.

2 Working conditions – for example, too many clients.

3 Emotional depletion.

4 Physical isolation.

5 Therapeutic relationships.

6 Personal disruption – the counsellor's own problems affecting the quality of his or her counselling.

7 'Psychic isolation' – lack of intimacy and emotional support.

On therapeutic relationships, Brady et al. (pp. 15–16) wrote (perhaps rather dramatically): 'We alternate between sleepless nights fraught with recollections of hostility and anxiety incurred from characterologically impaired patients, and fleeting moments of realisation that we have genuinely assisted a fellow human being.' They end their review on a *fairly* positive note: 'Most of us feel enriched, nourished and privileged in conducting counselling, but these benefits come at a significant cost' (p. 23).

## Some Rewards of Counselling

Counselling can be a very rewarding occupation. Helping someone overcome very difficult and challenging life circumstances can bring great personal satisfaction for the counsellor. Focusing on the life and experience of another person in ways that enable the healing of past emotional hurt, and encourage a more creative outlook for the future, is, in itself, a rewarding and worthwhile experience.

Other rewards are more indirect. Counsellor training involves the development of understanding and sensitivity towards others, and these qualities can be reflected in a counsellor's personal life and relationships. Having an awareness of the way in which destructive behaviour is often a result of damaging life experience can help us to become more tolerant and understanding of others. Knowing that it is possible to transform such behaviour, together with underlying attitudes and values, into something more constructive and creative helps us to remain optimistic for ourselves and others.

Counsellor training also involves the development of self-awareness and insight into our own histories and characters, and these days trainee counsellors are expected to engage in some direct experience of being a client in counselling and all counsellors are expected to undertake at least 30 hours of continuing professional development (CPD) each year. Apart from helping us to appreciate the counselling process 'from the inside', our own personal counselling can help us to become more understanding of ourselves, and can help us change things that we don't like or that adversely affect our relationships with our clients and others.

## Some Issues and Practicalities of Private Practice

Some practitioners think it is unethical to run a practice and charge people directly for what could be deemed mental health issues more properly dealt with through the taxation system and the NHS (Pilgrim, 1993). Many believe that counselling is available generally only to those who can afford it and that it is offered by white, middle-class practitioners to middle-class clients. However, it is also interesting that most practitioners explore the possibility of private practice at some point in their career, and it does give them considerable autonomy. On the other hand, there are also numerous problems.

To start with, private practice means running a small business. Market research – finding out about likely customers, competitors and the probable demand for services – is an important first step. The practice location is a key factor as working in a sparsely populated or economically impoverished area is likely to ensure financial insecurity (Feltham, 2002). Business planning, accountancy, marketing, advertising and administration all play a significant part (Syme, 1994; McMahon,1994). There is also a range of professional issues to be considered, such as further training, supervision, communication outside the counselling session, privacy, security, confidentiality, punctuality, CPD, note-taking, accreditation, after-hours accessibility, the nature and form of contract between the practitioner and the client and the development of trust and care (McMahon, 1994; Shapiro, 2000). Factors such as the client group seen, whether to engage in open-ended or time-limited counselling, experience and stamina all affect the number of weekly client contact hours that can be safely undertaken.

Private practitioners will probably earn less in the first few years and, at the same time, have extra expenses – for their room, perhaps, telephone bills, postage, training, purchase of equipment, and professional body and registration fees. There are no paid holidays or sick leave, no employer's superannuation schemes and the majority of private practitioners work in isolation for most of the working week – no colleagues to help relieve the pressures of difficult clients or intense counselling sessions.

## Some Trends and Issues in Counselling

From many possibilities, we have chosen aspects of four: brief counselling, evaluation, specialisms and professionalism, including accreditation and statutory regulation.

### Brief counselling

Brief or time-limited counselling is generally understood to be around six sessions. Many agencies, including GPs' surgeries, see this as the limit, while others allow a review after six sessions, with an extension possible. In practice, most counselling relationships are for fewer than six weeks anyway (Feltham, 1997) but the obvious issue is: what about clients who need longer? Is their time in counselling to be limited by economics? Thorne's (1995: 35) view was that market forces are too influential, and barbaric in their effects: 'The creeping contamination of almost all areas of our corporate life by the forces of the market place means that more and more people experience themselves not as persons but as consumers or providers and as potential victims on the altars of cost-effectiveness and efficiency.'

On the other hand, it is unethical for clients to be encouraged to stay longer in counselling than they need – they may be being exploited, another client could be seen – and many people can be helped in a few sessions. Thorne (1999: 7) described an experiment on himself, stimulated by the thought that 'lives can be changed in the twinkling of an eye . . . The notion that meaningful change can only come about as the result of long and painstaking processes is clearly untrue'. His experiment was to offer just three sessions of person-centred counselling to clients with concerns such as delayed grief, the aftermath of rape, performance phobia and physical abuse. To his surprise he judged the sessions to be effective, and he was impressed by how much clients prepared for them.

However, at the same time Thorne wondered if it was really 'a charade, an abject capitulation to a mad world', if the counselling had worked only because it fits 'a world which is constantly on the hoof', a world of management values like short-term effectiveness performance indicators and accountability. His values are to put down roots, reflect, not be 'forever in a rush, consumed with busyness' and to know how to wait. These values lead to a further twist in his argument: he believes that they and related personal qualities are necessary for effective brief counselling.

## Evaluation

The fundamental evaluation issue of whether or not counselling works has been resolved (Bergin and Garfield, 1994; McLeod, 1998; Hubble et al., 1999; Department of Health, 2001a; 2001b). We do not yet fully understand *how* it works, though the finding that most approaches work most of the time – the Dodo bird verdict – strongly supports the 'common factors' view (Hubble et al., 1999). If so, then comparative outcome studies are 'costly experiments in futility' (Ahn and Wampold, 2001) and counselling research should focus on clarifying the various possible common factors and ways of making them more effective. A further implication is that the important elements of training are intensive practice of listening and respect for clients' strengths and ideas (Tallman and Bohart, 1999), and the emphasis therefore should be on interviewing skills, the therapeutic relationship and the core conditions. However, techniques matter too because they can contribute to the client's trust in the relationship and possibly because some techniques (and counsellors) are better matches with some clients than others (Hubble et al., 1999).

Evaluation of counselling can take many other forms – for example, reflecting on work with clients after a session has ended (McMahon, 1994), considering the social, cultural and organizational issues that could influence the therapeutic relationship (Lago and Thompson, 1996) and counselling supervision (Carroll, 1996). For those involved in research, it is common practice in workplace counselling settings for the client to provide feedback to the organization about the practitioner, his or her experiences of the therapeutic process and subjectively to rate perceived outcome (McLeod, 2001). BACP has, in recent years, thrown its weight behind the CORE system which is now being used in a number of therapeutic settings (Mellor-Clark, 2000) (CORE stands for Clinical Outcomes in Routine Evaluation). For the first time, data are being collected in a systematic manner over a number of years. The system allows for individual therapist work to be evaluated as well as providing larger-scale statistical insights, but the administrative costs are high.

Beliefs about the role of evaluation differ considerably depending in part on therapeutic orientation. Practitioners from a cognitive-behavioural background tend to see evaluation in a positive light, believing that it helps provide the client with greater control over therapeutic process and improves practice (Dryden *et al*, 1995). Practitioners from other orientations may see evaluation as damaging to the essence of the therapeutic relationship, as being more about performance than quality of being (Tudor and Merry, 2002). There is also a political argument that evaluation is more about justifying and maintaining financial constraints and political whims than it is about the needs of the client.

## Specialisms

Counselling is expanding very fast, too fast for some observers: 'Can there be too much counselling, too many courses, too many publications?' (Jacobs, 1995). And one of the ways in which it is expanding is by creating specialisms such as HIV/AIDS counselling and bereavement counselling. Two, obviously opposed, views on this aspect of expansion are: 1) that at least some of the specialisms are justified; and 2) that they are marketing ploys and specious.

At first glance, developing skills and expertise in working with particular groups of people (e.g. young people, the elderly, ethnic minorities) or with particular 'problems' (e.g. bereavement, alcoholism, sexual abuse) seems an obviously good idea. Particular people, or particular kinds of problems, the argument goes, need experts with specialist knowledge in order to respond to them effectively. Many counsellors do not have this specialist knowledge or experience, and such clients are best left to counsellors who do.

While this argument has some merit, and may be a better argument in some circumstances than others (McLeod, 1998; Bimrose, 2000), it is in danger of creating a profession that has abandoned the idea that counselling consists of a general set of values, attitudes and relationship skills that can benefit all people, no matter what the 'presenting problem'. Instead, counselling becomes a 'technology' based on the accurate identification of subgroups within society, and a whole raft of possible problems, each with its own counselling response. Moreover, there is often as much variety within subgroups as there is between subgroups. Being a member of a particular group does not necessarily mean that an individual is typical of that group, or representative of it in any real sense. Identifying subgroups can lead to stereotyping and treating people as if they are representative of their group, rather than as unique individuals who have some things in common with others, but who also have many differences.

A further argument against at least some specialisms in counselling is that their very existence can create serious self-doubt in the minds of counsellors and therapists who, perhaps mistakenly, believe that certain problems are beyond their competence. While this may sometimes be true (depending on the training and experience of the individual), it isn't always so by any means. A counsellor who is able to enter into deep, non-judgemental, caring and non-possessive relationships with others, and sustain them, can be effective across a whole range of groups and problems. If the point of view that the source of healing resides in clients themselves together with their experience of being understood in the kind of relationship just described is correct, then specific knowledge of specific problems or groups becomes far less important.

## Professionalism, accreditation and statutory regulation

Counselling has been becoming more and more 'professional' in the last few years, a trend which has been criticized as too controlling, too defensive (against possible litigation) and stifling (House and Totton, 1997; Thorne, 2002). A recent exception to this trend is the tone and number of BACP ethical codes for counsellors, supervisors, trainers and those who use counselling skills. Until last year they had become increasingly prescriptive and with an emphasis on what not to do. In contrast, the new *Ethical Framework for Good Practice in Counselling and Psychotherapy* (BACP, 2001) is much more positive, simpler in the sense of replacing all the other codes and, in particular, treats ethical problems as questions to be approached using principles (which may compete with each other) and as a process. It is thus more trusting and less controlling.

However, in 2002 the United Kingdom Council for Psychotherapy (UKCP) and the British Psychologyical Society (BPS) did not take this view of ethical codes and the overall trend is still towards tighter control. Thus more training courses are becoming accredited, and many people argue strongly for statutory regulation, which seems to be coming closer (Horton, 2002). There are also arguments against it (Horton, 2002; Thorne, 2002). Thorne, for example, argues that it does not protect the public better than voluntary self-regulation. Rather, therapists attracted by the power and arrogance which he associates with professionalism and statutory regulation are *more* likely to abuse their clients.

Other problems with statutory regulation are whether counselling and psychotherapy can be defined as an occupational group, and that there are competing professional bodies, with no sign of joint negotiations happening, financial issues and so on (Horton, 2002). More fundamentally, regulation implies that it is practitioner qualifications and skills, acquired in training, that are the most potent factors in positive outcomes. This is unlikely, as discussed earlier. However, and at the time of publication, the government has stated its intention to regulate, in some way, what they call 'the talking therapies'. Horton (2002: 61) concludes that 'The argument that at some stage statutory regulation is inevitable remains strong, however flawed and despite the dissenting voices'.

## Counsellor Education and Training

Counsellor education and training contain three elements: personal, practical and academic. The order here is deliberate and contrasts with traditional university values. It assumes that competence as a counsellor is more to do with the counsellor as a person than his or her knowledge of theory and research (though both these aspects matter). As a result, being a student on a counselling course can be unsettling and distressing because you are asked to reflect deeply on yourself and your attitudes and values. There is much more emphasis on personal development in counsellor training than in clinical psychology or psychiatry training. A general issue here, then, is that if increasing your self-awareness and working through feelings and reactions contributes to greater competence as a counsellor, why not for practitioners in the helping professions generally?

A related issue is whether or not personal therapy is a necessary strategy for personal development in counsellor training. The problems with it include cost (40 hours of counselling at an average £30 per hour is £1200), the lack of fit with some models of counselling (40 hours is too long for the cognitive approach, too short for the psychodynamic), and that trainees may not feel committed to an imposed requirement. Counter-arguments are that it's valuable experience in being a client and that 'real' clients are sometimes reluctant or resistant too. The research evidence is mixed but does not support (so far) a positive relationship with effectiveness as a counsellor (Macran and Shapiro, 1998).

However, the 40 hours' requirement may change, and BACP do offer trainees the alternative of citing 'an equivalent experience' to being a client, one which is 'consistent with the core theoretical model' of the particular training course. They deliberately do not give any guidance on what 'equivalent' means; it is up to the applicant to make a case. In the UEL course, the core model is an integration of humanistic and cognitive-behavioural approaches, and our view is that co-counselling (which apart from initial low-cost training is by definition free) and the course's form of journal work (applying the core model to oneself) are sufficiently equivalent experiences to counselling as defined by the course to contribute to the currently required 40 hours.

Further, nearly all aspects of a counselling course can stimulate personal development. For example, two of the essays in the UEL postgraduate Diploma ask students to apply, respectively, a model of transition and loss to a personal experience, and a personality theory to themselves. Clearly, both are very personal. The word 'I', banned from many undergraduate courses in pursuit of a spurious objectivity, is used often. In the same essays, students are also asked to be academically skilled: to evaluate the model and theory objectively as well as in terms of its relevance to themselves.

## QUESTIONS FOR REFLECTION AND DISCUSSION

1  What words and images do you associate with 'counsellor' and 'psychotherapist'? How realistic are they?

2  In what ways are counselling and friendship different?

3  A sexual relationship between a counsellor and his or her client is unethical. But what counts as sexual activity? And what about relationships with ex-clients?

4  How would you select people for counsellor training?

5  How would you assess someone's competence as a counsellor?

## Suggestions for further reading

Bayne, R., Horton, I., Merry, T., Noyes, L. and McMahon, G. (1999) *The Counsellor's Handbook. A Practical A–Z Guide to Professional and Clinical Practice* (2nd edn), Cheltenham: Stanley Thornes.
Brief entries on about 150 everyday aspects of counselling (e.g. beginnings, difficult clients, boundaries, sexual attraction and supervision). The entries on boredom, core conditions, brief counselling, congruence, emotions, empathy, multiculturalism, paraphrasing, silence and stress are particularly relevant to the PG Dip at UEL.

Macmillan, A. and Clark, D. (1998) *Learning and Writing in Counselling.* London: Sage.
This book discusses various 'tasks' and 'processes' involved in choosing a course, in training and in practising.

Yalom, I.D. (1989) *Love's Executioner and Other Tales of Psychotherapy.* Harmondsworth: Penguin Books.
This text presents vivid discussions of counselling with ten clients. It is fairly consistent with the UEL diploma's core model.

Feltham, C. and Horton, I. (eds) (2000) *Handbook of Counselling and Psychotherapy.* London: Sage.

McLeod, J. (1998) *An Introduction to Counselling* (2nd edn). Milton Keynes: Open University Press.
These two major textbook complement each other. The first brings together about 60 authors and over 100 topics with a largely practical emphasis. The second offers a more reflective consideration of some of those topics and others – for example, the role of research, the history of counselling and counsellor training.

## Training courses

For details of counselling courses accredited by the British Association for Counselling and Psychotherapy (BACP) phone 01788 550889.

# 9  The Professional Academic

*John Radford*

## SUMMARY

*Academic staff are normally qualified in a discipline and/or in a profession. Seldom, however, are they formally qualified in the large range of tasks they have to carry out, from teaching and research to administration. While the distribution of tasks varies, most academics will have to undertake most at some time. Nor are academics organized as such. They may owe allegiance to a discipline, a profession, an institution or, more recently, to a trade union. They signally lack the power and prestige of established professions such as law and medicine. Some of the causes of this situation, and possible changes, are discussed. It is argued that psychologists in particular ought to be at the forefront of developing an academic profession in that, of all disciplines, psychology is the most fundamental to education. A significant move has been the foundation of the Division for Teachers and Researchers in Psychology, within the British Psychological Society. This creates a route to the status of chartered psychologist for those whose main activity is teaching or research. The main dangers of professionalism are arrogance and rigidity, but it is argued that these can be avoided, while the benefits, to both the client and the practitioner, are very clear. There are, however, many obstacles in the way, which may prove insuperable.*

## Introduction

> If you are a real scholar you are thrust out in the cold. Unless you are a money-maker, I say, you will be considered a fool, a pauper. The lucrative arts, such as law and medicine, are now in vogue, and only those things are pursued which have a cash value (John of Salisbury, died 1180).

> To the members of the most responsible, the least advertised, the worst paid, and the most richly rewarded profession in the world (Ian Hay, dedication to *The Lighter Side of School Life*, 1914).

> Academic salaries are pretty comical, especially when you reflect on what your average academic has to do these days. . . . It is no secret that many of our best academics have left Britain to go where their work is appreciated, where they are freed from bureaucracy and where they are better paid (Susan Bassnett, Pro-Vice-Chancellor, University of Warwick, *The Times Higher Educational Supplement*, 1 March 2002).

*Plus ça change*, one might say. Ian Hay was writing of public schools, but there was a continuity of ethos, curriculum and personnel between these and the two ancient universities, and to an extent still is. The last remark is true, but the fact is that academic malaise is worldwide (Boyer et al., 1994; Altbach, 1996). To many it seems that they are no longer 'richly rewarded' in any terms. Certainly their status is far more ambiguous than that of the other professions featured in this volume. Indeed to some the words 'professional' and 'academic' may seem ill-matched. A decade ago Barnett and Middlehurst (1993) claimed that 'In the United Kingdom, the higher education community is being deprived of components of its professionalism just when it is clarifying to itself the nature of that professionalism'. Or rather, 'academics are changing from being a status group to being a proletariat without ever having been a profession.' Others have written of 'workers in the knowledge factories' (Smyth, 1995).

Some have eagerly embraced this role. Sally Hunt, newly appointed as General Secretary of the Association of University Teachers, states bluntly: 'I am a trade unionist, and I want what is best for the members. It is as simple as that' (*The Times Higher Educational Supplement*, 12 April, 2002). Some may feel this is the way forward; others, clinging to delusions of duty, service and professionalism, may find it profoundly depressing. Students, who tend to see a simple black and white picture of bosses versus workers, may not realize that, without such delusions, some of them might not graduate at all.

## The Academic 'Profession'

There are no universally recognized criteria for what constitutes a profession (see, for example, Warren Piper, 1992; Eraut, 1994; Radford, 1994; 1997). But there are frequently cited characteristics, including: formal and intellectual training and qualification, based on a shared body of knowledge, both practical and theoretical; a commitment to acting in the best interests of the client, and acceptance of codes of conduct, enforceable when necessary; exclusion of the unqualified; accountability for what is achieved rather than for specific actions (one does not ask, indeed usually cannot tell, whether the surgeon is using the right instrument or the barrister quoting the right precedent); responsible, autonomous work without direct supervision; and autonomy and self-regulation of the profession itself.

The tradition in the UK has been for emerging professions to develop their own regulatory mechanisms, through professional associations, and at some stage seek to enshrine these in national legislation. This was the path followed by both law and medicine, and it is also that adopted by psychology. The British Psychological Society (BPS) began as a scientific society in 1901 but, in the course of the century, became also a professional one, rather unusually continuing a dual function. In contrast, in many countries professions are regulated directly by the state, a tradition stemming (in Europe) largely from Napoleon, and this has extended to academia, with universities being under more or less close governmental control. (When years ago my colleague Kjell Raaheim was first appointed professor at the University of Bergen, Norway, the instrument had to be signed by the King. This is no longer so.)

It is obvious that academics meet only some of these criteria. The vast majority are 'professional' in a general sense. They are paid at least something (unless emeritus). They work long and conscientiously without direct supervision or sticking rigidly to rules or hours, although such behaviour is constantly being eroded by sheer numbers of students, combined with ever-increasing bureaucratic demands. They still frequently put their clients' interests ahead of their own, willingly giving up extra time to keen, or weak, students. On the other hand academics are hardly organized at all as such and, consequently, lack self-regulation; they cannot exclude those unqualified (indeed many would strongly object to such an idea); and they are in general untrained. It has long been pointed out that it is odd that those who are in a sense the gatekeepers of all professions should not themselves constitute a profession (for example, Perkin, 1987; Elton, 1989; Radford, 1994). Perkin points to some of the reasons. Their loyalties are often divided among discipline, institution and occupation. They have in the past often failed to guarantee the worth of what they have to offer, and to make the public aware of it. They relied for too long on an assumption of 'effortless superiority' and (up to about 30 years ago) on a comfortable security in a pleasant and reasonably rewarding (both financially and personally) occupation. Such was the situation reported in Halsey and Trow's (1971) classic study *The British Academics*.

## Academic Preparation

'Academics' are a somewhat motley crew, with only a partial common identity (Henkel, 2000). There is, in the UK, no legal restriction on who may teach in a university. Many, including the present author, would wish to retain such freedom as a matter of principle. In practice, nearly all those appointed have either academic or professional qualifications or both. The former now nearly always includes a PhD. But the latter are hardly ever in the field they are actually employed in – that is, in the host of things that make up the daily work of a member of the teaching/research staff of a university – what in the USA is more neatly termed the faculty (but I shall retain the British usage). A social worker or a lawyer will be qualified in that occupation, but not in producing future members of the profession. Burgess et al. (1998) remark that until recently there has been relatively little discussion of postgraduate education in the UK. The nearest approach to a professional academic qualification is the PhD. This marks, at least ostensibly, a training in research, which is one function of some staff. Even in this, it is often rather notoriously inadequate (for example, Noble, 1994). PhD students may work in a productive group, or virtually alone, with minimal supervision; may receive almost no training in methodology, and may learn little more than is needed for a highly specialized project; may take excessively long to completion, or drop out altogether; and in any case may well learn little if anything of all the other activities required of a 'faculty' member (although now some untrained teaching is usually included, largely to relieve pressures on the regular staff). Still less likely are they to learn anything of the broader educational and cultural contexts within which they will work.

Almost a side-effect, although a crucial one, of the lack of formal training of academics is that they are constantly overtaken by events. Lacking any historical perspective, they are unaware of what universities are or have been, or might be, and why. With no grounding in educational principles, they are at the mercy of every pedagogical fad and fashion. (The words 'module' and 'semester' spring to mind. Both have been adopted almost overnight with minimal justification or awareness of their original context or appropriateness, and despite little evidence of positive and some of negative outcomes – see Rothblatt, 1991; Newstead, 2000.) Without any grasp of educational philosophy, academics find themselves intellectually helpless against a spate of political shenanigans and prejudices.

## Changing Circumstances

Probably at no time or place has higher education not been subject to change. But it is generally accepted that the pace has increased vastly in the last half century. Without going into the reasons behind this, I have elsewhere (Radford, 1999) listed the main changes, in no particular order and surely completely uncontroversially, as these:

1 An increasing demand for higher education, and a proliferation of institutions.
2 The participation of women in higher education up to, and beyond, parity with males.
3 Rising costs, especially due to growth in science and technology.
4 An increasing gap between costs and available funds.
5 A progressive extension of centralized government control of both finance and curriculum.
6 An emphasis on research as the primary activity of academics.

Some of these, such as the first, have been present since the start of western universities, indeed most likely since anything recognizable as higher education, probably the priesthoods of the earliest cities. Others such as the second and the last begin effectively only in the later nineteenth century. They are common in varying degrees to higher education around the world, and various solutions have been offered to the problems they pose. Currently, most observers of the UK fail to discern any very marked success here.

It is always risky to predict the future, but it does seem reasonably safe to say, as being already the case and likely to continue, that academics are going to have to undertake a widening range of tasks under increasingly adverse conditions. For most of these they are ill-prepared. They will have a wider range of students, in ability, social class, age, mode of study and cultural background including religious dogma at odds with the western tradition (McKenzie, 1987; Levine, 1997; Light and Cox, 2001). For the majority, research will not be a major component. There simply will not be the funds or the time. Trow (1987) pointed out that:

the past has shown that no genuine mass higher education system anywhere has been able to expand research in universities in line with expansion in teaching. Either separate institutions have developed for the two forms of mass and elite education, or both have been provided within the same institution.

The idea of training, not just for research but for other academic functions especially teaching, has been around for some time (Elton, 1989). In our discipline, the Association for the Teaching of Psychology, the first such organization in the UK, was the result of an initiative by the present author and the late James Breese in 1970. It was not, as sometimes thought, originally mainly concerned with pre-degree courses, in particular GCE A-level, which was introduced at the same time. It was the subject, not the level, that was the original defining characteristic. I can recall from my own student days not so far before that, however, the view of one lecturer that teaching should not be too good, as it would blur the natural distinction between the more and the less able.

More recently, the Dearing Report (National Committee of Enquiry into Higher Education, 1997) recommended training for academics, explaining:

the essence of professionalism is a thorough and up-to-date grasp of the fundamental knowledge base of the occupation; sufficient understanding of the theoretical principles to be able to adapt to novel circumstances and to incorporate research findings into practice; and appropriate practical skills and professional values.

Exactly. The main specific outcome so far has been the creation of the Institute for Learning and Teaching (ILT) which, in March 2002, recruited its 10 000th member. This has the following requirements for membership (summarized):

*Core knowledge*: 1. subject knowledge; 2. appropriate methods for teaching and learning; 3. models of how students learn; 4. methods for monitoring and evaluating one's own teaching; 5. implications of quality assurance for practice.

*Professional values*: 1. commitment to scholarship; 2. respect for individual learners; 3. commitment to the development of learning communities; 4. commitment to encouraging participation in higher education and equality of opportunity; 5. commitment to continued reflection, evaluation and improvement of one's own practice (Race, 2001).

Dearing has probably also accelerated the provision of inservice training courses for new staff, and most universities now provide these, some of up to 500 hours and some compulsory. Many are accredited by the ILT. Badley (1999) reviews the various attempts to improve teaching, including the Teaching Quality Assessment. However, training for academics does not, so far, seem to arouse their general enthusiasm. Leitner (1998) reported it unpopular, especially in the German-speaking world, and Radford et al. (1999) found similar attitudes in a detailed study of two universities in Britain and Norway, respectively. As to the assessment exercise, this has suffered from precisely the fault that underlies weakness in the performance of academics themselves – namely, ignorance of, or bland indifference to, all that research and the experience of centuries has taught us about how to do such things. Howarth (1993), in a widely circulated paper, drew attention to this knowledge, but it swiftly became apparent that politics, not facts, were the over-riding determiners. As, indeed, they generally have been in higher education (Carswell, 1985). At the same time, changes are constantly being made, and one must hope that some of these turn out better.

## Academic Tasks

In any case, teaching is only one function of academics, although it can be held to be the most central (Altbach, 1991). An institution with little or no research might still claim to offer 'higher education' if it maintained adequate levels of scholarship. A purely research one could not. It may also be the case that many, perhaps most, academics do find their way to becoming at least adequate teachers, especially given the enthusiasm for their discipline that brings them into it in the first place. This is not to say there is not much room for improvement.

There is much research on what academics do. Surveys of how they spend their time usually rely on a relatively small number of categories – for example, 'teaching', 'research', 'other' (Altbach, 1996; Enders and Teichler, 1997; Martinez et al., 1998). The purpose of these studies is to give a picture of the academic workload. But in considering preparation for a career, it is not so much a matter of time allocation as of the whole range of skills that may be required. 'Teaching', for example, varies from lecturing to several hundred, to one-to-one tutorials, small group work, laboratory and fieldwork supervision, workshops and so on. I am not aware of any detailed occupational analysis of academic work, but a short reflection shows that most academics will need to carry out, in varying degrees and at different times, most of the following:

+ *Research* in the refereed journal sense.
+ *Scholarship* and study.
+ *Professional practice* in an applied field, including consultancy.
+ *General writing*, course materials, textbooks, mass media, etc.
+ *Membership of professional bodies* with varied duties and functions.
+ *Teaching* in multiple modes, with concomitant preparation and marking.
+ *Counselling* and individual student guidance and advice.
+ *Course development*, including curriculum and syllabus design.
+ *Internal validation* processes and 'quality assessment'.
+ *Student recruitment* and selection.
+ *Assessment*, including formal examinations, course work, qualitative assessment, etc.
+ *Administration*, from record-keeping to co-ordinating the work of colleagues or assistants, timetable construction, ensuring supplies of equipment or source material, etc.

✦ *External relations* with the general public, parents, schools and colleges, employers, professional bodies.

✦ *Internal politics* and negotiations, including committee work as member, chair or secretary.

✦ *Clerical work*, especially wordprocessing and filing.

✦ *Meeting demands of external accreditation bodies*, rapidly developing into a virtually full-time occupation; and perhaps taking part as an assessor.

This is no doubt an incomplete list, but each item has two characteristics. There is a well established body of relevant knowledge and experience available. And academics are almost entirely ignorant of it. When it comes to administrators and policy-makers, it appears we can omit the 'almost'. But that is beyond the present brief. A newly appointed PhD is familiar, in all likelihood, with only the first two activities on the list. A social worker in a first teaching post may know only the third. Interviewing an applicant for such a post, I asked what he expected students to know at the end of, say, the first term or year. He replied, 'You can't express it!' I am not convinced that if the teacher cannot express it, the student will learn it. And of course there is a very substantial body of research-based expertise on teaching even such ineffable subjects as social work. Raaheim et al. (1991) offered a review of what helps students to learn, and the authors would claim that their conclusions still stand after 10 years' further research.

Psychology graduates will at least have learnt a good deal about learning and memory, some of it concerned with practical applications, but not much about conveying information to others. Graduates in other disciplines will lack even this knowledge. Similarly when it comes to, for example, the setting and marking of formal examinations (Newstead, 1992). Even among trained psychologists, such fundamental concepts of assessment as standardization, reliability and validity are seldom if ever mentioned (Radford, 2002). To most other graduates they will be unknown. Anyone who has worked in the GCE/GCSE system, itself very far from perfect, cannot but notice a far more professional approach there (brought about, admittedly, largely by the enormous numbers these systems deal with). Often academics must design a curriculum, or take over an existing one; seldom are they familiar with different models that have been used or their relative advantages and disadvantages (Radford, 1992).

## Higher Levels of Knowledge

Beyond any such list, as already suggested, there are higher levels of knowledge and skill necessary if professionals are to determine their own destiny at least to some extent, both individually and collectively. Academic leadership will fall to some, requiring special qualities (Moses and Roe, 1990; Middlehurst, 1993). Heads of departments are now frequently offered 'management training'

(Eley, 1994), but this is not always appropriate to higher education, and leadership in any case may be needed well before that exalted role is reached. Academics, especially younger ones, lack the confidence and the skill to resist the more grossly absurd demands upon them, and the knowledge to show why they are unacceptable and what is a better way. They need to be able to defend the rationale of their professional practice. As things are, all too often they are driven hither and thither by pressures that seem as capricious and uncontrollable as the British weather. Still further, changes in both society and technology are already presenting new challenges and problems, or opportunities: distance (in fact, worldwide) learning; private and corporate higher education; continuing education; new patterns of knowledge, and of enrolment and study; and so on (Taylor, 1999; Salmi, 2001).

And there are yet wider questions that concern the whole purpose of higher education, questions which go back at least to Confucius and Lao-tse (Chaplin, 1978; Tweed and Lehman, 2002). Far-reaching decisions are made about education based on unchallenged assumptions held by those making the policy. It is surely the role of academics, if anyone, to take a wider view. Nearly all the vast literature devoted to the purpose of higher education stresses values and qualities beyond formal training and qualifications. Every institution, probably, now has a more or less high-flown 'mission statement' (Allen, 1988). Thus the psychologist, Karl Jaspers (1960): 'Instruction and research must aim for more than the bare transmission of facts and skills. They must aim for formation of the whole man, for education in the broadest sense of the term.' There is not space to debate such issues here (see Radford et al., 1997). But if there is anything at all in these wider views, then at some point in their preparation, future academics must become systematically aware of them. Nothing like this happens at present. Modular degrees may produce graduates with no overview even of their own discipline, and specialized research doctorates result in what has been labelled 'the uneducated PhD' (source unknown).

## Education for Academics

How these lacunae may be dealt with is open to question. There is a flood of books offering more or less relevant advice. Provision of short courses, inservice training, etc., may help, but it can be argued that far more radical changes are needed, although at the same time they are most unlikely to come about. If, at the simplest, most staff will not be doing very much research, steps must be taken to ensure satisfactory career progression is not dependent upon it. Of course not all promotions are research based; but many are, and for many academics research prestige, and a research career, are what really count. Indeed, it is often these, or more selflessly a fascination with the discipline itself, that brought them into the university in the first place. Somehow such fascination, admirable in itself, must be balanced with the reality of the demand for mass teaching, and all that goes with it.

There is a case for a specialized, and improved, Postgraduate Certificate of Education (PGCE; normally a one-year course). There is a case for the development of a full professional qualification more appropriate than the PhD (Radford, 2001). One can conceive of a Doctorate of Higher Education which might include discipline material at a higher level than a first degree (particularly in view of the disjointed nature of modular degrees); history and concepts of (especially higher) education; psychology of teaching and learning; pedagogy, theoretical and practical; appropriate aspects of psychometrics, counselling and selection; and, of course, a research element. One might even envisage a common first year of mainly taught courses with the PhD. In psychology, such a course would be quite analogous to the professional qualifications in other branches of applied psychology, as described in this volume.

## Psychologists

Indeed it can well be argued (Radford, 1994; 1997) that psychologists should be the leaders in such developments, in as much as our discipline is fundamental to education, more so than any other. While training for education will draw on many disciplines such as philosophy, anthropology, history, etc., psychology is specifically concerned with mental and behavioural development, learning and thinking, social relations and social skills, assessment and measurement, communication, in short the basic processes of education. And in all these we can claim established knowledge that provides a sound base for practice; certainly a far better one than uncertain memories of one's own student days, which is all that most academics have to rely on.

There are encouraging signs that the importance of developing a profession of academic psychologist is being recognized. A fundamental step within the BPS was the creation in 1997 of the Division for Teachers and Researchers in Psychology. For non-members, the formal significance of this is that Divisions are the professional subsystems within the society. Qualification for one carries the status of Chartered Psychologist, and this can be gained by various routes, one of which involves obtaining the society's Diploma in Teaching Psychology (which is also accredited as a direct route to membership of the ILT). A natural progression would be for the diploma to be advanced to a higher degree, as has been done in other branches of applied psychology. The diploma involves precisely applying psychological (and other relevant) knowledge to the profession of teacher and researcher.

A recent statement by the Division Chair refers to 'recognising and supporting the professionalism of the practice of Psychologists who teach psychology and publish psychological research' (Booth, 2002). As usual with professions, this has two major aspects: protection of the public and advancement of the profession itself. The first arises directly from the society's Code of Conduct, which 'acknowledges that all Members . . . bear responsibility for the psychological impact on individuals and organizations of all their uses of their higher education, their professional training and continuing development, and their practitioner experience'. On the second aspect, it would be disingenuous, and unjustified, to ignore the fact that formal qualification and organization are generally closely linked to status and financial return, both matters of pressing concern for academics.

## Pros and cons

Certainly determined professional organization over a long period has helped to give medical and legal personnel a degree of wealth and prestige which academics can only envy. (Physicians have even high-jacked the academic title of 'doctor', that is, teacher, from Latin *doceo*, for their own basic qualification.) Yet the expertise of academics, at least in their own discipline, is at least equivalent to that of doctors and lawyers. It is true that professions in general have been subject to sharp criticism, even attack, from government, for some decades now, at least in the UK. Even doctors are reported to be 'unhappy with their lot' and, as with academics, this is a worldwide problem (Hawkes, 2002). With minor changes the words could apply to higher education:

> A key factor seems to be a change in the psychological contract between the profession, employers, patients and society, so that the job is now different from what doctors expected . . . Once . . . doctors were promised a reasonable balance between life and work, autonomy and job security, and deference and respect. Today they faced greater accountability . . . less autonomy . . . evaluation by outsiders, and a growing blame culture. The relationship with government also needed to change. Self-regulation had been undermined and autonomy weakened by treatment guidelines that doctors had little opportunity to influence.

There are still rewards, even in the life of academics. Perhaps most are originally motivated by an interest in, even a passion for, a particular branch of inquiry, and a wish to pass on their knowledge and enthusiasm to others. These do remain their primary functions, and can yield great satisfaction. But they are becoming ever more difficult to carry out satisfactorily, while other conditions are also deteriorating. There is, for example, some flexibility in working hours, but often at the cost of very long days. And as with all professionals, there is an obligation to be present when needed regardless of personal convenience. The famous 'long holidays' are largely spurious.

The tendency of all administrations, no doubt, is to think that more government is better. This is currently fairly explicit in the UK. But professionalism is essentially a matter of self-regulation and of balance between competing interests. The problem is not new. In 1776 Adam Smith argued that if university teachers are responsible only to the 'body corporate' of their fellow-teachers, they will all have a common interest to do as little as possible. On the other hand if authority is external, it will at best ensure that teachers go through the motions, it cannot enforce quality: 'An extraneous jurisdiction of this kind, besides, is liable to be exercised both ignorantly and capriciously . . . it is arbitrary and discretionary, and the persons who exercise it . . . are seldom capable of doing so with judgement' (Smith, 1776). This may sound familiar today.

The worst negative qualities of professionalism are arrogance and rigidity. It is all too easy for the qualified to be rude, patronizing or unfair to the client or, still worse, to cause real damage, and then to attempt to cover up what happened. A series of recent medical scandals has brought this sharply into focus. It is a natural tendency, too, to enshrine current practice to the point where innovation is stifled. Possibly for academics this would be the greater danger. Academic staff do on occasion abuse their position with individual students, but in their teaching can hardly cause damage on a medical scale. But higher education is essentially (I would argue) a matter of open inquiry, or it is nothing. It would be potentially disastrous if professional qualification of academics led to exclusion of unpopular individuals or censorship of controversial material. Both these have happened all too readily even without a professional framework. Many academics, besides, feel intuitively that 'professional' implies 'control'. Within psychology, there is a long history of tension between the BPS and (some) academic psychologists who saw it as interfering with academic freedom. Yet these, like nearly everyone, would, when seriously ill, surely prefer the attentions of a qualified physician to those of a quack.

What is necessary is a robust constitution with appropriate checks and balances. There is no reason why we might not expect academics to possess a pedagogic qualification, while at the same time possessing complete freedom to teach and research. On the whole the British model of professionalism has achieved fairly well a balance between the interests of the professional and those of the client; between control and rigidity. One of the basic principles, that of peer review, can already be seen in the mediaeval *ius ubique docendi*: the right of graduates of recognized universities to teach in others. It was applied to research within the Royal Society from 1660, and it served well as the basis of the external examiner system, and then of the accreditation methods of the Council for National Academic Awards. Professions should take responsibility for regulating themselves, subject to the law, but incorporate independent and effective monitoring. They need mechanisms for continual review, renewal and innovation. Universities have in the past succeeded in doing these things, if at times slowly (in contrast to, for example, the early Islamic equivalents). The policy now should be to learn from the past and develop further for the future.

## Conclusion

It should surely be beyond question that, as Altbach (1991) puts it: 'Without a well-qualified, committed, and adequately compensated professoriate, no academic institution can be fully successful.' Whether it will be possible, at this late stage, to evolve a true breed of professional academics is dubious. Vested interests, power struggles, politics on a large and small scale, the low point of awareness and influence from which academics themselves start, and sheer inertia in the educational system, all militate against it. Then again, there are at least some in academia, and within psychology specifically, who are actively working for something that I hope will be considered rather better than currently obtains.

## QUESTIONS FOR REFLECTION AND DISCUSSION

1  Academic psychologists: parasites, priests, proletariat or professionals (Radford, 1997)?

2  Why are academic salaries so low?

3  What would be the ideal preparation for an academic career, in your view?

4  Have we anything to learn, from a professional point of view, from academia in other countries?

5  What, if any, practical steps can academics take to improve their status?

## Suggestions for further reading

There is a spate of books discussing the state of universities worldwide and the changing role of academics. A glance at the catalogue of SRHE/Open University Press is recommended. Also, many of the issues are most explicitly dealt with in papers, as listed in the References. The titles of most of the following are self-explanatory.

Altbach, P.G. (ed.) (1996) *The Academic Profession: An International Study*. Princeton, NJ: The Carnegie Foundation for the Advancement of Teaching.
One of several large-scale studies of the profession worldwide.

Allen, M. (1988) *The Goals of Universities*. Milton Keynes: SRHE and Open University Press.
This book presents analyses of a large number of 'mission statements' – that is, what universities at least explicitly claim to be about.

Halsey, A.H. (1992) *The Decline of Donnish Dominion: The British Academic Professions in the Twentieth Century*. Oxford: Clarendon Press.
Compare this text with Halsey and Trow (1971) and the situation today.

Light, G. and Cox, R. (2001) *Learning and Teaching in Higher Education: The Reflective Professional*. London: Paul Chapman Publishing.
This book presents one view of some of the major professional aspects discussed in this chapter.

Raaheim, K., Wankowski, J. and Radford, J. (1991) *Helping Students to Learn: Teaching, Counselling, Research*. Buckingham: SRHE and Open University Press.
This text reviews personal experience and research. The authors would maintain that their views still stand.

# 1 Diary of a Research Student

*Anne Ridley*

## Introduction

What's it like to do a PhD? Perhaps a snapshot of my time as a research student will help throw some light on this question. I am a mature student in the final year of my thesis, researching the effects of anxiety on eye-witness testimony. One of the most crucial things to ask yourself when considering whether or not to take a PhD is 'will I enjoy it?' From my personal experience, I would say that if you enjoyed the research elements of your undergraduate degree then you will enjoy doing a PhD, but you do have to be motivated and fairly independent, because you are not spoon fed to the same extent. Another consideration is what you hope to achieve from it. A career change took me to a first degree where I discovered that I enjoyed academic life, so a PhD seemed a natural progression. When I've finished, I hope to get a job as a research fellow or a research-active lecturer. The next year or so will be interesting as I return to the world of work but, in the mean time, here are extracts from my diary for the last two years, showing some of the highs and lows of psychology research.

## Day 1: Early in First Year of PhD

Went to the library, searching for journal articles both electronically and in person – great though they are, online listings always seem to miss something! On the other hand, maybe I just don't use the right combinations of keywords in my search. Had a meeting with my supervisors to plan my first study. Was told my registration application was successful. (Registration requires the submission of a written research proposal a few months after enrolment. The aim is to ensure that you have embarked upon a viable programme of research.)

## Day 2: Early in First Year

My supervisor told me we had a query from the ethics committee regarding my first study. Oh, no, bureaucracy! This means a delay in starting my research, although it should be easy to resolve. Not planning to give any electric shocks after all.

## Day 3: Late in First Year

Started testing participants for Study 2 – some turned up, some didn't, most did. On balance, a satisfying day – 5 tested, 75 to go! Dealt with emails and phoned or emailed the next day's participants to remind them. Should get the data collected within 6 weeks. Heard we've had a paper accepted for publication. My name in print at last! So excited I spilled my coffee in the post room . . .

## Day 4: Early in Second Year

Went in early today with the sole purpose of testing my last five participants. Not one of them turned up. It is *so* frustrating when you get 'no shows' like that. The other post-grads in the room all had similar tales to tell. Getting participants is one of the most frustrating aspects of psychology research. Spent the rest of the day entering data. Tedious job, so not the best of days.

## Day 5: Middle of Second Year

Went to the University of East London (UEL) university-wide conference about the future of research. Postgraduates from all departments were invited to submit a poster of their research for a competition. I was a runner up in the competition which was wicked, particularly as I'm not noted for my artistic talent.

## Day 6: Middle of Second Year

Meeting with supervisors to discuss results of Study 3. Yet again, my results have failed to replicate. It's not *all* bad news as my research is complicated and some common themes are emerging between the three studies to date. However, inter-pretation is difficult and we're not all in agreement over what to do for the next study. Spent the rest of the day preparing overheads for my first research presen-tation at a conference in Lisbon next week.

## Day 7: A Week Later

Sitting drinking beer in a Lisbon bar with fellow conference delegates recovering from the stress of first experience of public speaking! It didn't go too badly, although nobody asked any questions – not quite sure what to make of that. Have met a lot of interesting people at the conference, so now have more con-tacts in my area of research.

## Day 8: End of Second Year

Went to a UEL research seminar for postgraduates. There was a talk by a successful PhD student. She obviously had never encountered any problems. This was not much help, as I am feeling my PhD is in the doldrums at the moment. I'm trying to replace my second supervisor, who was unable to continue, and I'm waiting on different people for different things which means I can't get on (OK, I could be reading that paper I found but I'm not in the mood today). Went to the pub at lunchtime with other researchers. Some good news today though. AP had has just emerged from her viva and it went really well – she will soon be Dr P, so it can be done and I *will* do it.

## Day 9: End of Second Year

Meeting with first supervisor. (My new second supervisor is external so does not come to all meetings.) Have now upgraded from MPhil which means my research is adequate to proceed to PhD. (This involved writing a summary of what I have done and my future direction, which helped me to organize my thoughts on the PhD, so it was very useful.) I'm still not doing enough reading (gentle hint from my supervisor), so I know I'm going to find my literature review really hard. Everybody else I talk to seems to find the reading the easy bit and the writing the difficult bit. With me it's the exact opposite.

## Day 10: Early Third Year

Great news! Had a positive reply from MZ (one of the research gurus in my area saying I can use her experimental materials). Must get on with a detailed proposal for the study and start running it before all the undergraduates disappear on exam leave.

## Day 11: A few Weeks Later

Results of Study 5 were really good and have tied up many of the loose ends of my earlier studies. This really was an amazing feeling – although the results are what I expected on the basis of how I interpreted the findings of the earlier studies, I still can't believe it worked out so well. It means I've probably finished collecting data for my PhD. Everything seems to be going really well at the moment, long may it continue into the writing-up phase. What's more, today I was asked to write part of a chapter for a book, about doing a PhD . . .

# Acknowledgements

To Brian Clifford, my supervisor, with thanks for all the support and wise advice. To Michael, Nick and Jo, for putting up with the mood swings. To all the other researchers in Room 141 and beyond, for being there too.

# 2 A Note on Continuing Professional Development

*Christine Doyle*

## What is Continuing Professional Development (CPD) and Why do we Need it?

It is often said that we in the west especially, are living in an age when there is an 'explosion' of knowledge and a 'revolution' in the nature of work and information. Much of this is driven by rapid technological advance. Castells (1997a; 1997b; 1998) believes we are on the verge of a network world. This revolution in the technology of information processing has allowed the creation of a global economy and of virtual teams which can communicate and work together on opposite sides of the world. Intranets within organizations give employees wide access to information which was previously the preserve of just a few specialists and anyone with a computer, modem and phone line can access the Internet and a limitless supply of information. This information is dynamic, interactive, mutually generated and globally shared in a way that was impossible with any previous technology. In addition to these technological changes, in the UK at least, there has been a move from a manufacturing to a service economy with a consequent rise in the numbers of 'knowledge workers' – people who earn their living by using their knowledge, skills and competences to provide a service to clients. Chmiel (1998) documents a sharp decline in manual jobs and a great increase in cognitively demanding work.

The days when people could train for an occupation when young and then become more proficient simply by doing the job are long gone. There is a need for lifelong learning to cope with technological change, to keep abreast of developments within one's area of expertise, to innovate and learn of innovations which enhance the service to clients, to develop one's skills and competences. In short there is a need for constant CPD throughout one's career.

Psychologists are no different from anyone else when it comes to lifelong learning and CPD and, in addition, the British Psychological Society's (BPS) Code of Conduct specifies that 'Psychologists shall endeavour to maintain and develop their professional competence to recognize and work within its limits, and to identify and ameliorate factors which restrict it'. Thus undertaking CPD is an ethical obligation. Keeping a personal log of CPD activity was voluntary but in preparation to a move to statutory registration of professional psychologists, the BPS membership voted in 2000 to make the recording and monitoring of CPD mandatory.

As I write, the BPS is conducting a consultation exercise on the guidelines which will govern CPD. In the consultation document it is suggested that CPD is a process which should be planned, undertaken, recorded and evaluated and that psychologists should undertake a range of CPD activities according to individuals' needs and the nature of their roles and work. The proposed generic guidelines stipulate that chartered psychologists must undertake the number of hours of CPD activity as specified by the division to which they belong. (For instance, the Division of Occupational Psychology currently specifies 120 hours over a three-year period with a minimum of 20 hours in any one year.) Those who belong to more than one BPS division must satisfy the CPD requirements of each division, although some activities may be common to several divisions. Suggested CPD activities include the following:

+ Post-qualification training courses.
+ Received or conferred professional supervision in an area of psychology.
+ Presentation or attendance at conferences.
+ Research.
+ Learning skills and information from others.
+ Preparation of new/updated material for teaching, training or publication.
+ Attendance at courses according to the individual's needs.
+ Peer-group discussion.
+ Professional committee work.
+ Reading.
+ Personal psychological counselling for professional purposes.
+ Systematic reflection on practice.

## The CPD Process

This list is not exhaustive but from this it can be seen that CPD can take a very wide range of forms. Much CPD may also occur in the normal course of one's work. For instance, an occupational psychologist may be asked to design and deliver a new training course or selection procedure which may entail familiarization with new areas of content, techniques and psychometric instruments. However, the sheer variety of CPD activities can lead to the danger that it becomes fragmented and piecemeal with too much attempted in too little time and nothing truly mastered. For this reason it is essential that CPD is undertaken as a systematic process although flexibility is also important. CPD opportunities may arise unexpectedly or new circumstances may create new development needs. There must be a clear plan but it needs to be monitored and updated.

The first step is to identify your learning needs in the context of your current roles, the requirements of your organization and your future career goals. The aim is to maintain or enhance your existing professional competence and/or to develop new competences. According to the BPS draft guidelines, one way to do this is to start by identifying the following:

✦ The services you are delivering.

✦ Likely demands for new services in the immediate future.

✦ Key areas of these services which require development.

✦ Priority objectives for these key areas.

The next step is to prioritize your development needs according to the resources you have available (time and money) and to select activities which will meet your learning goals. This can be done by considering your current levels of knowledge and skill, the importance of this knowledge and skill for your current roles, future work and your organization's priorities. You will also need to take into account your BPS division's requirements. For instance, the Division of Occupational Psychology requires a balance between activities which enhance knowledge, skill and competence so simply enhancing theoretical knowledge would not be sufficient. It is also a good idea to consider what development activities might fulfil more than one learning goal since time and resources are finite. Having done this, you need to set SMART objectives – those that are:

✦ Specific – you know exactly what you are trying to achieve.

✦ Measurable – so you can check progress and know when you've reached your goal.

✦ Attainable – challenging but achievable.

✦ Realistic – practical, within your resources of time, money, etc.

✦ Timetabled – without dates and milestones we all get lost.

You then need to put the plan into action, modifying it as appropriate in the light of experience, changing circumstances and unplanned opportunities for development. Successes and failures can be used as opportunities to learn from experience.

Finally you should record and evaluate the effectiveness of your CPD activities. This can be done as you complete each activity and evaluate learning outcomes for the extent to which they met your objectives. As this is an ongoing process any failures to achieve your goals fully become the basis for the next round of CPD activity. Completing a summary personal log is not an onerous task. The generic examples given in the BPS consultation document are quite brief but you also need to keep evidence of the activities you have undertaken and their learning outcomes. These can be as simple as a set of OHPs generated using PowerPoint or a certificate of attendance at a conference. Or it can be as extensive as a thesis submitted successfully for a professional doctorate or details of a training course from training needs analysis through design, delivery and evaluation. It all depends on what your development goals were. The good thing is that large CPD projects such as a professional doctorate can fulfil a large number of development needs simultaneously and will thus more than fulfil your CPD obligations for a period. (The full process is illustrated in the case study of three years of CPD in Box A2.1.)

> **Box A 2.1  A case study of CPD in occupational and academic psychology**
>
> *Name*:
> Christine Doyle
> *Membership of BPS Divisions*:
> Division of Occupational Psychology
> Division for Teachers and Researchers in Psychology
>
> **General considerations**
> As a member of two divisions and someone with a busy schedule and limited financial resources, I need to maximize the learning outcomes from each activity so that as far as possible it fulfils the requirements of both divisions. As an academic, I am more concerned with the training needs of student clients taking the MSc in occupational and organizational psychology and of practitioner clients undertaking the professional doctorate in occupational psychology than with providing a service for the general public or organizations. However, through the quality of my teaching, the doctoral programme and my research supervision, I am vicariously responsible for enhancing the quality of service offered by both MSc and D. Occ. Psych. graduates. In the context of my organization I am committed to providing a first-class preparation for a career in occupational psychology and, via the doctorate, to enhancing the development of practitioners and, through them, to the advancement of the profession and evidence-based practice. I also wish to celebrate and increase diversity within our profession. In these senses, I see no conflict between my roles as a teacher and researcher in psychology and as a chartered occupational psychologist concerned with the theory and practice of occupational psychology.
>
> **Initial development needs**
>
> 1   Increase my knowledge of the theory and evidence base of Occupational Psychology
> 2   Develop skills as an academic author
> 3   Enhance skills as a teacher
> 4   Develop skills as a researcher
> 5   Develop skills as a practitioner

# Developing Objectives

The development needs listed above are not SMART since they are not specific, measurable, achievable or realistic (they could take several lifetimes!), and there are no timescales attached. Thus a refined list of objectives might include the following (see also Table A2.1):

**1** Write an academic textbook in occupational psychology (within three years; objectives 1 and 2).

**2** Attend BPS occupational psychology conference every year and an additional international psychology conference whenever possible (ongoing; objective 1).

**3** Learn how to use PowerPoint to improve presentations (three months; objective 3).

**4** Achieve membership of ILT and read at least one article per month in journals devoted to teaching and learning in higher education (ongoing; objective 3).

**5** Develop knowledge of qualitative methods of inquiry and analysis by arranging workshops (one year; objective 4).

**6** Gain Level B (Intermediate) Certificate of Competence in Occupational Testing (within one year; objective 5).

**Table A2.1  Developing objectives: a log-book**

| Date | Development need no. | Development objective | Development activity | Outcome | Reflective evaluation | Hours |
|---|---|---|---|---|---|---|
| January 1999–June 2002 | 1 & 2 | Write textbook to increase knowledge of discipline. Develop skills as an academic author. | Literature searches, Internet searches, conference attendance. Writing, revision, creating indices, liaising with editor and publishers. Obtaining copyright permissions. | Book is in press, due out September 2002. | Writing was an onerous but very enjoyable activity; I now have a very extensive up-to-date knowledge of the discipline (including growth points). I have gained confidence as an author and have published numerous articles in addition to the main text; I now have much more knowledge of the publication process. | Very difficult to estimate but maybe 1 day per week over 3½ years – mostly evenings and weekends but I even took the work on holiday!  1575 hours. |
| January 1999, 2000, 2001, 2002 | 2 | Attend conferences to increase knowledge of discipline. | Attendance at BPS occupational psychology conferences. | Knowledge gained has fed into my teaching and writing my text-book. Led a work-shop on the role of professional doctorate in CPD in 2000. | Very valuable for keeping up to date and spotting emerging trends/issues. Have also gained by giving presentations and reflecting on the future of the profession. | 4 × 2 days.  64 hours. |

| Date | Development need no. | Development objective | Development activity | Outcome | Reflective evaluation | Hours |
|---|---|---|---|---|---|---|
| July 2001 | 2 | | Attendance at European Congress of Psychology at the Barbican, London. | Gave two poster presentations of professional doctorate research – invited to present at a Warsaw conference in June 2002 as a result. | Made valuable contacts. Learnt about diary study research and incorporated the technique into own research. | 4 days. 32 hours. |
| September 2001 | 4 | Learn to use PowerPoint to improve quality of OHP slides. | Pay colleague to give initial tutorial, then learn by preparing conference/open-day posters and OHPs for lectures. | Gained skills and successfully completed slides for conference posters, etc., and lecture OHPs. Can now produce colour transparencies. | Still more comfortable using OHP slides – need to learn how to give online presentations and how to produce charts, graphs, etc., and incorporating photos, etc., into displays. | Initial learning: 4 hours. Practice: 10 hours. |
| April 2001 | 4 | Achieve membership of ILT. | Wrote application. | Granted membership. | Reflection on practice was useful and staying within word limit was an exercise in writing discipline. Not much other benefit so far because the ICT system doesn't allow me access to the restricted site but I do receive … the journal 'Active Learning in Higher Education' and thus access to HE research. | 4 hours. |

| 1999–2002 | 5 | Develop knowledge of qualitative research methods. | Read books on introduction to qualitative methods. Attended workshop on grounded theory. Supervised doctoral students and assisted in turning rep grid data into psychometric instrument. Gave numerous rep grid workshops. | Gained general knowledge of qualitative approach and detailed knowledge of grounded theory. One-day workshop on discourse analysis and use of narrative planned for May 2002. | I now know a lot about the theory but do not feel confident about the practice – I need to use these techniques and associated computer programs. | Difficult to estimate since this has been an ongoing process but a minimum of 20 hours so far. |
|---|---|---|---|---|---|---|
| June 2000 | 6 | Gain Level B (Intermediate) Certificate of Competence in Occupational Testing. | Course attended and passed. | Now qualified to use the Hogan Personality Inventory. | No opportunity to put this knowledge into practice. Have great reservations about the instrument. Need to gain competence in more 'mainstream' instruments, e.g. 16PF5 and MBTI. | 50 hours. |

*New objectives 2002–3*
1 Learn to use WebCT in my teaching.
2 Produce core book/pack for Level A Certificate of Competence in Occupational Testing course.
3 Use qualitative techniques in research or gain 'hands-on' experience.
4 Attend conference on teaching and learning in higher education.
5 Join Virtual Environments research group within school (see also Objective 4).
6 Attend at least one BPS Occupational Psychology Affiliates Group training day.

# Part 2
# GENERIC ISSUES

# 10 Research: The Ubiquitous Handmaiden of Professionalism

*Brian R. Clifford*

## SUMMARY

*This chapter makes the case that research underpins all professional activity because change is ever present, both in the discipline and in the level of professional expertise exhibited by the exponent of the service provided. It makes the case that, while research execution is as much art as science, none the less certain basic considerations are present in all exploration of human behaviour and experience. Having established these basic considerations the various research approaches are presented and their strengths and weaknesses detailed. A major debate within research methodology is then presented and the core elements of the dispute are laid bare and their implications for the research approach adopted spelt out. The chapter closes by arguing that whatever the pretheoretical assumptions are that one adopts, there are certain principles of operation in research that cannot be ignored and that must be adhered to if the research product is to have validity, reliability and replicability.*

## Introduction

Irrespective of which profession you seek to enter there is one component of your education that will always appear in whatever course you undertake: research. This is necessarily the case because no discipline or practice is static: new frontiers are always being opened; the envelope is always being extended; and past and present work must always be evaluated for validity and reliability and, hence, usefulness for incorporation into new practices, policies and mechanisms in your profession of choice. Evidence-based or, at least, evidence-guided practice is becoming the watch-word of all professions. Thus, research becomes seminal in all professional induction.

## Research

So what is research? Research means different things to different people and in different professions. Broadly, it extends all the way from *re-searching* extant knowledge, practice or theory, to the *creation* of new knowledge, practice or theory. Its focus can thus be retrospective or prospective; it can be empirical or rational; it can be creative or it can be algorithmic.

At this point it may seem that research and scholarship are synonymous. However, they are not. The basic difference is that scholarship is concerned with fully understanding what someone else has said and possibly reformulating the accounts given. Research, on the other hand, is concerned with the production of new knowledge, new insights, new laws, mechanisms, procedures or processes. The distinction may be formulated as the ability to wonder (scholarship) versus the ability to know (research). The former is essentially open ended whereas the latter is essentially closed. Research is closed because to conduct research which is meaningful requires the adherence to a number of methodological 'rules' and 'tactics' which are generally accepted by the research community as rigorous, meaningful and productive of knowledge or understanding.

Now to talk of research as closed is not to be pejorative and proscriptive. The various research methods found across the professions of clinical, occupational, educational, health and forensic psychology are many and varied. Often this variety is forced by the topic of inquiry; often variation is forced by compromise and research becomes as much art as science in its execution. However, underlying the myriad varieties of research that exist can be detected the strain towards the canons of research. Whatever the topic of research, whatever the field of inquiry, none the less there is the strain to maintain the principles of research design, implemented within a framework of ethical acceptability. To paraphrase Medawar (1972) research begins as a speculative adventure, an imaginative pre-conception of what might be – a thought that goes beyond anything you have logical or factual authority to believe. It is the power to wonder, the invention of a possible world. You then expose your thought, idea or conjecture to critical scrutiny – by way of a critical literature review or practice audit. Having established a prima facie case for your idea you are then set to take the next research steps. This involves clarifying your concepts, identifying the variables of interest and then setting about exploring the hypotheses you feel justified in holding.

Now this appears so clear cut and ordered to the beginning researcher: you start with a desire better to understand some phenomenon; by the application of some selected systematic means you obtain meaningful data; then, following careful reflection and interpretation, you end up with conclusions concerning your initial phenomenon of interest. However, unlike this 'reconstructed logic of science' (Kaplan, 1964) that you will meet in the published literature, real research is often messy, intensely frustrating and fundamentally non-linear. As stated above, it is as much art as science, as much compromise as design, especially in the applied, real-world context.

## Background considerations

Despite the above acknowledged gulf between the rhetoric and the reality of research, once you are clear on the question(s) you wish to address the next question is how to proceed. This is a difficult question because the available methods are numerous. However certain guidelines are available to render the task of selection manageable.

The basic aim of research is to gather empirical data to support (verify) or challenge (falsify) or clarify (understand) your idea: this emphasis on empirical data is what differentiates psychology from, for example, philosophy. However, as has been said, there are many methods available, which unfortunately have become more or less synonymous with overall approaches to psychology. Thus cognitive psychology emphasizes experimental data; occupational psychology, psychometric data; developmental psychology, longitudinal data; social psychology now emphasizes qualitative methods and data. Applied psychology in general, because of the difficulty of conducting 'true experiments', emphasizes interviews, observational methods, field research and quasi-experimental designs. So where do you begin?

If truth be told the professional area you enter, and the department within which you study, may have a 'preferred method' and you will be dragooned into utilizing this approach. Allowing for this pragmatic solution to research design selection you should, none the less, be aware of the various approaches available and the overall problems that attach to any and all approaches by virtue of psychology's unique subject matter – human beings. These overall problems emanate from the fact that neither the respondents nor the researchers are inert beings.

## Participant effects

Coolican (1998) argues that human *participants* exhibit a number of biases. The well-known Hawthorne effect exhibits participant's reactivity. The Hawthorne effect showed that whatever was done to workers in an electrical factor (positively or negatively) their productivity went up. This indicates clearly that humans are not inert; rather they are thinking, feeling sentient beings who will react in different ways if they 'know' or think they are being evaluated. As Coolican indicates, in real-life research naturalistic or participant observation methods are means of getting over this.

Social desirability responding is another human reactive phenomenon whereby participants attempt to present a public image of social respectability. Clearly all self-report measures run the risk of eliciting this response, but so do any questions in questionnaires that request views on socially sensitive matters. Related to this aspect of reactivity, but different from it, is the observer effect. People who know their behaviour is being observed will almost certainly react in subtly or grossly different ways, depending upon the observed's perception of the reasons for the observation. Human participants are active, sense-making beings. They will pick up cues as to what the research is about, and the usual norms of social interaction will come into play – for example, co-operation. This is the so-called demand characteristics of a research method.

The placebo effect serves to demonstrate that humans who 'know' they have received a treatment, intervention or a manipulation, will behave as they believe they are expected to behave. Related to the placebo effect is researcher-evaluation apprehension. This is shown by participants' eager inquiries regarding whether the research is likely to work, and 'how did I do?' 'Yeah saying' and response acquiescence set refers to the tendency of participants to respond in one direction, and usually positively. This response set can be detected and controlled for by inserting 'opposite' questions and including a lie scale (for example, as in the EPI).

## Researcher effects

Complementary to participant bias in human research is bias in *researchers* and *research designs*. The self-fulfilling prophecy is the clearest demonstration of this bias. Labelled people will actually being to demonstrate the labelled behaviour. This is also referred to as the Pygmalion effect – researcher's expectations or hopes have actual effects upon participants. The standard control procedures for this effect are single, or better still, double-blind techniques whereby neither the participant (single blind) nor the data gatherer (double blind) know which condition(s) the participants are in. Another well-known research effect is the halo effect whereby an examiner or assessor's overall positive or negative evaluation affects his or her evaluation of a specific trait, ability or response.

These and other, more structural and procedural, confounding effects will be further addressed when we look at quasi-experimental designs. For the moment, suffice to say that in *any* research there are a multitude of possible confounding effects and a great deal of effort and thought must be devoted either to eliminating or statistically controlling possible confounding variables as explanation.

These *participant*, *experimenter* and *structural* biases are potentially present in all research so, while they act as a backdrop to considerations of specific method selection, they do not serve to make that selection. As has been said, tradition, local predilection and sheer necessity frequently force the choice of method. So what methods are available?

# Research Methods: Specific Techniques

## Experiments

At the positivist end of research the true experiment is the method of choice. Here participants are allocated at random either to the control or the experimental group. These two groups are treated identically except that the experimental group undergoes a treatment whereas the control group does not. Both groups are then measured on the same variable. The manipulated variable is referred to as the independent variable and the measured variable is called the dependent variable. With all other variables controlled the manipulation of the one variable is assumed to be the cause of any observed consequent change in the dependent variable. This is Mill's (1874) 'method of difference'. Note that what has been described is the archetypal experimental design. In reality several independent variables can be manipulated simultaneously (for example, a multifactorial design) and several dependent variables can be measured (for example, multivariate designs). However, the logic of causation remains the same.

Within the experimental method further decisions will have to be made concerning repeated measures (within-subject) designs, matched subject designs and factorial (between-subject) designs. The deciding factors here will be economy of time and/or respondents, and control of variance (variability). Finally, it is possible to conduct mixed designs where some variables are manipulated within-subjects, while others appear as between-subject factors or variables. This gives rise to the so-called split-plot or mixed design.

The experimental method is not without its detractors. A frequent criticism is its artificiality and its lack of ecological validity or mundane realism or, in forensic psychology, its legal verisimilitude. In short, it is frequently argued that, while the experiment has good internal validity, it has poor external validity. As we will see later, the ontological, epistemological model of the human that underpins the experimental method is currently under attack.

## Quasi-experiments

Quasi-experimental methods are available for research purposes when conditions pertain that exclude the conducting of 'true' experimentation. A great deal of research in the professional literature is of this type. The interested reader is directed to Campbell and Stanley (1963) for what still remains the best account of the many quasi-experimental designs available.

Broadly, quasi-experimental methodology is employed when either you cannot randomly allocate participants to conditions or you have less than perfect control over the independent variable, or both. Thus a great many experimental studies conducted *in situ* are quasi-experiments where either intact groups have to be used under different conditions or variables cannot be manipulated but either happen infrequently, by chance, or not at all. In addition, while a study may begin as a true experiment, reality may intrude and the researcher has to be creative in salvaging his or her research and engage in damage limitation.

So what are quasi-experimental designs and how valuable are they? Fundamentally, their value resides in how well or badly they retain internal and external validity. Internal validity is the basic minimum without which any experiment is uninterpretable. Essentially, did the treatment(s)/manipulation(s) make a difference? External validity refers to the result's generalizability – to other populations, settings, treatment and measurement variables.

With respect to internal validity in quasi-experimental designs eight different threats have to be guarded against. The first threat is *history* – uncontrolled specific events outside the experiment can happen at the same time as the experimental manipulations or interventions are being undertaken. The second threat is *maturation* – micro- and macro-changes in the respondents can occur coterminously with the manipulation. The third threat is *testing* – the effect of taking an initial test (to establish a baseline) can have an effect upon the scores of a second testing. Threat four is *instrumentation* – unnoticed changes in either the measuring instrument, the scorers or the participants over time. The fifth threat is *regression* to the mean – a statistical phenomenon whereby extreme groups move closer to the overall mean of the two groups on second testing irrespective of what was done to them. Threat six is *selection* artifact – these are caused by differential selection methods being used for the different groups or treatments. Threat seven is *experimental* mortality – across time a differential rate of loss of participants can occur in comparison groups. This would not be a major problem if it had been possible randomly to allocate participants to groups. The last threat to internal validity is *selection–maturation* interaction. Here different intact groups may be undergoing different changes unrelated to the experimental manipulations.

All these threats are threats of confounding. The researcher can mistakenly assume that observed change or difference is due to the manipulation whereas such change or difference may, in reality, be due to these various extraneous factors.

External validity or representativeness of quasi-experimental designs is jeopardized by four main threats. The first is *reactive* or interactive effects of testing. For example, pretesting may influence eventual responsiveness which would not vary if pretesting had not been undertaken. A second threat to external validity is *interaction* effects of selection bias and the experimental variable. The third threat is *reactive* effects of the experimental arrangements. For example, non-reinforced or control groups may become resentful (resentful demoralization or, more prosaically, the 'screw you' effect). The last threat is that of *multiple-treatment* interference. Prior treatments/manipulations are usually not erasable. In the true experiment this can be controlled for by counterbalancing: in quasi-experimental designs it cannot.

Campbell and Stanley (1963) document some 16 research designs, only three of which are true experimental designs. The interested reader should consult this source as, almost certainly, the researcher seeking qualifications in professional psychology will rarely be capable of running true experimental designs. The research psychologist (MPhil or PhD postgraduates) should have more scope for executing the true experiment.

It is when the true experiment is not possible that students begin to realize that research methodology is as much an art as a science. Research is not carried out in a vacuum; rather, it is frequently the outcome of compromise, creative construction and plausible recoverability.

## Correlational methods

Apart from the practical impossibility of running a true experiment or even a quasi-experiment, there are other reasons for opting for a method other than the experimental. Ethics may not allow the conducting of an experimental study. However, we can still explore the relationship between variables of interest. This is achieved by selecting a correlational rather than an experimental methodology. Correlation methodology explores the co-variation between two or more variables (via linear and multiple regression techniques). Now while it is a truism that correlation can never disclose causation, modern techniques can certainly approach it. Several correlations compared across time, known as a cross-lagged design, can tease out the directionality of association, and path analysis can indicate the magnitude of different associations.

In the development, forensic, occupational, health and clinical fields correlational studies are frequently the bases of longitudinal and cross-sectional group comparisons. Both these group comparison methods have their problems but, all other things being equal, the longitudinal design is to be preferred to the cross-sectional. In terms of practicalities, masters and doctoral theses usually allow only cross-sectional designs, the more time-consuming longitudinal studies being reserved for post-masters or post-doctoral studies.

## Interview methods

Another major research methodology is that of the interview. The interview can be face to face, over the telephone, by email or over the net. Additionally, the interview can range from structured to unstructured. The structured interview will be characterized by containing exactly the same questions for all respondents and a closed – probably Lickert scale – response format. The semi-structured interview uses more open-ended (rather than closed) questions, but is still designed to obtain similar types of information from each interviewee. The semi-structured interview is more respondent led and is designed to allow the interviewee's unique perspective to emerge clearly and comprehensively. The non-directive interview is designed to allow the respondent as much freedom as possible when addressing the research topic of interest, and to ensure a rich and 'thick' response to emerge. Despite being interviewee led the researcher must retain some degree of specifiable focus if meaningful data are to be captured.

Clearly the benefits and costs of these different types of interview method must be weighed carefully. The more structured the interview the more reliability there will be, the easier will data be to compare across individuals or groups and the greater will control be. The more unstructured the interview the richer the data but the less comparable will any two respondents' data be. Depending upon your metatheoretical assumptions and research orientation, quantification possibilities may not be an issue. However, some framework of understanding will have to be 'imposed' on the accumulated responses if sense is to be made of the data. Thus, as in most research, a compromise has to be made.

In the case of interview data, that decision will be between obtaining rich, full and comprehensive accounts, and obtaining data that can be organized and understood within a well prescribed, and communicated, research topic. Discourse analysis, content analysis, thematic analysis, grounded theory and conversational analysis are likely research techniques that will be brought to bear upon these interview data. As we will see below, statistical and software packages now exist to aid 'sense-making' and to ensure tractability of the data that can arise.

## Questionnaires and surveys

These research methods form a large part of postgraduate research output. Basically this research method can range from simply asking (research-related) open, exploratory, believed-to-be relevant questions to administering tests which have a theoretical and normed underpinning, such as aptitude, ability, personality, intelligence and attitude tests and questionnaires. It is unfortunately the case that postgraduate students frequently perceive research based upon questionnaires as an 'easy option'. Nothing could be further from the truth. Major problems of reliability and validity must be addressed if constructed measuring instruments are to be of any value. Reliability is a question of consistency: external reliability asks whether the same results will pertain with the same participant at a later date; and internal reliability asks whether the test is internally consistent. This in turn can be assessed by split-half reliability, item analysis and Cronbach's alpha. Validity refers to how well the test or questionnaire tests what it purports to test. Validity can be checked by face validity considerations, content validity, criterion validity and construct validity. A consideration that is rarely if ever met in postgraduate work with new scales, questionnaires or tests is standardization. Without standardization of a measurement instrument we can never be fully confident in its reliability and validity. As has been said, this research choice is not an easy option!

## Observational methods

Observational research methods exist and are exploited fully most noticeably in educational, occupational and developmental research. As Coolican (1998) indicates, observational studies can be ranged along four dimensions: structure (whether data are recorded within a predetermined framework and scoring system or are open ended); setting (whether contrived or naturalistic); level of observer's participation (uninvolved, participant observer or observing participant); and, lastly, disclosure (participants are aware or not of being observed). Clearly such studies involve major considerations of what to measure, where to measure, how to measure, when to measure and whom to measure. In addition, in such open-ended flexible research, problems of interpretation and reliability loom large.

### Case studies

Case studies have been an enduring research method within psychology and yet their status is somewhat ambiguous. While Bromley (1986) points out that they are the 'bedrock of scientific investigation', they seem to contravene the canons of experimental psychology (random allocation to groups) and, by definition, they lack external validity (because unique). Case studies involve the intensive study of one individual, group or organization, usually *in situ*. Within experimental psychology, and especially cognitive neuropsychology, they are frequently referred to as '$n=1$' studies. For example, a person exhibiting a rare cognitive deficit is examined intensively and an independent variable of interest is manipulated. By utilizing such an *n*=1 or case study an existence proof can be established of some process or mechanism as being of importance in normal functioning. In applied psychology research generally, case studies can provide extremely rich data but they do lack generalizability and replicability, by definition.

## Diary methodology

Diary studies require participants to keep more or less detailed and comprehensive records of their thoughts, behaviour or emotional reactions to people, events or happenings. These types of study are frequently used in clinical (for example, panic attacks), cognitive (for example, autobiographical memory), health (for example, smoking cessation) and forensic psychology (for example, post-traumatic stress disorders). Again rich and fully meaningful data can be produced but again the dangers are human frailty in terms of forgetfulness, reliability and, it must be said, honesty, together with a lack of research control and objectivity.

## Archival studies

A last approach to be detailed is archival research. This can be conceptualized as a secondary form of observation. Scientifically, however, the data are 'frozen' and no manipulations can be applied although the extant dataset can be repartitioned and reanalysed in a number of interesting and research-directed ways. Research can be conducted on other people's research data (secondary analyses); on official or unofficial public and private documents (for example, court cases or medical records); and, finally, any published or unpublished source material whatever.

# A Major Research Methods Debate

The perspicacious reader of this chapter will have noted that I have studiously avoided the use of the term 'scientific'. Just 10 years ago this chapter would have been easy to write: it would have simply documented the scientific method with its emphasis on understanding, explanation, prediction and control and the scientific approach which allowed these four aims of science to be achieved. Today, a chapter on research is much more difficult to write because, within psychology, a deep philosophical disputation, frequently obscured by highly charged emotion, threatens to polarize the discipline of psychology, cause schisms within schools or departments of psychology, and alienate colleagues within subdisciplines. So what is the nature of this debate?

The headline dispute is between qualitative versus quantitative methodology as the better way to proceed in coming to understand human behaviour. However, the dispute goes beyond method to strike at the very heart of psychology's foundation – science. Broadly, the debate rests on four pillars – ontology, epistemology, concepts of human nature and methodology. Fundamentally, two views exist of social science generally and psychology specifically. On the one hand, we have the view that social sciences are essentially the same as the natural sciences and are therefore concerned with discovering lawful relations regulating and 'determining' individual and social behaviours. On the other hand, the opposing view, while still concerned to describe and explain human behaviour, emphasizes how people differ both from inanimate objects and from each other. These two views eventuate in very different ways of viewing social reality and of how to interpret it.

The first issue is how to conceptualize the essence of social phenomena – is social reality external to the individual or group or is it the product of individual thought and action? This is the ontological debate – found in philosophy as the nominalist–realist debate. The realist position argues that objects have an independent existence and are not dependent for their existence on a knower. The nominalist position argues the opposite.

The epistemological debate centres on the question of how we gain knowledge, and its nature and form. Are the objects of knowledge real, objective and 'out there' and capable of being apprehended, or is knowledge subjective, based on experience and of a unique personal nature? Is knowledge extant or is it emergent? Depending upon one's stance on this epistemological question, one will stress the researcher as an objective observer, with a dedication to the methods of science or, if knowledge is seen as subjective, personal and constructed, the researcher should be a participant and highly involved with his or her respondents.

The third pillar of the dispute is the conception held of the respondent or participant – is he or she 'determined' and responding almost 'mechanically' to outside forces, or is he or she initiator of his or her own actions and thoughts? This debate is most clearly focused in forensic psychology (but in other professions as well) where a key issue at trial can be whether the defendant is a product of his or her environment and conditioned by it (or his or her genes or psychological structure) or if the defendant is capable of free will and thus master of his or her own destiny. This is the longstanding debate between determinism and voluntarism: determinism and free will.

The fourth pillar is a product of the foregoing three: different research methods are called for depending upon the choice one makes among the contrasting ontologies, epistemologies and models of human beings available. Most generally, one will adopt a positivist stance or an anti-positivist stance. If one adopts the positivist stance then one adopts the view that the social world is similar to the natural world and exists independent of the experiencing individual, and will thus adopt but also adapt the existing methods, tactics and procedures of the natural sciences. The aim will be to establish regularities and relationships between factors of interest and the approach to analysis will be predominantly quantitative. In a nut-shell, this choice will be for the normative stance and for a nomothetic approach, selecting from among the plethora of research methods that fall within the scientific method.

However, if one adopts the alternative ontology, epistemology and model of the human being, different consequences flow. If subjective experience in creating the social world is held to be important the methods of science will be eschewed for other techniques or approaches already available in sociology and currently being developed in social psychology and cultural studies. These methods will be geared to understanding how individuals create, modify and negotiate meaning in the world. As such the methods will be qualitative rather than quantitative, and designed to document what is unique and particular to the individual (or group) rather than what is universal and general. Because of its stress on the individual and the particular, this approach will adopt the interpretive stance and the ideographic approach in research, selecting from among the numerous qualitative approaches now available. Wherever possible the imposition of external form and structure will be avoided since this would reflect the viewpoint of the observer as opposed to that of the actor directly involved. Theory and meaning extraction will be grounded in data generated by the research act, and theory will follow, not precede, the research.

Researchers of this persuasion point out that positivism failed to notice key differences between human beings and inert 'things' or objects: 'Social Science, unlike natural science, stands in a subject–subject relation to its field of study, not a subject–object relation; it deals with a pre-interpreted world in which the meanings developed by active subjects enter the actual constitution or product of the world' (Giddens, 1976: 146).

Social science is thus a subjective undertaking rather than objective one. But more than this, because of our self-awareness and power of language, we must view social interaction as a different order of complexity from any other and thus no other system is capable of providing a sufficiently powerful model to advance our understanding of ourselves.

As early as 1934 people like Mead were arguing that anti-positivists were going too far in abandoning scientific procedures of verification and giving up hope of discovering useful generalizations about behaviour. Some have questioned whether there are not dangers in giving up the methods of science for methods more akin to literature, biography and journalism, and Coolican (1998: 727) points out that skills of analysis must rise above common sense or more or less well executed journalism. Others have asked 'is it possible to move from the interpretation of one specific action or event . . . to a theoretical explanation of behaviour' (Dixon, 1973: 4–5).

## Commonalities in the Research Report

If the most distinctive feature of science is its empirical nature, its second most noticeable feature is its set of procedures which serve not only to indicate what was done but also to allow replication by other researchers in the field. Having said this it must be made clear that there is no one scientific method – no single invariant approach to problem-solving: 'What is important is the overall idea of scientific research as a controlled rational process of reflective enquiry, the interdependent nature of the parts of the process, and the paramount importance of the problem and its statement' (Kerlinger, 1970: 17).

Having said that, however, all research, of whatever persuasion, must cohere with canons that stand as criteria against which a study can, and will be, evaluated. These canons are, according to Lincoln and Guba (1985), 'truthfulness', applicability, consistency and neutrality. Within the experimental, quantitative tradition, these canons are met by considerations of internal validity, external validity, reliability and objectivity, respectively. Within the qualitative approach the equivalent considerations are credibility, transferability, dependability and confirmability, respectively. Within the latter tradition, personal and functional reflexivity and triangulation of data, method, investigator and theory are important considerations in assessing the achievement of the canons of 'good research' (see Banister et al., 1994).

## And so to Analysis

Assuming that the researcher has selected his or her preferred stance and consequent method, and executed the research programme efficiently and effectively, eventually he or she arrives at the data-handling, analysing and interpretation stage.

For those researchers who capture their data in, or reduce them to, numerical form – and even those who don't (see below) – statistical packages of great scope and power are now available. The industrial standard is SPSS. Just as important, there now exists a blizzard of 'idiot guide' handbooks that guide the fledgling researcher through data preparation, data entry, statistical test selection and, eventually, output interpretation. While most researchers will be familiar with versions of SSPS from their undergraduate curricula, none the less at postgraduate level they will have to learn the more complex and advanced statistical techniques involving multivariate analyses.

But for all its power and precision SPSS is incomplete as a researcher's tool. Progressively literature reviews – the sine qua non of all research – are becoming statistically rather than verbally based. This is achieved by meta-analysis. SPSS does not have this facility and the researcher (or the department) will need to purchase one or other of the few bespoke meta-analysis packages currently available. Likewise, power analysis is becoming an important consideration for journal editors and dissertation examiners but, once again, SPSS does not have this facility and it has to be purchased as a stand-alone package.

In addition, much professional applied research employs designs which are best handled by structural equation modelling (SEM) or path analysis (PA). Again SPSS is not the best statistical package with which to attempt these analyses. Specifically designed SEM and PA packages exist, and these techniques will become an essential part of the researcher's armoury.

When is qualitative methodology quantitative? When they use Q methodology (Stephenson, 1953). This methodology is undergoing a renaissance, and for good reason – it straddles the ever-widening divide between quantitative and qualitative approaches to research. For those who use it, statistical packages exist which factor analyse by subject (PCQ3 and PQMethod, and new Window-based versions). Thus the richness of qualitative data can be given precision by the application of numerical techniques. Likewise, content analysis, discourse analysis and other theme-based qualitative methodologies can be contained and informed by currently available statistical and software packages such as NUDIST, ETHNIGRAPH and QUALPRO.

Increasingly, then, for all researchers, of whatever persuasion, computer-based data handling will become important and a necessary skill that has to be acquired in order to be counted as a competent professional.

## QUESTIONS FOR REFLECTION AND DISCUSSION

1 Are there any fundamental differences in the research that is likely to be carried out under the rubric of clinical, occupational, educational, guidance, counselling or forensic psychology?

2 Has the qualitative vs. quantitative debate generated more heat than light?

3 Research methodology has a number of criteria by which its value is evaluated. What are they and can they be prioritized, or are the criteria context dependent?

4 Pick out some political assertions that appear to be 'scientific' and subject them to the scientific sieve. Do any of them survive?

## Suggestions for further reading

Cook, T.D. and Campbell, D. (1979) *Quasi-experimentation: Design and Analysis Issues for Field Settings*. Chicago, IL: Rand McNally.
   Given that most real-life research does not conform to the true experiment or its conditions, this book on quasi-experimental designs is essential reading for any professional concerned to conduct research that is designed to have maximum impact on knowledge accumulation or policy development.

Cryer, P. (1996) *The Research Student's Guide to Success*. Buckingham: Open University Press.
   Designed for the PhD student, this book nevertheless is a mine of helpful hints for all researchers. In the OU style the book is replete with self-test questions and tasks that ease the learning and development of research skills and tactics.

Kinnear, P.R. and Gray, C.D. (2000) *SPSS for Windows Made Simple. Release 10*. Hove: Psychology Press.
   An absolute must for any researcher who has to analyse quantitative data and requires computational assistance. SPSS is the industrial standard for parametric and non-parametric analysis, and this book really does live up to its title *Made Simple*.

Robson, C. (1993) *Real World Research*. Oxford: Blackwell.
   The generalist's best introduction to types of research that any professional person is likely to need to know about. It covers models of the research process and deciding upon research questions. Methods of data gathering are discussed for a variety of research designs and approaches, and it takes you gently into data analysis and report writing.

# 11 Beyond Evidence-based Practice: Rethinking the Relationship between Research, Theory and Practice

*David Harper, M. Rachel Mulvey and Mary Robinson*

## SUMMARY

*In this chapter we examine the relationship between research, theory and practice in the life of the applied psychologist. Current UK policy initiatives stress the importance of basing professional practice on firm evidence – what has become known as 'evidence-based practice'. The notion of the applied psychologist as a scientist-practitioner is one model of relating practice to evidence. However, such models present a number of dilemmas for the applied psychologist. If we only ever do what is deemed effective, how do we develop innovative approaches? How can knowledge of groups help us in deciding how to approach an individual case? Do practitioners really base what they do on the research literature? If not (and surveys suggest that many practitioners are not as influenced by the literature as we'd like to think), why is this? There are often tensions in this debate between practitioners and academic researchers – for example, about what kind of knowledge counts as evidence. We need to ask whether the research that is currently done is the most useful for helping people in practice. Do we need to move towards more practice-based research rather than research-based practice? Other models of the relationship between theory, research and practice have been proposed including that of the reflective practitioner who draws on research evidence but combines it with past experience and other knowledge. We argue that, at the very least, we need to move away from narrow modernist notions of science to embrace a broader range of research methodologies while remaining both accountable for what we do as professionals and able to give a rationale for practice that goes beyond assertion but is based on a wide variety of kinds of evidence.*

## The Rise of the Evidence-based Practice Movement

The last decade has seen an enormous rise in the priority given to 'evidence-based practice' in all areas of applied psychology. Within the NHS in the UK, for example, a focus on the importance of supporting evidence for interventions has led to the development of such journals as *Evidence-based Medicine* (www.ebm.bmjjournals.com), founded in 1995, and *Evidence-based Mental Health* (www.ebmentalhealth.com), founded in 1998. Within the UK criminal justice system, there have been a number of policy initiatives for reducing reoffending, such as *What Works. Reducing Re-offending: Evidence-based Practice* (Home Office, 1999). Such initiatives have the potential to focus public services on providing only those interventions for which there is firm evidence. This seems a laudable aim. Moreover, applied psychologists are in an excellent position to evaluate interventions. However, there are a number of dilemmas for applied psychologists in thinking about the relationship between research, theory and practice.

One dilemma is best expressed as a question: whose evidence? In other words, who gets to decide what counts as evidence? For example, the UK Department of Health's *National Service Framework for Mental Health* (DoH, 1999a: 6) lists five gradings of evidence:

> Type I evidence: at least one good systematic review and at least one randomised controlled trial.
> Type II evidence: at least one good randomised controlled trial.
> Type III evidence: at least one well-designed intervention study without randomisation.
> Type IV evidence: at least one well-designed observational study.
> Type V evidence: expert opinion, including the opinion of service users and carers.

Note that what service users and carers think is here relegated to the lowest category. In contrast to this kind of position, some commentators have argued that, in mental health, for example, those who use services have an important stake in the kind of services they are offered and thus the kind of criteria which are important to them need to be represented. Thus Perkins (2001) has noted that a reduction in psychiatric symptoms may not be the only or even the most important criterion of success in mental health services from a service user's point of view. Rather she argues that services need systematically to ascertain the goals of service users (as they define them) and accord them the status currently enjoyed by the views of professionals. She questions whether many interventions would look effective if outcome was measured by service users' scores on scales like Rogers et al.'s (1997) measurement of empowerment.

A related dilemma for applied psychologists can be expressed as: what kind of evidence and of what? In other words, what gets to count as evidence? In the field of health care, as we have seen, the randomized controlled trial (RCT) has come to be seen as a gold standard of evidence. In these trials, research participants are allocated to different interventions in a randomized fashion in what should be a 'double-blind' procedure. In other words, neither the participant nor the staff involved in their care should be able to tell what experimental condition they are in. In the USA there have been moves towards classifying psychotherapeutic interventions according to whether they are empirically supported or validated. But what is meant by 'empirical' here refers only to evidence from RCTs (Roth, 1999; Chambless and Ollendick, 2001).

There are a number of problems with the use of RCTs in the kinds of areas in which applied psychologists are likely to work, not least the practical and methodological difficulties of attaining double-blind procedures in practice (Moncrieff et al., 1998). Moreover, while they are able to answer a small number of important questions, RCTs are inappropriate for other questions practitioners might want to ask (Slade and Priebe, 2001; Williams and Garner, 2002). Thus while an RCT might be able to say that with X group of participants (and research samples are usually a highly selected group) experiencing Y problem, intervention W appears to work better than other interventions or no intervention at all, they are usually less able, if at all, to answer questions like what kind of people with these problems might benefit most or least and what kind of practitioners might be most and least able to use this intervention. Since RCTs are based on group means they tell us very little about individuals but, in practice, applied psychologists need to be able to work out what will help them in a particular situation. Roth (1999) has suggested the introduction of clinically meaningful analyses like the number needed to treat (NNT) criterion – that is, how many people would need to receive the experimental condition for one person to gain a benefit he or she would not have obtained from receiving the control condition. While noting that much research continues to focus on comparisons between 'brand name' therapies, Roth argues for the further development of pan-theoretical research which focuses on factors like the importance of the therapeutic alliance and the skilfullness with which interventions are implemented. In order to give a flavour of how applied psychologists negotiate a relationship between research, theory and practice in their different fields, we will next focus on three areas of applied psychology.

## Rhetoric, Reality and Practice: Three Perspectives on Evidence-based Practice in Applied Psychology

### Clinical psychology

Within clinical psychology the currently dominant model for relating research, theory and practice is that of the *scientist-practitioner* (for example, Barlow et al., 1984) first outlined following the conference of those associated with US clinical psychology training in 1949 at Boulder, Colorado. In this model there was a desire to train practitioners to apply the scientific method to understanding and aiding diagnosis and treatment, although in the UK the involvement of clinical psychology in treatment was much slower than in the USA (Pilgrim and Treacher, 1992). It was clear even at the time that this model was essentially a compromise position to prevent a split in the young profession between courses which emphasized either the scientist or practitioner side of the model (Pilgrim and Treacher, 1992). Even 50 years on there is a lively debate in clinical psychology about this model (for example, see the February 2000 issue of the *American Psychologist* for a variety of views); for a detailed examination of the different interpretations of the model, see Long and Hollin, 1997; Clegg, 1998; John, 1998; Milne and Paxton, 1998; Corrie and Callanan, 2000.

Pilgrim and Treacher (1992) have argued that the scientist-practitioner model serves a rhetorical function for the discipline of claiming the authority of science while, in practice, research has little impact. There is some evidence to support this. For example, few clinical psychologists actually *do* research if it is defined as publication in scientific journals. Norcross et al. (1992) noted that the modal number of publications for UK clinical psychologists was zero, with 8% of clinical psychologists producing approximately half of published work although 76% had published at least once in their careers. Moreover, few clinical psychologists *read* research: Milne et al. (1990) reported that only 20% of their sample had read an academic journal each week (although 45% did monthly); only 14% attended national scientific conferences; and only 16% thought published research had 'a lot' of influence on their work. Even when there is research, it is increasingly of a professional nature (for example, audits – see Clegg, 1998). In addition there have been a number of more conceptual criticisms – for example, of the implicit if not explicit individualistic and pathologizing focus of much research. Thus despite extensive research demonstrating that the concept of 'schizophrenia' has little reliability or validity, it continues to be used as a variable in much clinical psychology research (Boyle, 2002).

Despite these continuing problems, trainers on clinical psychology courses, trainees and regional NHS psychologists still tend to endorse the scientist-practitioner model in surveys, particularly if the notion of science is interpreted broadly (Kennedy and Llewelyn, 2001). It seems that there are issues of how clinical psychologists construct their professional identity at stake here as well as whether or not research is conducted (Corrie and Callanan, 2000; 2001). Clinical psychology thus faces a number of choices for the future in relation to the scientist-practitioner model and to evidence-based practice in general.

One option is to maintain the model but simply to broaden what we mean by 'research' to include a wider variety of studies, including so-called 'quick and dirty' projects (for example, Milne et al., 1990). This would fit with the comments of some that the model represents 'an attitude to practice rather than a commitment to participation in the academic community' (Kennedy and Llewelyn, 2001: 77). Milne (1999) has developed this option further by differentiating between the different kinds of relationships practitioners can have with research – for example, as scientist-practitioners (who conduct the often unattainable ideal of PhD-type research) or evidence-based practitioners (who conduct research with others in line with NHS research and development objectives). Roth (1999) has warned of the dangers of going down the US path of identifying 'empirically supported therapies' because of the way this has been used to restrict practice, especially by managed-care organizations. In the NHS there has been more of an emphasis on the development of clinical guidelines which involve both evidence and professional opinion (for example, Roth and Fonagy, 1996).

Another option is to have a much broader and inclusive notion of 'science' and 'evidence' and to step away from simplistically modernist and naively realist views (Corrie and Callanan, 2001). Thus Larner (2001: 40) has argued that 'the choice is not between psychological science and non-science, but between an exclusively logical-positivist and a critical science'. However, while it is important not to set up false oppositions between theoretical paradigms, it is equally important to understand potential conflicts and contradictions between different orientations and paradigms (Harper, in press). A third option is to move to different models altogether, some of which will be discussed below – for example,

Schön's *reflective practitioner* (1987); the *critical practitioner* (Larner, 2001); a practice-based inquiry (for example, Hoshmand and Polkinghorne, 1992); or towards a narrative-based practice (for example, Greenhalgh, 1999; Roberts, 2000). It remains to be seen where UK clinical psychology will go. Most likely is that it will do what it has usually done as a discipline and aim for a compromize solution. Thus one clinical psychology course has recently stated that it conceptualizes the clinical psychologist as a 'reflective scientist practitioner' (Clearing House for Postgraduate Courses in Clinical Psychology, 2001: 103).

## Educational psychology

For the educational psychologist the current UK government view of education as central to the drive towards social inclusion has brought the issue of theory, research and practice into sharp relief. Working within the disciplines of education and psychology and at the individual, group and institutional levels, educational psychologists are aware of the importance both of keeping abreast of current research and of contributing to the body of evidence consulted by policy-makers.

The spread of consultation approaches to work with schools and other institutions (Gutkin and Reynolds, 1990) has coincided with the need for more transparency in the application of specific interventions and the need to satisfy public accountability initiatives such as best value – reviewing services in terms of organization and value for money (DefEE, 1997b). This concern with the effects of intervention is apparent in both national and international contexts in educational planning, the current government focus on targeted spending in education and the broader search for a rationale for policy-making in areas of major social expenditure such as health, social care, education and criminal justice.

Evidence-based practice represents an approach to decision-making about the most effective intervention that is transparent and accountable. It focuses on the current best evidence about the effects of particular interventions in both the short and longer term and has implications for practitioners working with an individual child and policy-makers charged with the responsibility for the well-being of the whole community.

The broad definition of educational research outlined by the Organization for Economic Co-operation and Development (OECD) clearly indicates an interest in intervention beyond that which is simply concerned with raising achievement. It sees research as:

> [S]ystematic original investigation or inquiry and associated development activities concerning the social, cultural, economic and political contexts within which educational systems operate and learning takes place; the purposes of education; the processes of teaching, learning and general development of children, youths and adults; the work of educators; the resources and organizational arrangements to support educational work; the policies and strategies to achieve educational objectives; and the social, cultural, political and economic outcomes of education (OECD, 1995: 37).

The educational psychologist is well placed to look beyond measures of efficacy and to consider the impact of particular interventions on issues such as self-concept, social interaction and the emotional well-being of client groups.

Individual pieces of research can present a confusing and conflicting picture of 'what works' in terms of any intervention. Within education, the current focus on research has resulted in greater attention being paid to systematic reviews. Such reviews seek to interrogate research evidence to gain answers to questions such as 'do children who learn phonics in nursery read independently at a significantly earlier age?' or 'does a reduction in class size improve children's academic performance?' Systematic reviews which involve identifying research reports and 'assessing them in an explicit and standard way so as to produce accessible syntheses of research findings' (Evidence for Policy and Practice Information and Co-ordinating Centre, 2001) have the advantage of protecting against bias and providing a mechanism for accountability. The approach is open to abuse (for example, conducting the interrogation in such a way so as to justify what is happening), but it represents the most realistic opportunity to base policy on the best available evidence.

The current UK government focus on social inclusion places education at the centre of investment in the future and nowhere is this more evident than in the early years where the aim appears to be the establishment of 'an ideal of early years provision as a well managed enterprise producing products to meet the needs of consumers and doing so to predictable and predetermined standards' (Moss, 2001: 79). Because of the scarcity of educational provision to preschool children, some quite strong studies of particular approaches have been carried out. The best known initiative to be scrutinized in some detail is Head Start, a US project aimed at breaking the cycle of deprivation. This long-term project generated numerous studies in the 20 years between 1965 and 1985, 210 of which were subjected to a meta-analysis by McKey et al. (1985). The results are summarized by Sylva (1994) as placing the general benefit of this kind of preschool experience beyond reasonable doubt.

In the UK the Sure Start initiative (for rationale and background, www.surestart.gov.uk) represents a key element of the government drive to tackle child poverty and social inclusion. This is an early intervention programme aimed at integrating services to young children and their families in order to break cycles of deprivation. Planning included notions of 'getting it right from the start' (Ball, 1994) and consideration of what works in early years provision. It was based on many of the lessons learnt from Head Start but with more of an emphasis on community involvement and the need to fit the initiative into particular local priorities.

Prior to the actions of the UK DfEE to co-ordinate and integrate services in the early years (through the development of Early Years Development and Childcare Plans in each local education authority) this area was considered a 'Cinderella service' where the emphasis was on 'care' and the serious work of educational planning started with entry to school. Provision of early years education was patchy, variable, subject to frequent reverses of fortune and generally viewed as less important than 'real' education of the school-age population. Responsibility for provision in the early years rested with local authorities or the private sector. The rapid growth of early years provision has afforded educational psychologists an opportunity both to reflect on the evidence status of some of the beliefs held by those in early years planning about what is critical in early development and learning and to highlight the need to establish a comprehensive evidence base upon which future policy development can rest.

While little is explicitly written about the theories underpinning this rapid development, assumptions are made about child development; the factors influencing progress in learning; and how learning can best be organized for young children. Moss (2001) questions the dominance of developmental psychology in early childhood policy and practice at the expense of other perspectives such as social constructionist theories. Many psychologists (for example, Parker-Rees, 1997; Mortimore, 2001) question the shift in emphasis from play to learning in some of the curricular initiatives. The specific interest of the current government in raising standards has led to a highlighting of the teaching of literacy and numeracy. This emphasis seems to be based on the assumption that providing specifically focused literacy and numeracy from an ever earlier age will lead to the raising of standards. Aubery (2001) sees this as an example of how research and the efficacy of holistic child learning can indicate the dangers inherent in a narrow curriculum which overemphasizes literacy and numeracy.

Is it sufficient for an intervention to have proven long-term benefits for it to be included in policy determination? MacDonald and Roberts (1996) would suggest that the optimal intervention combines a good 'here and now' experience with good results. The responsibility of the early years provider and those contributing to meeting the needs of children in the early years is that, as far as possible, we are providing an effective intervention in a child's life. If we accept that practice should, wherever possible, be based on evidence, we need to ensure that the evidence we need is available, widely disseminated and debated. The awareness of what has been shown to be effective can then be balanced alongside professional judgement and knowledge of a particular child or context and the need for innovative practice in order to develop and extend the interventions needed to bring about change in children's lives. It is not suggested that evidence-based practice is an alternative to the exercise of clinical or professional judgement; rather, it suggests that this judgement is made in the knowledge of the wider-scale implications of a particular approach.

One positive aspect of increased central planning in education presents an opportunity for educational psychologists to be more proactive in relating theory, research and practice. The development of the EPPI Centre (Evidence for Policy and Practice Information and Co-ordinating Centre, 2001), based at the University Of London's Institute of Education, represents a rare opportunity for ensuring that theory remains central to research activity. The centre has been set up to undertake research synthesis by supporting a network of review groups undertaking systematic reviews in different areas of education (including early years provision) and presents practitioners with an opportunity to contribute to research at all levels and ensure a sound theoretical underpinning. It is part of the responsibility of the educational psychology profession to ensure that the research evidence considered clearly differentiates between assumption and evidence and includes holistic and child-centred perspectives on what is considered to be the most effective approach.

## Careers guidance

As policy initiatives have come and gone with successive political administrations, those working in public service (that is, in organizations whose main source of income is from the public purse, delivering professionals' services either free or subsidized at the point of delivery) have had to shape their practice to the wheel of policy imperative. There has been evident pressure on careers service professionals as a result of policies which do not fully represent the knowledge base that underpins careers guidance practice. As a result the performance indicators devised for contract compliance do not really measure the work practitioners actually do. Such tensions between policy and practice are also to be found in further education (Randle and Brady, 1997).

It is clear that the fundamental relationship of practitioner and client has been affected by the target-driven or audit culture now commonly found in public service delivery. Every practitioner has had to make choices about how to practise in response to funding and audit requirements. Whether conducted in public sector or private practice, to fee-paying or non-paying clients, the careers guidance interview is no longer a process shared only by the professional and the client. Rather, there is a sense of an uninvited guest where policy hovers in the interview, vying with the client for the practitioner's attention.

Whether competing in the open market or delivering to a contract, companies provide professional services to ever more sophisticated and demanding clients. As a result there is likely to be pressure for that service to be more complex and more closely tailored to individual customer demand. Ideally, this customer challenge requires employees who can both think around complex problems and work across disciplines to provide appropriate answers to novel problems. An organization which seeks to simplify its business and routinize its workforce is neither equipping its staff or itself to respond to a complex and unpredictable external environment. Success in such an environment might be sought through commitment to staff development, even though really encouraging employees to innovate means allowing them to try something new and occasionally to fail. Above all, however, staff development requires that the people themselves recognize what they have learnt from their experience. This kind of reflection has to be resourced, at some real cost to the company; but only through this kind of true investment in people can they and the organization learn.

Like educational psychology, careers guidance has been shaped by recent government policies based on an agenda of 'social inclusion' (Social Exclusion Unit, 1999). The policy is aimed at all young people aged between 16 and 18 but targets in particular those not in education, employment or training. The policy introduces a new kind of service in which personal advisers work with individual clients to deal with whatever need they present, from drug dependency to careers guidance, with the intention of providing the best start in life for every young person (DfEE, 2000b). With effect from April 2002, personal advisers are to work within Connexions partnerships. One interesting possibility afforded by this radical reorganization is that it gives practitioners and managers alike the chance to reflect. Indeed, the draft standards explicitly encourage such activities (DfEE,

2001). Beyond the advantages for employees and organizations, reflection on practice fulfils an important role in the claim to professional practice: 'If CEG [careers and educational guidance] practitioners want to be seen as professionals, reflective practice and, by direct implication, developing a research culture are essential' (Careers Research and Advisory Centre, 1998: 6). The emphasis is firmly on 'evidence-based practice' although there is little clarity about what is meant by the term other than 'ensuring that new interventions are based on rigorous research and evaluation into what works' (DfEE, 2000: 33). The emphasis on the evidence base is related to earlier criticisms of research in education by Hargreaves (1996) for lacking a cumulative approach. His argument is that there needs to be systematic testing of a body of knowledge to extend and enhance what has already been researched.

## Tensions and Dilemmas in Negotiating the Relationship between Research, Theory and Practice

In the previous section we gave examples of how applied psychology and applied psychologists in different settings have tried to relate theory, research and practice. We have seen that there are many theoretical debates and practical ups and downs. In the final section we will summarize some of the key issues and suggest possible ways forward; here we note, however, that it is clear that bringing theory, research and practice together is far from easy and, if it appears to be easy, it is probably because one is not doing justice to one of these areas. Simplistic and scientistic approaches to the relationship could be said to be founded on notions of 'expert knowledge' which either devalue or professionalize lay and service user knowledges. Clegg (1998), for example, has noted that such models draw on modernist ideas of 'technical rationality'. Moreover, for better or worse politicians and policy-makers are not persuaded by empirical investigation only (as a speaker at one conference put it 'we're a long way from evidence-based government'), and research is not the only show in town in planning services (Cook and Shadish, 1986, Kane, 2002). Moreover, 'theory' and 'practice' are often institutionally separate: for example, on many courses in the applied psychology disciplines academic teaching is separate from practical placements; journals tend to have either a research or practice focus; and there are different conferences and books and so on (Potter, 1982).

## Beyond Evidence: Research as a Form of Learning within the Community of Practice

As a result of the kinds of pressures found when trying to apply research findings to practice, some applied psychologists and others have started to think about how to construct research that would be most helpful to practitioners and users of services. In other words, instead of the usual top-down approach of questioning why practitioners do not do more research we might try a bottom-up approach and ask what it is about how research is usually conceived that prevents practitioners engaging in it. Thus commentators like Hoshmand and Polkinghorne (1992: 60) have talked of the need for new forms of knowledge and inquiry – a 'knowledge of practice'.

In order to deal with the complex and unfamiliar situation, the applied psychologist needs to broaden and develop his or her repertoire. In other professional disciplines, notably health visiting (Fish, 1991) and social work (Winter, 1989; 1991), practitioners have made conscious attempts to ensure that the professional reflects on his or her working practices (Kolb, 1984). The intended outcome of such reflection is to create a virtuous circle, where the learning outcomes from an individual's reflection on his or her practice can inform future action, which in turn leads to further learning and a further iteration of the reflective learning cycle.

Eraut (1994: 9) lists the components of responsibility to be found within the professional domain:

+ A moral commitment to serve the interests of clients.

+ A professional obligation to self-monitor and periodically to review the effectiveness of one's practice.

+ A professional obligation to expand one's repertoire, to reflect on one's experience and to develop one's expertise.

+ An obligation that is professional as well as contractual to contribute to the quality of one's organization.

+ An obligation to reflect upon and contribute to discussions about the changing role of one's profession in wider society.

Many professional bodies require their practitioners to undertake activities in line with these recommendations. For example, the Institute of Career Guidance (ICG) requires two ongoing commitments from practitioners who seek inclusion on the professional register. One is to practise by the institute's code of ethics, the other is to undertake continued professional development (CPD). The importance of CPD for the individual is that it ensures that practice keeps up with innovation. The importance of CPD for the profession is that the sharing of such learning ensures the development of the collective knowledge base, the next generation of learning for the profession (Engeström et al., 1995). For the individual practitioner, research may form part of a programme of CPD, and CPD may be a way for those who are not active researchers to learn from research about how to improve their practice.

In order to transfer what he or she has learnt from solving a problem in one context to a problem presented in another context, the individual practitioner will need to reflect on his or her practice and on what he or she has learnt from it. Winter (1991) lays emphasis on the upward spiral where a learner reflects on their working practice, identifies a learning outcome which then feeds into his or her professional practice, which is in turn the object of further reflection. The learner's practice is no longer predicated on a fixed body of knowledge but, rather, on a continuous development of the theory which underpins that practice.

A model which appears to embrace this kind of approach is that of Schön's (1987) *reflective practitioner*. This model differs sharply from notions of technical rationality (Clegg, 1998). This approach assumes that expert practitioners can easily be identified and agreed by peers in any given situation. Consensual agreement among practitioners on important factors often focuses on personal qualities such as wisdom, integrity and intuition. While research-based knowledge is accessed during this process it is combined with knowledge of other cases which bear some similarity and with subjective, emotional perceptions about the particular therapeutic relationship or context (Clegg, 1998). Here, then, there is an emphasis on an integration of theory, research and practice at a more personal level. It also assumes agency on the part of the practitioner. In this it appears to draw on an active philosophy of learning (see Figure 11.1). This ties in with previous work on philosophies of learning (for example, Kolb et al., 1974). It is possible to delineate different strands of reflection within Schön's model, and Fish (1991: 79) describes four which she suggests are essential to the effective supervision of practice in health visiting and initial teacher training:

1 *Factual* – description of the situation, then of the practitioner's feelings.
2 *Retrospective* – holist reflection on what was new and what was discovered.
3 *Sub-stratum* – cultural or contextual assumptions.
4 *Connective* – linking to further practice.

These strands are not linear or necessarily sequential, but the professional can weave them together in reflecting on a learning interaction either with a client/pupil or with his or her supervisor (as opposed to manager) or mentor. While Fish offers these insights into professional formation, she is adamant that they are not recommendations 'as that would be the technical/rational school of professionalism' and she prefers the 'professional artistry model' (1991: 79). Eraut (1989: 184) argues that critical control of 'largely intuitive aspects of practice' is essential for the transfer of knowledge practice to a wider range of situations, and is desirable for the improvement of performance in familiar situations.

There is, however, a counter-argument to the concept and practice of the reflective practitioner, which is that, while the autonomous practitioner indubitably works alone with his or her client, he or she is held responsible to his or her peers

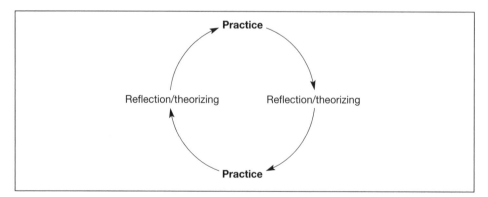

**Figure 11.1 An active philosophy of learning**

within the practitioner's community of practice. Very often, particularly in the public sector, professionals are employed and work in organizations. So while professionals practise alone, they never practise in isolation. Lave (1991: 64) depicts learning as 'a social phenomenon constituted in the experienced, lived-in world', and argues that, within a community of practice, there is a relationship between those who are well established and those coming into the profession. She argues that these two ends of the practice spectrum should be depicted not as teacher/pupil or expert/novice, but as 'old-timers' and 'newcomers' (p. 68). She also indicates the essential iteration within a community of practice, a circle of life, where 'newcomers' enter the community, are accepted and become 'old-timers'. She goes on to identify as a third category those who have completed this circle: the 'newcomers become old-timers'. The relationship between old-timers and newcomers is one of *mutual* dependency: 'the newcomers [are dependent] in order to learn, and the oldtimers in order to carry on the community of practice . . . success of both new and old members depends on the eventual replacement of the oldtimers by newcomers-become-oldtimers themselves' (p.74).

Engeström (1994: 11) suggests that the view of learning as receiving knowledge and practising skills by repeating the same tasks is misconceived. He argues that (p. 12) 'learning is constructing' rather than repetition and storing, and distinguishes three levels of learning. First-order learning is a form of conditioning, typically imitating. In first-order learning the focus is limited to the immediate task. Second-order learning identifies general patterns and embraces some investigative learning. Third-order learning happens when the learner questions the task and transforms the context itself. This questioning can occur as cognitive conflict, which is often the stimulus or basis for deep learning:

> Cognitive conflicts as a source of motivation creates a *context of criticism* at the beginning of the process of investigative learning. Students become aware of limits and contradictions in their practice and in the knowledge and tools they routinely use. Such a critical stance lays a vitally important groundwork for the construction of new knowledge and new forms of practice (Engeström, 1994: 24, emphasis in original).

While this relates primarily to the learning of the individual, there must be some widening from the individual to the collective to develop the knowledge base shared by the community of practice, and the impetus of conflict for learning is found in this wider context too. The 'collective zone of proximal development' (Engeström, 1994: 44) is the contested area between traditional practice and alternative future directions.

## From Evidence to Accountability

All professions can expect closer government interest in their self-regulation (Friedman et al., 2000; Phillips, 2001), and this should include social reporting as part of their evaluation and quality assurance procedures. In social reporting some voice is given to the end-users whose views are not always given as much weight as those of the professionals, as we argued earlier, in order to enable professionals to be accountable to their stakeholders. For professional services delivered at public expense, stakeholder evaluation will be critical, although this runs the risk of identifying a service which cannot be funded, in effect creating a demand which cannot be supplied. The Careers Research Advisory Centre (CRAC) predicts innovation will be the hallmark of successful careers companies and recommends investment to increase intellectual capital. It also connects competitive success with research: 'Successful innovation will almost certainly require CEG providers to have strategic planning processes which embrace the findings of external and internal research and evaluation' (CRAC, 1998: 2). Again, the Connexions partnership arrangements can be seen as an opportunity for careers companies to engage in evidence-based research in order to demonstrate added value and value for money. They may also help to set an agenda for other public services to invest real resources of time and money in order to allow for evidence-based practice from reflective practice at the level of the individual practitioner through to organizational learning at the level of the service provider.

However, we would argue that one of the important issues which appears to get lost in the debate about evidence-based practice is the reason we need evidence for what we do. Rather than fetishize 'evidence' we see the major issue here as about *accountability*. Applied psychologists need to be accountable to a wide variety of stakeholders (including the recipients of their services) for what they do and so we need to be able to justify and give a theoretically reasoned rationale for why we have used one intervention rather than another. If we keep this notion in mind it means that we need to move beyond narrow modernist conceptions of science in evaluating our work. Rather than simply relying on narrow criteria of reliability and validity we could, perhaps, evaluate our work according to the more inclusive but still rigorous criteria emerging in qualitative research (for example, Yardley, 2000).

In evaluating our theories we also need to draw on ethical principles and criteria to orientate us to what count as better theories and practices. Some have argued that we need to debate the values that underpin much research and have called for 'ethics before effectiveness' (Bracken and Thomas, 2000: 22). The American social constructionist psychologist, Ken Gergen, has suggested that we need to focus more on the *usefulness* of our theories (Misra, 1993). Of course, we also need to examine other ways of commissioning research and, increasingly, researchers are looking at partnerships with users of services rather than only with the traditional commissioners and purchasers of services (for example, Patel, 1999; Lindow, 2001; Faulkner and Thomas, 2002). We have argued here that we need to move away from simplistic conceptions of evidence-based practice and to seek a more dynamic and reflective conceptualization of the relationship between theory, research and practice. This entails not only developing real-world criteria for evaluating research evidence but also different ways of going about the research enterprise itself, embracing a wider variety of methodologies and kinds of evidence. Only then are we likely to find not just a more effective relationship between theory, research and practice but also a more ethical one.

## QUESTIONS FOR REFLECTION AND DISCUSSION

1   What is 'evidence-based practice' and what have been the implications for applied psychology of the rise of the evidence-based practice movement?

2   What kinds of evidence could psychologists gather, apart from that found in randomized trials?

3   What are some of the criticisms of a narrow conception of evidence-based practice?

4   What alternatives are there to models like that of the 'scientist-practitioner', and what are their pros and cons?

5   As well as effectiveness, what additional factors might psychologists need to bear in mind in making judgements about the appropriateness of particular interventions? How might they go about investigating these factors?

## Suggestions for further reading

David, T. (ed.) (2001) *Promoting Evidence-based Practice in Early Childhood Education: Research and its Implications*. Volume 1. Oxford: Elsevier Science.
A good overview of current research in this area.

Clegg, J. (1998) *Critical Issues in Clinical Practice*. London: Sage.
A critical examination of different approaches to thinking about theory, research and practice. Written by a clinical psychologist but easily applicable to other areas of applied psychology.

Priebe, S and Slade, M (2002) *Evidence in Metal Health Care*. London: Brunner-Routledge.
A good overview of some of the debates about evidence in mental health contexts.

Roth, A. and Fonagy, P. (1996) *What Works for Whom? A Critical Review of Psychotherapy Research*. London: Guilford Press.
A thorough overview of psychotherapy research but also includes a sophisticated model outlining how practitioners might draw on evidence in exercising their professional judgement – written by two clinical psychologists but, again, applicable to other areas.

Schön, D.A. (1987) *Educating the Reflective Practitioner*. San Francisco, CA: Jossey-Bass.
A good introduction to the reflective practitioner model.

# Sexism in Psychology and how to End it: Feminist and Critical Debates in Applied Contexts

*Irina Anderson and Bipasha Ahmed*

## SUMMARY

*This chapter focuses on the difficulties that an applied or professional psychologist may encounter when attempting to utilize research findings deriving from academic social psychology and it discusses such issues from a feminist perspective. We argue for the problematization of research findings in the context of sexism in research and, given this, how they may best be applied in practitioner contexts. Drawing on research conducted within the sexual violence research paradigm, we explore how the latent construct of sexism may (inadvertently) permeate academic research findings, creating difficulties for the professional or applied psychologist who works with the population groups to whom the very findings of this research apply. Although problems of applying this research may become apparent in any sphere, these may become particularly acute when, for example, an educational, clinical or counselling psychologist is trying to work with already disadvantaged or marginalized social groups such as sexual abuse or sexual assault survivors. The issue of sexism in social psychological research has been widely explored by feminist psychologists (Ussher, 1989; Griffin, 1995). However, this issue has not been tackled to such an extent in the context of research about sexual violence and, in particular, the implications that sexism in this arena may have for the practitioner have not been widely considered. This chapter evaluates some of the theoretical and methodological concerns that feminist psychology brings to the research agenda and, using rape perception studies as examples, examines the contribution that feminist debates can make not only to the ways in which both academics and practitioners assess research findings but also to our roles as practitioners in the context of sensitive topics of application such as sexual violence.*

## Sexism in Psychology

Psychological academic research has often been criticized for being prejudiced and for obscuring research findings based on these prejudices. For example, psychologists have challenged psychology on the grounds that mainstream social science is, among other things, racist (e.g. Howitt and Owusu-Bempah, 1994; Ahmed et al. 2000) and heterosexist (Stainton Rogers and Stainton Rogers, 2001). In addition, feminist psychologists have long argued that it is also essentially androcentric, producing knowledge about predominantly male behaviour on topics which are seen to be of interest mostly to men (Griffin, 1986), which are then generalized to 'people' in general. Psychology as a science has also been criticized by feminists for serving patriarchal strategic ends so that the scientific principles underpinning psychology work in the interests of (white, bourgeois, heterosexual) men. Researchers have argued that the scientific knowledges produced of men and women support the patriarchal status quo by constructing gender and gender differences as naturally occurring, therefore unchanging, as opposed to socially constructed, therefore malleable, categories. For example, psychologists prefer to see gender as a biological category where men can be conceptualized as, among other things, more active, stoical and intelligent than women. This viewpoint has been strongly contested by social constructionists who argue for the flexible societal negotiation of gender categories (Wilkinson, 1997). Thus, an allegedly value-free psychological science has produced supposedly objective evidence that women are, for example, naturally suited (only) to domesticity and mothering (Jordanova, 1989), are less intelligent than men (Bleier, 1984), are less capable than men of mathematical and spatial reasoning (Walkerdine, 1989) and are more prone to sickness and mental instability (Ussher, 1991). Given the many arguments that such findings are more expressive of a particular gaze or worldview (i.e. a patriarchal one) rather than being simply reflective of reality, they may present problems for practitioners who wish to incorporate such findings into applied contexts.

## Sexism in Sexual Violence Research

To illustrate our argument further, we will refer to sexual violence research in social psychology and, in particular, to rape perception research (see reviews by Pollard, 1992; Ward, 1995) as an example of how psychological research may be accused of sexism and what the consequences might be for those wishing to utilize such findings in practitioner contexts.

The rape perception framework is a loose term used to describe the many attributional and attitudinal studies which typically ask participants to read a hypothetical incident of rape and then answer a series of questions on it. These questions usually measure, on Likert-type scales, the amount of blame, fault and/or responsibility the participants attribute to the people involved in the incident such as the attacker and the victim, as well as other judgements such as their perceptions of the victim's or perpetrator's character, behaviour, bad luck, etc. Sometimes, the scales utilize a cumulative measure to gain an impression of the participant's overall attitude towards the rape victim and/or the attacker. Although a popular and highly productive research paradigm (for example, Pollard reviewed 110 studies in a 15-year period of 1975–90; also, many more studies were performed during this period which were not reviewed by Pollard), there are nevertheless a number of difficulties with the rape perception framework which, when scrutinized from a feminist standpoint (e.g. Wilkinson, 1988), often reveal highly dubious and ethically suspect methodological practices. For example, it has previously been illustrated how rape perception research may be disempowering to female (and to a certain extent male) participants. Anderson and Doherty (1997) suggest that inadequate attention to the detail of the methods used and the research questions asked in a typical rape perception study often leaves participants struggling to re-evaluate the victim's role in the rape even after it has already been decided that the perpetrator is to blame for the incident. Anderson and Doherty (1997) showed how some studies ask participants to attribute blame to the victim on a rating scale even though the incident they have just read clearly states that the victim was genuinely raped by the perpetrator and that she is therefore a legitimate victim of rape. In this case, it is argued by the authors that this practice occurs largely because researchers fail to orientate to their role as researchers of a highly gendered topic such as rape in a society characterized by unequal gender power. This is displayed by little or no attention that is afforded to the terminology that is used to describe the rape, where labels such as 'rape', 'victim' and 'perpetrator', despite their connotations regarding responsibility and blame, are freely included in the description. Similarly, little or no sensitivity is displayed towards participants' reactions and emotions when they are to be confronted with the task of being asked to 'blame' an apparently genuine victim. The participants may experience these practices as disempowering because in a research study such as this they are confronted prima facie with societal patriarchal assumptions that allegations of rape *are* problematic and continue to be problematic in spite of claims to the contrary (i.e. by the woman or, more specifically, the researcher who says she was raped). Society's reluctance to recognize the occurrence of rape in the first place is also reflected here, highlighting the difficulties that women typically experience in trying to get their claims of rape accepted and treated seriously.

Problematical methodological practices are also at the heart of the critique of sexism in rape perception research where rape perception researchers can be seen frequently to utilize dubious research designs. For example, a number of rape and pornography perception studies have measured gender differences in the degree of sexual arousal to rape depictions (e.g. Malamuth and Check, 1980). However, no theoretical reason is given for why *women's* sexual arousal should be measured as well as men's in these studies (Anderson and Doherty, 1997). Consequently, this practice is consistent with a common rape myth – that women secretly enjoy forced sexual intercourse (Brownmiller, 1975). This focus also privileges men as the 'proper' subject of 'malestream' psychological inquiry. Women participants are subjected to these tasks because of the requirements within positivist research for the counterbalancing of dependent and independent variables. Within the 'rigours' of unreflective positivist research (positivism refers to an approach to knowledge generation characterized by its strong belief that objective knowledge can be attained only through rigorous scientific procedures, particularly through controlled experimental manipulation of variables – see Fox and Prilleltensky, 1997; Willig, 2001), it is this requirement which takes precedence over the potential unease of participants confronted with this task. We, as well as other authors, believe that such practices within the rape perception tradition disregard the personal and political implications of engaging in potentially sexist practices.

There are other examples of sexist practices within rape perception research. Notwithstanding a very early study which set out to examine 'Are male bystanders confronted with a rape situation likely to help?' where 'The present study simulated a rape in a realistic setting' (Harari et al., 1985), many other studies also worryingly reproduce sexist and morally objectionable practices in their research process. Often, both the quantity and content of dependent variables used to measure judgements of the victim and perpetrator vary considerably. For example, in a study by Cann et al. (1979) six dependent variables were used to judge the rape victim but only two to judge the perpetrator. In this study, the content of these measures between the victim and perpetrator also differed substantially, as well as the sheer quantity of the measures whereby the victim was judged on such aspects as her 'behaviour on the night', 'type of person' that she is, her 'suggestive behaviour prior to the assault', 'her unconscious desire to be raped', her 'fault' and 'how believable her testimony is'. With respect to the perpetrator, however, the participants were only asked to evaluate the degree to which he was at 'fault' and the length his sentence should be. In a more recent study by Damrosch (1985), participants were asked to evaluate only the victim on eight dependent variables similar to the ones described in the previous study, despite the fact that the description clearly stated that the assailant used a knife to drive the victim to a deserted spot where the assault took place, after which the rapist stranded the victim by driving away in her car. Although such studies undoubtedly reflect the researchers' genuine orientation to knowledge generation about rape, they nevertheless reveal a sexist prejudgement of women where women by and large play a contributory role in their own rape.

Although this process may be an inadvertent one, these studies, in a similar process to a legalistic one, search for 'proxies for sluttishness' (Ellison, 2000; in the legal context these include dredging up previous abortions, drug taking history, mental health problems, etc.) that reflect the woman in a less than favourable light, that can be used to minimize her experience and legitimize the perpetrator's. In yet another study entitled 'Just because she doesn't want to doesn't mean it's rape', Shotland and Goodstein (1983) examined perceptions of the extent to which a rape may be perceived as genuine, as a function of the onset of resistance from the victim (early vs. medium vs. late), type of protest (verbal vs. verbal and physical) and degree of violence from the assailant (low force vs. moderate force). However, despite an extremely detailed description of the incident provided for participants entitled 'Sexual behaviour in a dating situation', where both the assailant and the victim play out a highly interactional dating situation, participants were only really asked to evaluate the victim and not the perpetrator. The dependent measures evaluating the victim comprised four items measuring her fault/responsibility for the rape (e.g. 'Diane is more responsible than Lee for the fact that intercourse occurred'), four items measuring her desire for sex scale (e.g. 'Diane wanted to have sexual intercourse with Lee'), while the perpetrator's role in the rape was only ever obliquely measured with the 'extent of the man's violence' scale (one item – 'Lee behaved violently towards Diane') and on the subjects' perceptions of 'whether a rape had occurred' (one item – 'Lee raped Diane').

## Implications of Sexism in Sexual Violence Research for the Applied Psychologist

Such practices have implications for the professional psychologist who may wish to utilize findings from rape perception research when applying them to a population group he or she may be working with such as rape victims. First, given the seemingly disproportionate amount of attention focused on the victim rather than the perpetrator in rape perception studies, the professional may be forgiven for also following this trend in his or her practice, by focusing on the victim rather than on the perpetrator. This may distort the perception that it is actually the perpetrator and not the victim who is at 'fault' and who 'causes' the crime. Such practices, rather than helping, may hinder the victim, who may experience secondary victimization (Williams, 1984) in the post-rape period not only from agencies such as the police or unsupportive family and friends but also from the very therapies that are designed to help. Secondly, applied psychologists such as therapists and clinicians, who may use findings from rape perception research, may, in the course of their practice, focus on the victim's characteristics such as her personality (e.g. the 'type of person she is') or her behaviour, rather than on the perpetrator's. This may again have the effect of minimizing the perpetrator's role in the rape while maximizing the victim's. A more insidious result of this practice, however, is that as a result of such studies, social change with respect to rape will be focused at the victim rather than the perpetrator. Thus, if the therapist derives from rape perception studies an internal, victim-focused assessment of the causes of rape, then the focus of the therapy will concomitantly lie with the victim's problematical personality, inappropriate behaviour, cognitive deficits or some other sup-posed vulnerability to rape. Thus, studies have already appeared dealing with the 'Coping ability of women who become victims of rape' (Myers et al., 1984). Myers et al. examine women's vulnerability to rape based on their mental health records (e.g. drug taking and psychiatric history) and their cog-nitive processes which exhibit external as opposed to internal locus of control (the hypothesis being that although 'external women want to avoid the assault as much as internal women, their cognitive processes do not provide alternatives to cope with the situation' – Myers et al., 1984: 73). They also examine personality dimensions, where 'women who successfully resisted rape were higher on Dominance, Social Presence, Sociability and Communality scales' (p. 73). The overall hypothesis of the study was that 'rapists select women for their apparent vulnerability and then proceed to the "testing stage" in which they determine if the potential victim can be intimidated' (p. 73). Although it does not deal directly with rape perception, this study is symbiotically related to rape perception studies, which also share a victim-focused orientation to the problem of rape. It is a short step from studies such as these to therapies which attempt to rectify the victim's apparent lack of certain desirable personality traits or her inappropriate lifestyle (containing as it may episodes of drinking and/or drug taking), or indeed which attempt to inculcate in the victim a different attributional style, by changing her internal to external locus of control. The crucial point is that the perpetrator is simply omitted or even forgotten in the researchers' and therapists' preoccupation with the victim, leaving the social crime of rape to be dealt with on an individual, victim-focused level. This process, far from disrupting sexual violence occurrences in society, actually perpetuates them.

In general, we argue that many of these problems occur due to a failure of researchers to engage in critical reflection which leads to a lack of recognition that this research is located within a context of gender power relations. Such research is therefore potentially disempowering to the participants (particularly female participants) and can sometimes result in trivialization of the experience of and issues around rape. Why have these research practices persisted? Often, these practices become apparent and indeed applauded in the light of objective data collection and analysis within *positivist epistemologies* – that is, theories about the nature of knowledge (epistemology refers to questions that one can ask about what and how we can gain knowledge about phenomena) which suggest that 'there is a straightforward relationship between the world (objects, events, phenomena) and our perception and understanding of it' (Willig, 2001: 3). Therefore positivist epistemologies require, for example, counterbalancing of dependent and independent variables, the subsequent treatment of participants as 'subjects' and an inadequate reflexive theorization of gender within strictly scientific theories and methodologies. Such problematic research practices therefore continue under the auspices of a search for objective truth.

The problems with positivist methodologies and the lack of critical reflection which lead to sexist research practices are issues which have been tackled thoroughly (though not necessarily conclusively) by researchers and practitioners working from a feminist standpoint. In the next section we consider both the claims and the solutions to some of these problems that feminist psychologists have brought to the research endeavour. The discussions of these issues have not necessarily led to 'once-and-for-all' solutions but have provoked debate not only between feminist researchers and 'traditional' researchers but also between feminist researchers themselves, thus creating a particularly vibrant forum for the discussion of such issues. We will argue that such debates may be useful when considering how practitioners should best contextualize and utilize academic research findings, as well as informing practitioners of some of the issues that they must tackle in their praxis as psychology therapists, applied psychologists and other psychology-related professionals.

# Feminist Theory and Method as Useful in Informing Research and Practice

Many debates within feminist thinking in psychology can be extremely valuable to those working in broader professional contexts, whether these are researchers working with participants, academics and lecturers working in academic institutions, clinicians working with clients or practitioners working with victims of sexual violence. Feminist theories and debates can also provide useful insights into our various roles as professionals. In this section, we will consider just some of the theoretical and methodological issues which have been discussed mainly when they have become apparent within the context of research but which, we argue, are clearly relevant in wider contexts, such as how we understand our roles as professionals. However, a cautionary note is needed here. Not all women who see themselves as feminist psychologists or feminist researchers are in agreement about all issues but, often, the tensions and contradictions which emerge in debating them can be fruitful in raising awareness about them. We will discuss more formally the two interlinking issues which we have already raised above and which have been identified by feminists as important. These, we argue, may be directly responsible for sexist research practices. The two issues are *the appropriateness of positivist research methodologies in knowledge generation* and the issue of *reflexivity*.

## 'Positivist' versus 'feminist' methodologies

We have already described many of the problems that occur due to the strict adherence to 'positivist' rules in research – the counterbalancing of variables, a wide power differential between the researcher and the research subject, etc., and their consequences for knowledge generation in a discipline. Not surprisingly, these rules have been heavily criticized by feminist writers. It is due to such criticisms that qualitative methodologies (including constructionist methodologies – see Willig, 2001) have emerged as part of a critique of the status of positivist experimental psychology (e.g. Harré and Secord, 1972) in psychology both past and present. Qualitative methodologies also have an added advantage for the feminist – they are also often seen *as* quintessentially feminist (Maynard, 1994). Many feminist psychologists have favoured such methods. By not relying exclusively on measuring psychological phenomena or on statistical analysis of data, they are seen to address the problems within some positivist methodologies that tend to fix meanings and ignore the role of context (Morse, 1992; Denzin and Lincoln, 1994). Meanings within social life are seen as variable and negotiable according to their context of use. It is also recognized within such methods that we are all part of the world we study, so acknowledging the role of the researcher in acquiring knowledge, rather than viewing his or her role as merely a 'neutral describer' of the world. In other words, many qualitative methodologies are concerned with 'reflexivity', with a recognition that 'Researchers are not tape recorders, ventriloquists or photographers ... [they] negotiate the data, wander the margins of local meanings, listen to and puzzle over words offered by informants and ultimately have the final word' (Maracek et al., 1997: 48).

So, should research psychologists unanimously adopt any one or even some of the myriad of qualitative or critical methods, and should the professional psychologist specifically seek out studies using such methods in their practice? There is no clear-cut distinction between quantitative and qualitative methods and their underlying epistemologies. It has been argued that there is no necessary connection between qualitative methods and any kind of progressive politics, such as feminism (Burman, 1994). Several writers, such as Sandra Harding (1987) and Mary Maynard (1994), suggest that while qualitative methods, social constructionist methodologies and relativism have often been seen as synonymous with critical theory and method, and positivism and quantitative methods have been seen as synonymous with the uncritical, the picture needs to be more complex than this if we are to reach not only a satisfactory understanding of knowledge generation about a specific topic but an ethically appropriate one as well. Instead, several authors have suggested that a distinction needs to be made among method (the actual procedure utilized to gather data), methodology (the theory developed within a particular piece of research which will then also imply the method of analysis to be used) and epistemology (a theory of knowledge incorporating questions seeking to explain what we can know and how we can know it with respect to phenomena of interest.). Only by making these distinctions and using our epistemological insights to determine our methodology and method will research question generation, data collection and reporting of results proceed in a reasonable manner. It is the way that methods are applied, stemming from a properly constructed epistemological inquiry, that determines politics. In other words, if a researcher is concerned with challenging sexism in research conducted with survivors of sexual violence, he or she must also be aware that the methods and methodologies he or she uses to study such groups do not re-produce or perpetuate such oppressive practices. Furthermore, this issue is something that should not just be confined to the realm of the academic. That is, practitioners should also be aware of the practices (such as the therapies) they use within professional contexts, how they are applied and how those practices themselves may determine their political commitments. In addition, quantitative methods can be just as useful as qualitative ones when wanting to be political (Maynard, 1994). In fact, several authors have argued how becoming over reliant on one type of method (i.e. qualitative methods) may obscure how politically limiting they can potentially be (Burman, 1990; Maynard, 1994). We need to think about the political commitments we make as well as the epistemological ones.

To illustrate the potential problems an applied psychologist may encounter if he or she commits only to one type of epistemology (and, subsequently, methodologies and methods as well), many feminist as well as other critical psychologists have, in the past, uncritically adopted a relativist epistemology such as one proposed by Edwards and Potter (1992) in their theory of discursive psychology, as a way of opposing traditional psychological epistemology and methods. However, this stance did not automatically confer criticality on the adoptee of this approach. While salutary in its anti-positivist and anti-cognitivist stance, this approach suffers from other problems which have been documented and debated for a number of years (Kitzinger, 1995; Wilkinson, 1997). One of the major problems with this approach, according to some perspectives (Parker and Burman, 1993) but not others (Hepburn, 2000; Anderson, 2002), is that it lacks a theory of subjectivity (Hollway, 1989). For example, while this approach uses interview material as data, they nevertheless, by virtue of their epistemological underpinnings, take a particular (and some would say, very peculiar) stance on how they theorize the status of their participants who actually produce these interview data. Specifically, the main concern is predominantly with the discourse produced, while who is actually doing the speaking is disregarded in subsequent analyses. For example, it has been suggested that:

> One advantage of the discourse analytic approach . . . is that, because it entails talking to people, it goes some way towards giving a voice to those silenced and in a sense helps 'empower' the subjects of traditional social research. There is however, a certain irony in this approach and its objectives. In an important sense, the participants themselves are irrelevant because it is the language they speak that is the site of investigation . . . It is therefore questionable whether the 'democratic' underpinnings of this research can be fully realised in practice (Widdicombe, 1993: 109–10).

Thus, it has been argued that by viewing the identities of their participants as constructed within the discourse rather than associated with those particular participants (e.g. a person may produce sexist discourse but there is no theorization offered as to whether the person providing such discourse can be considered sexist), discursive psychologists appear to marginalize or ignore those very voices that other critical psychologists are trying to empower (e.g. Gill, 1995; Kitzinger and Wilkinson, 1995). This in itself is seen as patronizing and oppressive, although others would argue that adopting a relativist methodology need not be seen as such (Hepburn, 2000; Anderson, 2002).

It can be seen, then, how there are many tensions between theory and practice, not only between epistemological (and subsequently, methodological) positions but also within epistemological standpoints themselves, that the professional psychologist may find overwhelming when attempting to select the 'best' type of research to inform his or her practice. Although not easy to resolve, we nevertheless caution against the unproblematic adoption of one or other epistemological and methodological standpoint. Each approach, whatever it is, can make a significant contribution to the professional psychologist's therapeutic or professional outcomes. Better still, a multi-method approach to evaluation of research may serve the practitioner well (Ward, 1995).

## Reflexivity and bridging the academic/applied divide

The second issue that the professional psychologist may wish to explore in relation to his or her practice is the issue of reflexivity, which we have already discussed in some detail. Here, we expand on some of these issues further.

Why should the applied psychologist be concerned with theoretical issues which arise in the context of academic research? After all, it has often been suggested that theory and practice are distinct from each other. In this respect, academic psychologists, including 'feminist psychologists', have been criticized by applied psychologists for being overly concerned with academic, theoretical and methodological research issues at the expense of the applied implications of their research. However, we have already discussed the kinds of implications which may arise not only for the academic psychologist but for the applied psychologist as well when, for example, researchers of sexual violence fail to consider their own location in the social context of conducting research on an emotive topic such as rape within the wider context of inequitable gender power relations. Neither have they been overly concerned with the effect that their theories and findings may have on rape survivors in the context of the relationship between counsellors and their clients in clinical settings. These issues are, and should be, of as much relevance to the professional psychologist who seeks to implement research findings in his or her work as they are to the researchers themselves.

Furthermore, although hotly debated in psychology and disciplines allied to psychology, many feminists have argued that the distinction between theory and practice is overstated. Indeed, many have argued that theoretical debates and how they may affect broader contexts (e.g. professional environments) are not and should not be thought of as separate and distinct from each other (Ahmed, 1997a). Identifying oneself as a feminist does not circumscribe feminist activity only to the academic context – our identities are consistent in this respect whatever the circumstances. As such, the questions that concern us in theory should also concern us in practice. This issue should be regarded as an important form of reflexivity.

One way to bridge the academic/applied divide, which has been proposed by feminists (Ahmed, 1996), is to be reflexive – to pay attention to the role that the researcher has in the research process and to be acutely aware that the way we characterize a phenomenon will change the way it operates for us (the so-called 'impossibility of objectivity'). A particularly important aspect of reflexivity, as has been illustrated with respect to research on rape, refers to a recognition of a self-awareness of who we are, what we're doing and how our actions might affect those with whom we are working. In another aspect, reflexivity is understood as the need to reflect critically on research practices to reveal assumptions and biases which are often overlooked (Ahmed, 1997b). These types of reflexive awareness can and should, of course, also apply to any practitioner working in an institutional setting/practice. The professional psychologist must take the issue of reflexivity seriously, not only when evaluating research findings in the context of his or her practice but also in his or her professional environment itself. If anything, this issue gains particular significance when clients' and/or patients' feelings are at stake.

The professional psychologist may be aided in his or her search for optimal reflexive awareness by referring to two types of reflexivity, which are key features of feminist standpoint research (Wilkinson, 1988). Although these refer primarily to research practice, they are equally applicable in practitioner contexts. First, the practitioner needs to be aware of 'functional reflexivity', which is a sustained critical reflection on research practice – how were research questions conceived, what approach to knowledge generation is used, what type of data are gathered and how are they gathered, etc. Not only can the practitioner use the concept of functional reflexivity to evaluate research findings but can also use it in his or her own work, when assessing issues such as 'is the client viewed as a set of cognitive processes/individual or as a social phenomenon/a product of his or her cultural and historical nexus', 'are the psychological and social processes which are being discussed viewed by the practitioner as predominantly socially constructed or as real', etc. The answers to these questions will clearly determine the types of practice (therapy, assessment, etc.). A second type of reflexivity that may be useful to the psychology practitioner in the context of his or her work is 'personal reflexivity', which refers to a critical reflection on the way in which the researcher's or practitioner's identity, interests and values may be expressed in the process of research or practice. For example, do the practitioner's beliefs in rape myths affect the type of therapy he or she selects for his or her client? Is the practitioner aware of the power differential between him and her and the client, which may lead to one type of therapeutic session/outcome rather than another? Critical reflection of this sort thus operates as a bridge between empirical research, and a practical and political engagement with social issues (Parker, 1994).

In an important sense, reflexivity, then, can be seen as a way of attempting to transcend power differentials between researcher and research participants (Woolgar, 1988), or client and analyst, educational psychologist and child, etc. The main reason for being reflexive, to care about the types of questions you ask and how your personal beliefs are involved in praxis, is because of the need to improve the quality of experience for the people involved in your practice – the clients, the children, etc. Only when these issues are considered will psychological research and practice be able to attain their ultimate goals – to offer solutions to human problems, to improve quality of life and to gain sound knowledge of just some of these human processes.

## Conclusion

Throughout this chapter we have discussed the problems of 'traditional' psychological research, in this case, sexual violence research and how such research perpetuates sexist practices. We discussed how this might cause problems for the practitioner wishing to utilize these research findings. We then argued for an evaluation of debates in feminist psychological research as being useful to the practitioner not only in assessing academic research practices but also in assessing the actual role of practitioners in applied contexts. In particular, we focused on two issues which both researchers and practitioners alike may find useful in their work: the appropriateness of (positivist) research methodologies and the issue of reflexivity. We highlighted how a lack of critical reflection in research can lead to sexist practices, which were illustrated with reference to sexual violence research. The crucial point we focused on is that findings from research, which utilize problematic research practices, may then be taken up by practitioners who work with vulnerable groups such as women who have been raped, children who have survived sexual abuse, etc. These issues were discussed in the context of feminist standpoint research, where these issues are continually debated and which have hopefully brought fresh insights to practitioner contexts. We urge practitioners, as well as researchers, actively to engage in these debates in an effort to avoid oppressive practices both in research and applied settings.

## QUESTIONS FOR REFLECTION AND DISCUSSION

1   How would an understanding of epistemology and politics in research be useful in applied contexts?

2   How might reflexivity be useful in understanding client/practitioner interactions?

3   How might sexism in research findings affect the way they are utilized in practitioner contexts?

## Suggestions for Further Reading

Ward, C. (1995) *Attitudes toward Rape: Feminist and Social Psychological Perspectives.* London: Sage.
An excellent overview of rape-perception research, its problems and how feminists have addressed these problems in feminist research and praxis. It provides some excellent examples of feminist-inspired therapies, etc.

Maynard, M. (1994) 'Methods, practice, and epistemology: the debate about feminism and research', In M. Maynard and J. Purvis (eds) *Researching Women's Lives from a Feminist Perspective.* London: Taylor & Francis.
This chapter provides a detailed and thoughtful discussion of the issues which arise when considering epistemology and methodology in feminist research.

Figg, J. (ed.) (1999) 'Feminist psychology: issues for practice', special issue of *Educational and Child Psychology*, 16(2).
A special issue that looks specifically at how feminist psychology may be useful (or not) to understanding educational psychology practice.

# 13 The Higher Education Context

*John Radford*

## SUMMARY

*Education and training for all the applications of psychology discussed in this volume take place within the context of higher education in the UK. While higher education worldwide faces problems, the situation in the UK is in some ways unusual. The reasons for this are largely historical, taking history up to the very recent past. The earliest British universities were, like those elsewhere, training institutions for the learned professions of law, medicine and theology. For various reasons this function was largely lost and, in the nineteenth century, the dominant ethos came to be a strictly non-applied general education, initially stressing moral and social values, specifically Christian, but later the development of the intellect as such. This, for some, still largely defines 'real' education, as opposed to training. In the twentieth century research came to be a dominant feature, and largely the criterion of institutional prestige and individual promotion. It also greatly increased the cost of higher education and contributed to the system of state funding and consequently control. Recent years have seen rapid rises in student numbers, but a relative decline in resources, together with massively increased bureaucracy. Government policy appears to have no solutions to the resulting problems and to be unwilling to look at other systems which perhaps do so. Within this framework psychologists have particular concerns. Among these are the massive preponderance of female recruitment and the imbalance between the large numbers taking single-subject psychology degrees and the relatively few who can go on to work in applied psychology. It is suggested that psychology in a mass system needs to contribute more to a general education, and to reject the dichotomy between education and training.*

## The Higher Education Context

Learning is both hindered and injured too by the ill choice of them that send young scholars to the universities, of whom must needs come all our divines, lawyers and physicians (Roger Ascham, *The Schoolmaster*, 1570).

Even if our Universities no longer exist to evolve Gentlemen, cannot our Players be educated men? (O.L. Zangwill, Professor of Psychology, University of Cambridge, 1960).

Of all the ways in which Britain squandered the unique post-war opportunity to reinvent itself as an industrial trading nation before its old economic rivals came back on stream, the failure to establish a world-class education and training system is surely the most disastrous. (Corelli Barnett, historian, lecture to the Royal Society of Arts, October 2001).

Roger Ascham's worry was about what sort of mind and personality were suitable for higher education, whereas Corelli Barnett's is about the 'wrong sort' of education; specifically, one that denigrates technology and commercial success. Oliver Zangwill seems at first to echo this, recalling the sporting era that ended only in the 1960s, when amateur gentlemen were somehow superior to professional players even though the latter usually won. However it could be argued that educated professionals (female as well as male) are precisely what are wanted, and what higher education should seek to produce in all areas.

This volume is concerned with one area in particular, psychology, its professional applications, and training and education for these. These must all take place within the context of higher education as a whole, and we should consider some of the constraints and problems of the current British system.

## Origins of Academia

Higher education worldwide is facing problems, but there are many variations, and the British situation is in some ways unusual. The reasons for this are largely historical, if one includes quite recent history. All advanced societies that we know of have had systems of 'higher' education, usually institutionalized (Wilkinson, 1969; Perkin, 1991). The western form of universities, with a continuous development to the present day, began in the late twelfth century, primacy being generally accorded to Bologna. It did not, of course, emerge from nothing but from surviving elements of civic life going back to classical times. Later, strong influences from that world, especially Greece, and to a lesser extent from Islam, did much to shape even our present-day concepts of higher education (see Radford et al., 1997).

Universities were from the start service institutions, the basic function being to prepare entrants to the then major professions of law, medicine and theology. These formed the 'higher faculties', possession of at least one of which was one of the marks of a mediaeval university. Such professional training followed after education in the liberal arts (all deriving ultimately from Greek originals), the *trivium* of grammar, rhetoric and dialectic, and the *quadrivium* of music, arithmetic, geometry and astronomy. Those who taught constituted in a sense a fourth profession, marked by another feature of the mediaeval university, the *ius ubique docendi*, the right to teach in other universities. Scholarship was intensive, but research, in the modern sense, did not exist (Powicke and Emden, 1936; Cobban, 1975). The arts course was a general fundamental education, emphasizing what would now be called 'transferable skills' such as *disputatio*, putting a reasoned case, and *dictamen*, which we might call drafting. Grammar was Latin, the common language of scholarship, administration, diplomacy and business. Rhetoric was persuasive communication; dialectic was logical argument. Mediaeval society was, at least superficially, very unlike ours, and it is easy to under-rate its intellectual achievements. But as Cobban (1975) remarks:

> The quality of training received at a mediaeval university, the rigorous, exacting nature of the academic courses designed to equip graduates to deal with the empirical and physical problems of living and of society, gave a centre and a unified purpose to university education that is lacking in the present centrifugal academic scene where the mastery of a discipline is commonly sacrificed to a piecemeal interdisciplinary approach leading in no particular direction.

The earliest universities were not, as is sometimes thought, religious foundations. Indeed, the early Church bitterly opposed advanced learning, only later embracing it. Bologna was formed by the body of students, mostly of law, who hired the masters to teach them. As the new organizations developed, however, both church and state made strenuous efforts to control them. Oxford came formally into existence when the Papal Legate, Nicholas de Romanis, stepped into a dispute between town and gown, and gave the Bishop of Lincoln the power to appoint a chancellor, who, however, eventually came to be chosen by the university itself, constituted as a corporation of masters, and then to be a purely honorary appointment, whence the vice-chancellors we still have as chief executives. Nor were universities the domain of the aristocracy, whose education aimed at military and political leadership. Students were mostly 'upwardly mobile' middle or lower class.

## British Higher Education

Over the following centuries universities proliferated, changed and diverged in ways too complex to detail here (see Aldrich, 1982; Perkin, 1991; Eustace, 1992; Radford et al., 1997). In what eventually became the UK there were, and remain, significant differences among England, Scotland, Wales and (now Northern) Ireland. But it is perhaps the first that has been most dominant, not least in shaping our concept of a university education. As is well known, for the greater part of English university history, Oxford and Cambridge stood alone, despite numerous attempts at other foundations, at Reading, Winchester, Salisbury, Northampton and elsewhere. After the mediaeval period, the centralizing Tudor state, which now incorporated the Church, sought also to control higher education. Regius professors were appointed to oversee what was taught, the old autonomous student halls were replaced by colleges and the tutorial system instituted to monitor students' moral and social behaviour. For this and other reasons the professional functions weakened. Legal training focused on the inns of court, medical on the emerging professional bodies and the great teaching hospitals. The new function of research was largely served by new communities, the first of all being the Royal Society (1660). The importance of theology declined in that there was no longer one universal Church, though at the same time the established Church of England remained intrinsic to the two universities.

By the eighteenth century Oxford and Cambridge reached a low point of prestige and scholarship (with individual exceptions). But in the next century came renewal and revival. New subjects, including most radically new sciences, were admitted (even psychology by 1897). The Church link was slowly disentangled and clergymen metamorphosed into dons (Engel, 1983).

A new ethos came to prevail as to the functions of a university. While there were various views (notably Newman, 1857), those of S.T. Coleridge were among the earliest and the most influential. His concept (1830) was of a classically educated and enlightened Christian elite, the 'clerisy', fitted for national leadership and a counter to the brutalizing pressures of industrialization and urbanization. Here we see of course not the origins, which were earlier, but the enunciation of the attitudes deplored by Corelli Barnett (discussed more fully in Barnett, 2001). A century later the University Grants Committee report for 1930–5 asked: 'When the young graduate puts on the gown and hood of his degree, of what inward and spiritual graces are these the outward and visible signs?' (Shinn, 1986). In between, the 'graces' had shifted from Christian morality and service to the intellect. Mark Pattison, Rector of Lincoln, proclaimed in 1876: 'It is no part of the proper business of a University to be a professional school. Universities are not to fit men for some special mode of gaining a livelihood . . . but to cultivate the mind and form the intelligence' (Sparrow, 1967). In 2002 Chris Woodhead, the controversial former Chief Inspector of Schools, maintains: 'A university ought to be an institution in which those young people who have the intellectual ability to benefit engage with the best that has been thought and written. That engagement has no bearing upon any end external to itself.' It is specifically not 'training'. All along, there were those who disagreed, feeling that tertiary education ought precisely to fit men (still no women of course) for practical professions and all kinds of advanced work needed in the leading industrial nation, and paying no heed to outdated ties with the Church. Their recourse was to found their own institutions, the first (1825) becoming eventually the federal University of London, and others developing into the great civic universities such as Manchester, Leeds and Liverpool. As before, many attempts were made and only some succeeded (Jones, 1988). Even when they did, however, they eventually lost the battle against the prestige of Oxbridge, which still continues (see Ellis, 1994), coming to be seen as second class rather than distinctively different (Barnes, 1996). Industrial disciplines, engineering in particular, never achieved a qualification structure and prestige comparable to the ancient professions.

To jump forward, much the same thing happened when the 'binary system' was created around 1970 (Davies, 1992). The rationale for this was almost entirely political, and based on assumptions which were almost entirely false. Nevertheless the new polytechnics were intended to offer practical high-level education, especially to hitherto disadvantaged classes of students, and without spending resources on blue-skies research. But a combination of student demand and competition with universities fuelled 'academic drift' towards a single system, which was instituted in 1992 when the polytechnics were created universities by statute: as Tyrell Burgess has put it, 'to disguise the fact that universities were becoming polytechnics' (Burgess et al., 1995). And no less, to advance the central control of the system which has been an apparent if not stated aim of policy for several decades. The opportunity was also taken to dismantle much of the relatively democratic system of internal government instigated by the Council for National Academic Awards (CNAA), under which the polytechnics operated (Silver, 1990).

# Research

In the mean time a new element had entered the equation, namely, research. This had at least two sources, practical and theoretical. The practical cause was the phenomenal growth of science and technology in the nineteenth century. New knowledge was at a premium (even though numerous British inventions were exploited elsewhere, for example aniline dyes), and universities, including Oxford and Cambridge, came to be major suppliers. The theoretical background was a new conception of what universities ought to be, due largely to Wilhelm von Humboldt (1767–1835) (Sweet, 1978–80). German universities were reshaped after the Napoleonic wars and, as minister of public instruction in the new German confederation, he conceived of the university as a community of teachers and students jointly dedicated to the pursuit of knowledge, considered in principle as indivisible, unified by 'philosophy'. This was in fact the origin of the modern doctorate of philosophy, though a far cry from the extreme specialism it now represents. Universities should offer both professional training and pure research, but not strictly practical training or technical and scientific studies, which were relegated to specialized colleges.

Much of this was taken up in the USA, while in the UK research became dominant only in the twentieth century, the first PhDs (actually DPhil, Oxon) being awarded only at the end of the First World War, and then largely because it had become impossible to go to Germany for them. The elevation of research as a major function of universities has had two crucial results. First, it made the costs of institutions so great that public funding became virtually unavoidable. It is worth remembering that this did not begin in the UK until 1889, and took in Oxford as late as 1923. With it came central control and demands for accountability, although for most of the twentieth century these were kept at arm's length by the University Grants Committee (Shinn, 1986). The other result was to make research the major index of institutional prestige and individual career progress, as it largely remains (Halsey, 1992). It has in a sense replaced the moral/religious dimension of the nineteenth century, and it has become an article of faith that research and university teaching are inextricably linked. Mary Warnock (1989) states unequivocally: 'The crucial distinction between university and other forms of education lies simply in its necessary connection with research.' Reviews of the evidence, however, for example, Hattie and Marsh (1996), find little support for this view. Besides, in practice, as Coate et al. (2001) point out, the two are often managerially distinct, and this is reinforced by external pressures. Little refereed research by teachers feeds directly into their own first-degree teaching. The fact is, as any sports star will tell you, that competing and coaching are two different things, and the best players seldom make the best trainers. And in any case, very few students will go on to become researchers themselves.

What research and experience do suggest is, first, that it is important for the health of a department that a significant number of people are engaged in some high-level practice, which may include consultancy, professional practice, scholarship, authoritative general punditry or indeed innovative teaching, as well as research in a narrow sense (see Elton, 1992). Secondly, that these activities have a general if intangible effect at first-degree level, in 'raising the sights' of students, especially if these are initially set too low. There is a much more specific effect in graduate study, where students are actually being prepared for professional work or research. At that level, practice, research, supervision and teaching may almost merge into one. And, thirdly, a high research profile does give prestige, and tends to attract more able students, who then naturally obtain better results.

## Continuing Trends

At the start of the twenty-first century, British higher education manifests a number of continuing trends, some recent and some going back to the very origins of universities or before. The public perception of universities, by students, intending students and parents, now is that they have two major functions, teaching and research (and/or scholarship) (Radford and Holdstock, 1993; 1996; 1997). Their functions do not include moral or personal development (though the latter may be an incidental benefit), nor meeting the needs of employers, and least of all should they serve to carry out government policy. Employers and governments naturally take different views.

Students, in general, primarily want what their predecessors wanted in twelfth-century Bologna, that is a useful qualification, one that will enable them to enter an occupation they find attractive. There is a built-in contradiction here in that they want this in ever-increasing numbers, as has generally been true all along. In psychology, perhaps a quarter of those with first degrees can go on to professional work in the senses used in this volume. Others enter fields in which their psychology will be useful but not essential, and this shades into treating the subject mainly as a general education (Van Laar and Sherwood, 1995).

The admission, and latterly preponderance, of women has shifted the emphasis of the sort of psychology that is popular, away from rigorous experiment and mechanical models, towards a more caring, subjective approach (Radford and Holdstock, 1993; Radford et al., 1999b). It has also in itself obviously doubled demand for higher education in general. Women exceed men in higher education in most advanced countries, a situation reached in the UK, belatedly, less than ten years ago. Government policy of the last 50 years has, with some pauses, been to increase student numbers; 135% up between 1981–2 and 2000–1 (*The Times Higher Educational Supplement* 8 March 2002). The target is now 50% of the 18–21 age group by 2010 (it is currently around 35%). Presumably, it is thought that this is electorally popular, and it keeps the unemployment figures down. The ostensible reason, as stated by the Minister for Lifelong Learning and Higher Education (Hodge, 2002), is that new jobs 'will demand skills and qualifications associated with a university education'.

But will they demand those of a psychology degree designed primarily to fit graduates to enter professional psychology? Still more questionably, of course, those of a research historian or classicist? All the relatively non-applied disciplines make strenuous claims for the all-round applicability of their general education, perhaps with more sound than evidence. Woodhead (2002) quotes from the Centre for Economic Performance a figure of 30% of adults in the UK overqualified for the work they are doing. And from the Construction Industry Training Board, a need for 29 000 plumbers and 35 000 electricians over the next five years. He adds that only 14% of UK employees have an intermediate-level vocational qualification, compared to 46% in Germany. Conversely, it is clear that inflation inevitably means devaluation. Very numerous first degrees must produce an increasing demand for higher ones. And it is beyond reason that courses designed essentially for an upper 10 or even 20% of the population (how-ever crudely and inaccurately selected) can be suitable for half the total population, some of whom must inevitably be of below-average intelligence. One wonders what Roger Ascham would have thought.

Attempts at central control of higher education have likewise always been a feature but have increased dramatically in the last three decades, arguably as a deliberate policy (Salter and Tapper, 1994; Jenkins, 1995). They lay behind both the creation of the binary system and, when both halves proved too independ-ent, its abolition and the simultaneous creation of new assessment procedures for the whole of higher education. Early studies of these are mixed (Brennan et al., 1997), and they are besides constantly being altered. But a crucial feature from the point of view of academics is that these systems on the one hand over-ride much of the traditional autonomy of the pre-1992 universities, and on the other hand replace the essentially peer review-based approach of the CNAA. The new systems constitute an inspectorial system which is in many ways the antithesis of professionalism. Open criteria, dialogue, assessment by respected fellow profes-sionals, judgements on the basis of total achievement, are replaced by what may be termed academic gas-meter reading. There is a difference, however, in that whereas the meter reader goes about his or her business unobtrusively, the vari-ous assessment systems have contributed largely to a vast increase in bureaucratic and administrative demands on academic staff.

At the same time a new binary or perhaps tripartite system is being semi-covertly introduced through the assessment and consequent funding of research, using in effect the well-known Matthew principle: to him that hath shall be given. For 2002–3, half the 79 English universities will get under four million each, a further third 5–16 million and four over 60 million each. But at the same time, institutions are striving to meet ever tighter criteria, including what counts as research, only to complain, with reason, that the goals posts have been moved (Elton, 2000). It is a rather typically British, and exceedingly demoralizing, method.

This also illustrates another persistent trend, an increasing gap between what higher education is expected to do and the funds available to pay for it (Ashworth, 1993). It is amply documented that students are finding it increas-ingly hard to pay their way (Sanders, 2002), especially those from poorer backgrounds, it having apparently escaped the government's notice that these tend to be the ones with least money. Practically every measure of academic job satisfaction is at 'rock-bottom' (Baty, 2002). Payment has declined drastically, from twice the national average (Halsey and Trow, 1971) to two thirds above in 1992 to one third in 2002 (Green, 2002). (Except, remarkably, for vice-chancel-lors, some of whom receive ten times or more as much as a lecturer.) Staff–student ratios have deteriorated significantly, and larger classes yield poorer results (Fearnley, 1995). Institutions are unable to maintain plant even at a steady level. 'UK science at risk as labs fall apart' states a headline in *The Times Higher Educational Supplement*, April 2002. Even Oxford and Cambridge, the only British universities with substantial endowments, are struggling to maintain international standards (Elliott and Waterhouse, 2002). Several lesser ones are heavily in debt.

## Other Systems

All this is only too familiar. It is instructive to compare the situation with that in the USA. Generally available higher education was from the start a principle of Jeffersonian democracy and, although until quite recently large sections of society were effectively excluded, access at the end of the nineteenth century was already far wider than most of the world achieved for nearly another hundred years. Currently around 60% go on to some form of post-secondary education, though there seems to be little enthusiasm for increasing this further. Of these, however, 54% are at two-year colleges – comparable to further education in the UK (Falk, 1990). Only about one student in five corresponds to the conventional British stereotype: age 18–22, on a full-time, first-degree course. Two thirds of all academics work in non-doctorate-granting institutions, which would not be universities in the UK (Clarke, 1997).

Scott (2001) describes three general approaches to mass advanced education. Most European countries have some form of binary system on the Humboldt model, which protects and privileges the universities, and at the same time provides the intermediate-level applied qualifications mentioned by Woodhead. In psychology, however, there are several quite different patterns of professional training (Lunt, 1998). In the USA there is a wide range of institutions with clearly defined functions (Kerr, 1990; Clarke, 1997). The third is the current British unitary approach, which Scott idiosyncratically considers 'has so far been a success'. It might better be called 'pseudo-unitary'. There are in reality, and always have been since Oxford and Cambridge lost their duopoly, many levels of higher education, whether called 'university' or not. Bligh et al. (1999) distinguish seven types of institution, and Tight (1996) sixteen, but it is probably the case that no two are identical in foundation, tradition, curriculum, catchment, staff, resources, quality of teaching and research and many other variables.

Another major difference compared to many countries is the absence of private institutions, ranging in the USA from the most prestigious such as Harvard and Yale to many specialized colleges. Similarly in Japan, which, with a take-up of 45% of the age cohort, is facing a possible change from the German to the American model: some 80% of the students are at private institutions (Altbach and Ogawa, 2002). In the UK there is only the University of Buckingham, and the view of both customers (students and parents) and staff is very clear that higher education should be state funded (Radford and Holdstock, 1997; Radford et al., 1990a), although simultaneously they are pessimistic about the availability of such funds.

It is difficult to see that this can be the whole answer, and government apparently hopes that other sources will be forthcoming. The buzz word is 'entrepreneurial' (Clarke, 2001), and the admired model that of the Massachusetts Institute of Technology. Such a model is most easily adopted by the strongest institutions, and Oxford is currently leading the way. But, as a leader in *The Times Higher Educational Supplement* recently pointed out (1 March 2002), it depends crucially on giving universities freedom to set their own fees, which has so far been resisted. Of course some, such as Christopher Ball (for example, 1992), have long urged the adoption of effectively the American system, with a small number of research universities and an end to the distinction between higher and further education. But as Trow (1987) remarked:

> What is still lacking is a general recognition that all degree-granting higher education is only a part, albeit a central part, of a broad system of post-secondary and continuing education, marked by a diversity of standard, mission and cost, which has as its mission the advanced education of a whole society and not just its leadership.

## The future

All the above remarks will be very familiar. The system, and its constraints, may or may not change significantly, for better or worse. It may well be that we need at least two or three, if not more, distinct types of institution; but there is the likelihood of them drifting together again. There is a case for foundation courses which most students would attend at a local university, each of which would also specialize in advanced work in a small number of fields. There is a case for accepting that the bulk of research will rest with a few universities, while a greater number would offer advanced professional courses. The assumption that these, and indeed first degrees, are inextricably linked with research would have to be abandoned.

At one level, those seeking to train students in any of the branches of applied psychology will simply have to do what they have so far done, that is make the best of it – whatever strange form 'it' may take from time to time. But it also behoves us to be aware, as far as possible, of the underlying forces of change, to know something of meteorology rather than just buying an umbrella (if funds allow). Hence, most basically, the need for a professional approach to academia. Psychologists in particular are, or should be, in a position to appreciate what makes for successful education, and at least put up a case for it. I have tried to express my own views in publications already cited several times above.

W.C. Fields is said to have been once seen stalking through the garden of his palatial Hollywood home, slashing at the roses with his cane and growling, 'Bloom, damn you! Bloom!' We seem fated to rediscover at regular intervals what successful teachers, from long before Roger Ascham and up to the present day, could tell you. Good education depends on good teachers, experienced and tolerably rewarded and going beyond the minimum terms of any contract. Professionals, not proletariat. Good teaching and good learning cannot be forced into existence, whatever those in charge may think. For some time now policy appears to have been based on the principle of carrot and stick for the donkey – mainly stick. But donkeys will never make good teachers, beat them as you may. This isn't airy-fairy do-gooding but simple pragmatism, backed by literally centuries of experience and volumes of research. Psychologists are at the cutting edge of such knowledge.

More specifically, psychologists face particular problems. Some may not think it one of these that the gender balance of psychology has changed radically over the last 50 years, from predominantly male to overwhelmingly female (around 80%). But the evidence suggests that this also changes the nature of the subject and the profession. And it would surely be more desirable on many grounds if we could achieve something more like parity. Whether new, additional courses and/or rebranding might help I do not know. Gender-based occupational choices appear to be very robust (Radford, 1998). I do think it is a professional problem (one shared, incidentally, with medicine).

Psychology, at present, continues to be a popular subject for study (*The Psychologist*, December 2001, reports a 36% rise in graduates in five years). I may myself claim to have initiated a movement (GCE A-level, together with its knock-on effect on degrees) which constitutes by far the greatest ever increase in students taking formal courses in psychology. I remain convinced that this can only be, on balance, a force for good. Some scientific understanding of human behaviour is among the greatest desiderata if our species is to solve the problems it faces – and has largely created. Psychology graduates follow a wide variety of careers, and one hopes that a training in literacy and numeracy and in objective investigation, an appreciation of the amazing variety of human behaviour and some understanding of its causes, are of help both in employment and in personal life. Personal anecdotes do support this, but to my knowledge there is little systematic investigation. And at a practical level, we need only a certain number of professional psychologists. We do not need several times that number of psychology graduates, at least if their degrees are based primarily on the assumption that they will all be among the few chosen for professional courses, still less for research. An informal survey I did some years ago suggested that, in any case, professional course tutors do not in practice rely on the specific knowledge that all their recruits supposedly possess. Perhaps some rethinking is desirable, in which a comparison with practice in other countries (and other disciplines, and other ages) might help. In theory, modular courses provide an answer, but in practice they are too 'bitty' to be much use in isolation.

And, of course, we do need plumbers as well as psychologists (many householders might say more so). I do not know the answer to this puzzle. I do think that psychologists need to think out what role they can play in a changing higher educational system, providing both general education to large numbers, and professional training. Psychology might well claim to offer modern versions of rhetoric, dialectic and *disputatio*, as well as our more recent skills of objective investigation and experiment, and specific professional techniques. I should like to think that it might contribute to what Oliver Zangwill may have considered second best, but which I regard as near an ideal: the truly educated professional.

## QUESTIONS FOR REFLECTION AND DISCUSSION

1 'More means worse.' What is to be said about this today?

2 Should university education be qualitatively different from any other and, if so, how?

3 What are the advantages and disadvantages of the current British 'unitary' system of higher education?

4 It is generally agreed that British higher education is badly short of funds. What remedies can you suggest?

5 What has academic psychology to offer to the three quarters of its students who will not become professional psychologists? (Facts are to be preferred to opinions.)

## Suggestions for further reading

*Note*: See (as for Chapter 9) the extensive list of SRHE/Open University Press.

Clarke, B.R. and Neave, G.R. (eds) (1992) *The Encyclopaedia of Higher Education*. Oxford: Pergamon Press.
This text contains several relevant chapters. There are also other rather similar encyclopaedias.

National Committee of Enquiry into Higher Education (1997) *Higher Education in the Learning Society* (*the Dearing Report*). London: HMSO.
Currently the official guidelines for the development of higher education.

Radford, J., Raaheim, K., deVries, P. and Williams, R. (1997) *Quantity and Quality in Higher Education*. London: Jessica Kingsley.
This book offers a concise history of the development of higher education and a discussion of what the authors consider basic issues.

Warner, D. and Palfreyman, D. (eds) (2001) *The Shape of UK Higher Education: Managing Change and Diversity*. Buckingham: SRHE and Open University Press.
A collection of recent papers reflecting the book's self-explanatory title.

Warnock, M. (1989) *Universities: Knowing our Minds*. London: Chatto & Windus.
The 'old establishment' view.

# 14 New Directions in Applied Psychology: A Roundtable

*Edited by Rowan Bayne*

The main aims of the roundtable were to have a broader range of views than could be expected even in such a large School of Psychology as the University of East London's (UEL's), and to have a more focused emphasis on possible futures for applied psychology. I invited psychologists whom colleagues and I think of as experts in one or more branches of applied psychology to write brief responses (up to 500 words each) to two questions:

1 What do you think is the most significant issue or new direction in your area(s) of applied psychology today?

2 What new direction(s) would you like there to be?

Their resulting comments would, I think, make excellent seminar topics – they invite or demand a response. At a grander level, they do indeed suggest some very promising new directions for applied psychology. They also forcefully and valuably restate some basic values and principles which are seen as neglected or in danger. However, the method used to choose the contributors obviously does not justify any statement on how generally held such views are.

The contributions are organized in a similar sequence to the rest of the book, but this order is more out of tidiness than reality. For example, work-life balance is a topic for counselling and health psychology too, and four of the contributions don't fit the general sequence:

1 Ian M. Cockerill's overview of sport psychology was particularly welcome because UEL does not currently teach in this growing area.

2 Ethical issues are, of course, *generally* relevant in applied psychology, and Geoff Lindsay spells out central aspects of an increasingly sophisticated approach.

3 I think Michael W. Eysenck's topic of the structure of personality should also be at the heart of many applications of psychology (Bayne, 1995). However, despite being researched and discussed at a high level over many years (for example, McAdams, 1995; Funder, 2001) it is still largely a mystery, and there are no masters degrees in it as far as I know.

4 Finally, Nicky Hayes takes a general (and optimistic) view about the increasing dynamism of modern applied psychology, which seems a good note to end this book on.

# Clinical Psychology

*Sue Llewelyn*

The most impressive thing about clinical psychology in Britain today has been its recent growth in power, breadth and sheer numbers. For instance, the number of new trainees expanded from 145 in 1980 to 453 in 2001 (that is, more than tripling in 20 years), while the standard of training has been harmonized at doctoral level. At the same time clinical psychology's contribution is seen as central in the effective delivery of a whole range of NHS policies and priorities. I think we have done this by having a sound and reasonably coherent set of theoretically based procedures and skills to offer to the NHS and its patients, as well as being reasonably competent politicians in being able to position ourselves to deliver these skills, within an ethically sensitive framework. The important question is: can clinical psychology keep on growing, both in influence and in range, and can it deliver what it promises? Further, can we consolidate the profession's achievements without either losing our critical, ethical edge or our clinical effectiveness, by weakening ties with our theoretical base?

So, in my view the most significant issue for clinical psychology today is managing and maintaining expansion while holding on to the profession's unique qualities. It seems to me that we have developed and are still developing theories and practices which could potentially meet many of the expressed needs of patients and staff in health care, and which could make a lot of difference to people's lives. This has been true in mental health for many years, for both adults and children. Given the increasingly ageing population and the prevalence of chronic conditions, my own view is that the most significant areas of application now are within clinical health psychology and primary care. We could be contributing directly or indirectly to the care of almost every cancer patient, every patient with heart disease or obesity, or diabetes, HIV, dementia, CFS and so on. We could also be contributing, directly or indirectly, to most distressed families, suicidal adolescents, confused or depressed older adults in the community and so on.

Crucially, the contributions that we make have been developed from theory, experience and research, and we need all these sources: clinical psychology is an applied science so must keep a firm base within academic psychology, as well as our critical edge which comes from close contact with patients' lives and the moral and ethical questions which are thrown up by suffering. It is probably the profession's problem-solving skills and breadth of conceptualization which explain our expansion, both in numbers and range. But also the profession emphasizes reflection and empathy, which draws us close to the experience of our patients. In the words of David Smail (1998: 24) 'the great value of clinical psychology has been in developing a critical understanding of the phenomenon of distress based on real experience. Real knowledge can only be gained and elaborated in this kind of "scientist-practitioner" context, and perhaps we just need to be a bit bolder and more assertive about saying so.' Hence I believe that the scientist-practitioner model is crucial and underpins the success so far of the profession. Interestingly this view was supported in the recent Delphi study, which Paul Kennedy and I co-ordinated, of the views of trainers, trainees and supervisors concerning the future of clinical psychology training in Britain (Llewelyn and Kennedy, 2001).

Finally, what new directions would I like to see? Most psychological distress is never presented to the mental health services, let alone to clinical psychologists, but instead is suffered alone or is presented to community services like GPs and in schools. In addition, high levels of psychological distress also exist in hospitals through institutional neglect of the emotional and psychological in favour of the physical. So . . . I would like to see clinical psychologists working routinely with GPs and community nurses and teachers, such that consulting a psychologist becomes an entirely commonplace event. I would like to see new mothers and older people having local services available in which their experiences of distress could be explored and their perspectives valued. I would like to see schools and voluntary services being able to call on psychologists to help approach children and families with problems as soon as they appear so that they do not become entrenched and intractable. I would like to see hospitals become psychologically sophisticated so that people would receive sensitive care when facing hard choices, hearing bad news or dealing with uncertainty. I would like to see the models we have developed for coping with pain, with traumatic events, fear, depression and so on being widely available so that people don't have to suffer needlessly.

Although we have expanded in numbers, it would be quite impossible for clinical psychologists to do all this on their own. So we have to work closely with our medical colleagues, nurses, allied health professionals, other applied psychologists and a variety of professional groups to encourage the adoption of psychologically helpful interventions. So I would really like to see my colleagues stopping worrying about skills sharing: there is plenty of work out there. I see no evidence of a lack of need for careful thought about human problems. The contribution of applied psychologists is our ability to think carefully, to use theory as an effective tool, to access the evidence base and to attend carefully to what our clients say to us. I would like to see more of it.

# Educational Psychology 1

*Irvine S. Gersch*

This is a most interesting and significant phase in the history of educational psychology. Educational psychologists (EPs) are facing major challenges in responding to changes in the world as a whole, to the educational climate and in respect of their relationships with parents, children and schools, and local education authorities (LEAs). The demands on them are both exciting and challenging, and much will depend in the future on how the profession as a whole responds to such changes.

Some of the significant issues for the profession of educational psychology can be viewed under the following headings:

1 The aims and emphases of educational psychology services and type of work EPs actually do.

2 The emphasis on individual clinical work and work with families.

3 Adapting to the new national and international landscape and new challenges, for example, health, drugs, crime, behavioural problems, inclusion and raising standards of achievement in schools.

4 Making a difference to children, particularly the most vulnerable, through the application of psychological skills, knowledge, understanding and research.

5 Developing specialist areas.

6 Working for new sources of employers.

7 Changes required to training.

To take each in turn:

1 EPs have to consider carefully what services they offer and provide, given the many calls on their time. EP services need to think carefully about what they are doing and why and, most importantly, what will make the biggest difference and have the most impact. Choices have to be made about the levels of work and on whether to spend most of their time in, for example, clinical work, direct work with children, consultation with school staff, on training others, undertaking systems projects, carrying out research, advising LEAs as a whole. Principal psychologists leading teams will need to be able to lead responsive and creative teams who respond effectively to local and national challenges, and who are perceived by schools, parents,

children, the LEAs and other users of their service as helpful, practical and down to earth rather than ideologues. Customers of the future will continue to have a greater voice than ever in what service they receive.

**2** In recent years EPs, in my view, have not always given sufficient public weight to their work with individual children and families. Yet it is just this sort of work which is so valued by young people, parents and schools, and it is this type of work that attracted many psychologists into the profession in the first place. The point was elaborated during a keynote address given by the writer to the Association of Educational Psychologists in Doncaster in 2001, and it is noteworthy that the conference planned for the following year (2002) particularly invited papers about individual casework. The tide appears to be changing!

**3** and **4** EP will prosper, in my view, if it continues to adapt to the changing world and applies what we learn about psychology to assist with the real-life problems faced by society.

**5** The growing trend towards specialisms is likely to continue, and a major issue will pertain to the type of specialisms that emerge.

**6** For the future, EPs are likely to work for employers other than LEAs, including charities, private companies and independently. Issues about the type of work and their total working context will inevitably arise.

**7** The DfES is currently reviewing the future of training. If it is extended to three years, as many hope will happen, to ensure appropriate standards of work, issues will arise about whether qualified teaching experience will still be required, how flexible such training might be and whether there will be a change in the profile of applicants who apply for training (perhaps to those who are younger than currently).

Perhaps *the most significant issue* relates to the future nature of work undertaken by EPs and the changes in training required to ensure that graduates are able to undertake such work effectively.

## New Directions

My personal preferred direction for the profession would be that it continues to meet the central challenges of the nation, that it offers a broad range of psychological services (rather than being too narrow), that the development in specialist areas continues to flourish and that there is greater focus on the *psychological* aspects of the work, in its skills, knowledge and application of research.

I would like to see EPs continuing to work at many levels, at the level of the child and family, but also helping schools as a whole. EPs can help schools as a whole to become more inclusive, more effective in support of children with special educational needs, to develop effective behavioural procedures and policies, in raising standards generally, for example, and meeting other challenges causing concern to school staff. They should also be of help in developing the policies of LEAs and local communities and, indeed, the nation. I would like to see EPs frequently invited to offer the government advice about relevant issues.

I would like to see more time spent on sophisticated and in-depth casework with children and families, including detailed assessment where needed and interventions both of a direct nature and in working with teachers and other professionals to help make a positive improvement to children's lives. This will require the readjustment of work from perhaps seeing a large number of children superficially for statutory reasons, to focusing specifically upon children whose problems appear to have got stuck, and who require creative and more in-depth assessment.

Currently EPs contribute much exciting and wide-ranging work, including individual casework, assessment, intervention, counselling, dealing with traumatic crises, conciliation, helping children learn, research and training for teachers and others. I would like to see such colourful and important initiatives continued but also ongoing checking that such work is effective and meeting the needs of the key people who are requesting EP services. It is important that such services are well evaluated and 'hit the spot'.

I would like to see EPs deriving benefits through having choice of employers. While many might choose to work for LEAs, others may elect to work for other bodies, and even themselves. The idea of groups of practising educational psychologists, with a portfolio of employment, offers exciting opportunities for the future.

The move to extended training to meet the needs of the twenty-first century is, in my view, well overdue. I would like to see a smooth transition to three-year training, at doctoral level, attracting the highest-calibre candidates for the future.

Finally, in all this, I would like to see a profession that is confident, independent, creative, dynamic, responsive and able to face head on the real challenges faced by individual children, families and society as whole. They would be sufficiently self-confident to challenge thinking and current systems and creative such that they are willing and able to 'think outside the box' and offer new, fresh ideas which go against traditional patterns. In short, they should be able to respond to the demands and challenges of the future.

# Educational Psychology 2

*Sheila Wolfendale*

## Initial and Continuing Training of Educational Psychologists (EPs)

There is now an urgent need for the initial training of EPs to be extended beyond one year – see Chapter 2 for an outline of ideas and issues in EP training. The present one-year masters' level course provides an excellent induction and opportunity to be introduced to theory and practice issues but, with a range of increasing competing demands upon contemporary EPs' time and skills, there is a need for extensive grounding of these issues and for opportunities for trainee EPs to acquire repertoires of specialisms and skills as part of their apprenticeship and particularly for them to emerge from training as confident practitioner-researchers.

Continuing professional development opportunities for EPs need to be extended, acknowledged and formalized as a job entitlement. The growth of professional doctorate courses for practising EPs has been recent and rapid (Wolfendale, 2001) but there are still many employers (mostly LEAs) who do not yet encourage and support their employee EPs to avail themselves of these opportunities. The government is just beginning to recognize teachers' need for occasional sabbaticals and professional enrichment, and it is to be hoped that systems under discussion could include EPs.

## Practice Orientations

Chapter 2 describes a wide range of EP duties and activities; there is still too much emphasis upon EPs carrying out assessment of special educational needs within the parameters of the SEN Code of Practice and the Special Educational Needs and Disability Act 2001, at the expense of EPs being regarded and used as practitioners applying psychology to education, child development and to social policy issues. EPs are uniquely placed to apply a range of hypothesis-testing, problem-solving approaches to a myriad of issues to do with children's development, learning, education, welfare and well-being.

There is a part for EPs' professional organizations to play in lobbying central and local government with regards to a broader role for which EPs are well equipped.

## Emerging Directions of Practice

Again, Chapter 2 examines a number of trends and offers a number of visionary, 'blue skies' areas of EP practice. I would just like to highlight a couple of these areas here:

1 Consistent with government emphasis upon collaborative, 'joined-up' inter- and multidisciplinary ways of working, EPs need to position themselves to make a full and powerful contribution to such collaborative ventures. There are an increasing number of interagency initiatives (Atkinson et al. 2002) and, as these continue to proliferate, EPs need to be in the vanguard, contributing their broad knowledge bases and skills to best effect.

2 Linked with point (1), a challenge for EPs is to derive and apply working practices with children and their families that are truly partnership ventures, operating upon principles of reciprocity, equality, parity and mutuality of esteem, cross-fertilization of equivalent expertise and sharing planning and decision-making on behalf of children (Carpenter, 2000; Wolfendale, 2002).

## New Directions: A Wish List

EPs have had to be adaptable and have survived, in recent times, the vagaries of local government reorganization, the advent of a National Curriculum, local (financial) management of schools, OFSTED inspection of schools and LEAs, financial delegation and, currently, the opportunities and threats of (private and financial initiatives) as alluded to in Chapter 2. Some of these policy applications have threatened EPs' existence in their present form, but (to take an evolutionary metaphor) the EP 'species' is currently very strong and buoyant.

Looking back over a working lifetime of being an EP and closely associated with the profession either as practitioner or EP trainer, I perceive a number of 'bedrock', core functions as enduring and others as having evolved, symbiotically, in response to a changing socio-political scene, encompassing changes in family structure, shifting political and ideological climates and ever-evolving policies on provision for children.

For the future I am confident that EPs will continue to adapt creatively. Survival skills inherently epitomize a lifelong learning model (Field and Leicester, 2000), and it is consistent with a life-span developmental perspective that professional practice is predicated upon concepts of progression and continuity as well as change.

The adaptable EP will retain core principles and values about applying psychology for the benefit of children, who will be the adult citizens of tomorrow, while embracing the latest technologies (Mackin, 2002) to further these aims.

# Work-Life Balance

*Cary L. Cooper*

The last half-century has seen an enormous change in the nature of society and of the workplace in particular. The 1960s epitomized the limitless possibilities of change, with the British prime minister of the time proclaiming that the white heat of technology was about to transform our lives, producing a leisure age of 20-hour weeks. This was followed by the 1970s, a period of industrial strife and conflict in much of the developed world. The workplace became the battle ground between employers and workers, highlighted by Studs Terkel (1972) in his acclaimed book of the period, *Working*:

> Work is by its very nature about violence – to the spirit as well as to the body. It is about ulcers as well as accidents, about shouting matches as well as fist-fights, about nervous breakdowns as well as kicking the dog around. It is, above all, about daily humiliations. To survive the day is triumph enough for the walking wounded among the great many of us.

Out of the industrial relations turmoil of the 1970s came the enterprise culture of the 1980s, a decade of privatizations, merger mania, joint venture, process re-engineering and the like, transforming workplaces into free-market, hot-house cultures. Although this entrepreneurial period on both sides of the Atlantic improved economic competitiveness in international markets, there were also the first signs of strain, as 'stress' and 'burnout' became concepts in the everyday vocabulary of many working people.

By the end of the 1980s and into the early 1990s, the sustained recession, the move towards the privatization of the public sector and the ICT technology revolution laid the groundwork for potentially the most profound changes in the workplace since the Industrial Revolution. The early years of the 1990s were dominated by the effects of recession and efforts to get out of it, as organizations downsized and flattened their structures. There were fewer people doing more work and feeling more job insecurity. The rapid expansion of information technology also meant the added burden of information overload and the accelerating pace of work, with people demanding more and more information, and quicker and quicker. From the middle 1980s throughout the 1990s, we also saw the massive expansion of women in the workplace, with a noticeable pushing of the 'glass ceiling' further upwards. The changing role of men and women at work and at home added another dimension to the enormity of change taking place in the world.

The downsizing and the rapidity of change had certainly taken their toll in the 1990s. While this scenario is cause enough for concern, the underlying trend towards 'outsourcing' is leading towards a more insidious work environment –

the 'short-term contract' or 'freelance' culture. This has led to what employers refer to euphemistically as 'the flexible workforce', although in family-friendly terms it is anything but flexible. The psychological contract between employer and employee in terms of 'reasonably permanent employment for work well done' is truly being undermined as more and more employees no longer regard their employment as secure and many more are engaged in part-time working and short-term contracts. Indeed, the Institute of Management/UMIST survey (Worrall and Cooper, 1997–ongoing) (which has and will continue to survey 5000 managers each year over the next five years) found some disturbing results among Britain's managers: 1) organizations at the end of the 1990s were found to be in a state of constant change, with over 60% of this national sample of managers having undergone a major restructuring over the last 12 months and in each of the next three years; and 2) these changes led directly to increased job insecurity, lowered morale and the erosion of motivation and loyalty.

Most of these changes involved downsizing, cost reduction, delayering and outsourcing. Yet the perception was that, although inevitably these changes led to a slight increase in profitability and productivity, decision-making was slower and, more importantly, the organization was deemed to have lost the right mix of human resource skills and experience in the process (Worrall and Cooper, 1997–ongoing).

So what are the consequences of this change? First, as more and more people work from their home, whether part time or on a short-term contract, we will be increasingly creating 'virtual organizations'. The big corporate question here is: how will this virtual organization of the future manage this dispersed workforce, with the communication difficulties already apparent in existing organizational structures? Secondly, with two out of three families/couples already two-earners or on dual careers, how will working from home affect the delicate balance between home and work or, indeed, the roles between men and women? Indeed, with employers increasingly looking for and recruiting 'flexible workers', won't women be preferred to men, given their history of flexibility?

Thirdly, since the Industrial Revolution, many white-collar, managerial and professional workers have not experienced high levels of job insecurity; even many blue-collar workers who were laid off in heavy manufacturing industries of the past were frequently re-employed when times got better. The question that society has to ask itself is: can human beings cope with permanent job insecurity without the safety and security of organizational structures which, in the past, provided training, development and careers?

## New Directions for Research

Research in the field of occupational and organizational psychology needs to address a number of the questions raised above. First, research is currently being undertaken in exploring the psychological contract between employer and employee, and the consequences of this changing relationship, but this needs a better conceptual framework and research methodologies. Secondly, although much has been written about the virtual organization, there is little empirical work and few good practice examples have been explored or highlighted. As we use new technology increasingly over the next decade, we need to know more about what works and what doesn't, and what training and development people will need to cope with these changes. Thirdly, we have to explore the changing gender roles of men and women in the workplace and in the home, and how these may affect work life and the new ways of working. Fourthly, how do we encourage men to be more flexible in their working practices and to adopt a more discontinuous career path if that is appropriate to their skill base or family needs? Fifthly, what are the skills people will need in the new world of work and who will provide this training? Since we are moving towards a short-term contract culture, how do we learn to market ourselves, to get the updated training we need, to network with potential clients/colleagues, to learn to work with temporary networks, to develop our ICT skills base, etc.? And, finally, how do we begin to live with intrinsic job insecurity?

# Occupational and Organizational Psychology

*Clive Fletcher*

Unfortunately, there are perhaps more issues than new academic directions and developments in this field in the UK at the present time. In one sense, everything is rosy. Occupational psychology in the UK has boomed over the last 10–15 years, with a huge increase in the number of students coming through MSc programmes and findings jobs. This in turn reflects the steadily increasing demand for psychological services in this field from individuals and organizations. One indicator of the development in this area is that the British Psychological Society (BPS) annual occupational psychology conference in the early and middle 1970s would typically have had around 120–150 delegates, split more or less evenly between academics and practitioners. Now, the annual conference regularly pulls in over 600, with a heavy preponderance of the latter group. That shift in the balance to a practitioner-dominated professional group gives rise to the first set of issues.

There has been much criticism from some practitioners that their needs are not met by the traditional forms of meeting and discourse provided under the auspices of the BPS. They have felt that these are 'too academic' and not sufficiently focused on their interests and professional issues as applied psychologists. This has reached the point whereby a separate group, the Association of Business Psychologists, was set up in 2001 and held their own conference that year. To some extent this is understandable, as the focus of practitioners is not the same as that of academics. However, one has a strong feeling, listening to the comments (and complaints) of consultants and others, that the real problem is that the academic side is just all too difficult, and what they actually want are meetings and publications that are little more than experience exchanges and presentations of the latest tool-kits for consultants. Certainly, if one talks to the typical practitioner in occupational psychology, they have usually read very few if any recent journal articles. For them, continuous professional development seems to be about learning to use new tests or hearing about the latest business development practices, rather than enhancing and updating the scientific knowledge base which is the foundation of their professional identity. The practitioner-researcher work divide has been commented on extensively elsewhere (Anderson et al., 2001).

There is great danger here in that, should practitioners in this field allow themselves to get too divorced from that scientific knowledge base (after all, a condition for their chartership is that they completed a first degree in psychology, with all that it entails, before they went on to do an MSc), they run the risk of becoming little more than general human resource consultants. In other words, that scientific background and its maintenance are crucial to their validity, to the integrity of what they do and to their professional identity. Should they downplay it, lose touch with it or de-emphasize it, in the longer term the field as a whole is likely to lose credibility and support.

Alas, alongside this problem is another one that in many ways offers some parallels to it. This comes from the academic side and stems from the impact of successive research assessment exercises (RAEs). These are held every five to six years and involve the assessment of every academic department and their staff in terms of their research output, ostensibly through a peer review process. Each department is accorded a rating on the basis of this assessment, which greatly affects the funding of the department and, by implication, its prestige. There are many good reasons for having the RAE, but the way is has operated in psychology has given rise to some very undesirable side-effects. One of these is a tendency to devalue the contribution of research in occupational psychology. Indeed, the last RAE panel did not even have a chartered occupational psychologist as a member, but still felt it did not need to consult with external experts in judging the value of research in this field. The perception in psychology departments across the country has been that applied psychology in general is not a route to getting a high RAE rating.

The result of this is to drive occupational psychology research and academics to the business schools as their home. The RAE panel in this domain, unlike its psychology counterpart, most certainly does value organizational psychological research. In many ways, this drift to the business schools (which has also been observed to happen in the USA) has lots of advantages – perhaps it would make the members of the Association of Business Psychologists happy because of its inevitably more applied emphasis. But there are some significant downsides to this. Undergraduates in psychology will be less and less likely to be exposed to occupational psychology and will be less able to evaluate it accurately as a potential career option. But worse is the likelihood of this branch of applied psychology becoming more detached from its roots in mainstream psychology and ongoing developments coming out of it. Nor is this a one-way process because detachment from occupational psychology influences will impoverish the breadth of perspective and relevance of mainstream research.

So, there is a train of development that sees occupational psychology being divorced, both in academia and among its own practitioners, from its psychological and scientific roots. It is my contention that this process is unhealthy for the profession. To look on the positive side, the RAE process may have run its course, not least because of the problems of allocating funds in line with its assessments in any meaningful way. In time, then, its distorting influence may lessen. But, in the meantime, academic occupational psychologists need to challenge the kind of thinking enshrined in the psychology RAE panel. For the practitioners and their concerns, more needs to be done – but on both sides. One would hope that some publications (either in journal, book or electronic format) will be launched on to the market that will help practitioners keep themselves abreast of latest research and theory in an understandable and efficient manner. Traditional journal articles do not meet this need, and the BPS Division of Occupational Psychology could perhaps take the lead in promoting the development of such publications, perhaps in association with a commercial publishing house. However, this still requires practitioners to show the commitment and professionalism to acquire and digest the publications offered.

Finally, and largely unrelated to the above concerns, it will be important for this field of psychology to show an increasing awareness of cultural and diversity issues. For far too long we have been content to live off the outpourings of American organizational psychology research, which have demonstrably little relevance in many other cultures (Triandis and Brislin, 1984; Triandis, 1989). With the increasing internationalization of business, and political developments such as the strengthening of the identity of the European Union, occupational psychology needs to be wider and less USA-orientated in its perspective.

# Occupational Psychology

*Chris Lewis*

The momentum that, at present, is carrying occupational psychology along has two major sources. These are, first, the training and expectations of students who are making their way along this professional development route; and, secondly, the demands of the marketplace.

## Training and the Expectations of Students

Since the end of the 1980s the introduction of a royal charter for British psychologists has led the Division of Occupational Psychology of the BPS to put into place strict content rules to be followed by courses that train aspirant chartered occupational psychologists. On the whole these are masters programmes run at British universities. No course would be viable without BPS accreditation. Therefore the content of this applied discipline is clearly structured and, while allowing for some local interpretation of emphasis, universally followed. Every trainee occupational psychologist is expected to gain knowledge in the eight areas, as described in Chapter 3 of this book.

Despite a kind of disclaimer by the Division of Occupational Psychology that no listing of the fields of occupational psychology can ever be perfect or complete, these are, none the less, the determinants of the shape of this applied discipline in the eyes of most trainees. This is further reinforced by the criteria laid down for the remainder of the chartering process. What is lost sight of is that the purpose of this imposed structure was to ensure that all trainees receive a broad theoretical grounding across the whole applied discipline. It is not there to label discrete professional specialisms. The aim is to give trainees width of perspective, not to narrow their focus.

However, trainees do tend to see their strengths and weaknesses in terms of the prescribed structure. For example, they may consider themselves, when practitioners, as best suited to work in the field of assessment and selection and, at the same time, quite happy to give the human factors area a wide berth. Others may take the exact opposite view.

Where occupational psychology is going, therefore, is being determined by which of eight tracks new entrants want to go down. The rigidity that the prescribed structure has installed means that occupational psychology is, in broad terms, going nowhere particularly new. The developments tend to stay within their own areas, discourage eclectic creative solutions and lead to an increasing plethora of prescriptive approaches. The professional occupational psychologist is left only with the decision as to which one to take off the shelf.

## Demands of the Marketplace

As a generalization, the consumers of occupational psychologists' skills find it very hard to distinguish these from the skills of the human resources professional. Occupational psychologists have colluded with this confusion by adopting techniques emanating from business writers based on insightful common sense rather than psychological theory. In most of the occupational psychology areas the trend is for the two professional groups to move closer together. This does not bode well for the applied psychology discipline. The distinguishing features that the trained occupational psychologist ought to possess (namely, evaluation skills and the underpinning psychological knowledge) are undervalued. At the same time the comparative lack of a dedicated business focus is overemphasized. There is a distinct danger that, as a professional expert on human behaviour in the workplace, the occupational psychologist will be relegated from technologist to technician. The idea that occupational psychologists should rebrand themselves as 'business psychologists' would only serve to increase the danger.

At present occupational psychology looks as if it is destined to become more narrowly prescriptive, uninspiring and less exciting for the practitioner. It has drifted away from a focus on the 'needs' of business to that of their 'wants'. This is a real threat to long-term viability of the profession.

## Occupational Psychology: Where Should it Go?

A cynical view might be that occupational psychology has gone from being a young profession to one that is quite old and tired without passing through a long, active and influential mid-life. This is not the case, but it could happen if it does not start to recognize its strengths. The basic body of knowledge on which the discipline rests needs to be revisited so that it can be recognized and valued for the essential role it plays in making this profession distinctive and influential. Occupational psychologists are, first and foremost, psychologists. However the content of most of the masters' programmes in occupational psychology (again aided and abetted by the requirements imposed by the BPS Division of Occupational Psychology) does not obviously dovetail into the undergraduate experience of the students. The general scheme of things is that the students are expected to make the links themselves, but only if they find it useful, and they know how. Many don't and the two components of their higher education remain unconnected.

What this fuels is the narrow compartmentalization into the eight areas referred to above. Each has a practitioner-based body of knowledge, and that seems to do. What is overlooked is that the basic academic discipline of psychology does not use the same compartments. It has a different structure. This means that a single undergraduate topic area may have something to contribute to most, or even all, of the areas of occupational psychology. This awareness means that the compartments are linked. This in turn should facilitate more creative, less prescriptive solutions to work behaviour problems. A simple example would be that the study of individual differences and social psychology might lead to a 'selection' problem being redefined as one of 'organization development'.

The professional occupational psychologist should therefore look to the body of psychology for a solution when faced with a work-based problem. To refer to that from occupational psychology alone might help to classify the problem and point to a prescriptive solution, but this is the activity of a technician. To be really harsh, it is occupational psychology 'by numbers'. You do not need six years of training to do it. Just to be aware of different psychometric instruments and how to interpret them; to know how to design a competency framework; to be able to construct and run an assessment centre; are skills that are extremely useful and valid for an occupational psychologist working in the assessment field. But these are not enough if they see themselves as a psychologist. They need to have considered the psychological concepts and constructs that justify their use. This is one way that the occupational psychologists can put conceptual distance between themselves and human resources professionals.

Linked to this is the other feature that distinguishes those who have studied the discipline of psychology from other observers of human behaviour. It is the recognition that the evaluation of a solution is as important as its implementation. Being able to carry out the 'so what' test is where the occupational psychologist really adds value in the business sense.

The way forward for occupational psychology is to put trainees and fully fledged professionals back in touch with their psychological roots. Get them to see that something like attachment theory, which up to now was just a topic that they answered questions on in a developmental psychology exam in the fairly distant past, might just be crucial in considering the career development of managers.

# Counselling

*Colin Feltham*

Psychology has probably been the dominant academic influence on counselling theory and training, certainly if one includes psychoanalytic and humanistic psychologies. Long discredited, introspective psychology remains a significant implicit feature of counselling, and counselling theory is informed for better or worse by the quasi-scientific discourse of much psychology. Key counselling/psychotherapy theorists have been mainly (white, male, American) psychologists by training and affiliation, even if they have later rejected or seriously modified their views derived from traditional academic psychology. A majority of counsellors in Britain probably have a broadly ambivalent attitude towards psychology (for example, Van Deurzen-Smith, 1993) and, anecdotally, one can say that most psychology graduates undertaking counselling training have to *unlearn* their scientific mind-set and learn to trust experiential modes of knowledge and practice: self-awareness, immediacy, intuition and reflexivity. Nevertheless, empirical psychology does act as a necessary challenge to and brake on the often runaway subjective, romantic and faith-orientated characteristics of counselling and counsellors.

One of the most significant directions in which psychology has nudged counselling is evidence-based practice. Many counsellors are now obliged to evaluate and justify their practice using psychological research instruments. Since cognitive-behavioural practitioners began to advertise their evidence-based successes, humanistic and psychodynamic counsellors, particularly those working in publicly funded settings, have felt the pinch and moved towards greater investment in empirical research. This has been a significant new direction in the 1990s and 2000s but not necessarily the most significant or most welcome. A future area for pertinent research development would be empirical comparisons of psychologically trained counsellors with non-psychologically trained.

Two areas in which psychology has had some degree of welcome impact, I believe, are developmental and social psychology. There is some tendency for counsellors to be a little woolly, indifferent, opinionated or hostile about certain issues, such as the 'nature–nurture' debate, the nature of memory, long-term effects of early childhood experiences, age-related cognitive abilities, motivational states and the components of power and social influence in the counselling relationship. These are all areas in which psychologists have made careful and worthy studies and have something to offer counsellors. Even where they disagree, counsellors must benefit from debate with psychologists who put forward research-based challenges about the accuracy of recall, the effects of psychotraumatic experiences, the possibility of clients' merely outward compliance and so on.

As for *the* most significant new direction to date, my money is on evolutionary psychology (EP). This may seem strange coming from a counsellor, since EP tends to confirm genetically determined traits that are quite resistant to personal change efforts and hence to counselling. I think counselling lacks a depth explanation of the universal human proclivity towards suffering (and the relative difficulty in helping people to change counterproductive behaviours) and EP is one of the most promising such explanations on offer. Most psychology is somewhat atomistic in its focus and avoids grand theory and universal depth explanations. EP (and evolutionary psychiatry and psychotherapy), particularly as expounded by, for example, Stevens and Price (1996), Baron-Cohen (1997), Ratey and Johnson (1997) and Gilbert and Bailey (2000), offer persuasive explanations for the stubbornness of self-destructive behaviour and the reasons for certain genetically disadvantaged individuals and groups of people being hard to understand and treat successfully. The fact that such developments are vigorously opposed in certain quarters (for example, Rose and Rose, 2000) need make them no less compelling.

## What New Directions Should there Be?

First, I want to honour the contributions of some psychologists who have made useful contributions before going on to suggest that the best new direction might be towards an anti-psychology or post-psychology future for counselling. Individuals like Carl Rogers stand out as opposing the conventional psychologies of their time and place. More recently, in Britain, psychologists like David Smail (1993) and David Pilgrim (1997) have forced a social and political focus on to the agenda for clinical psychologists as well as counsellors, psychotherapists and other mental health workers. Neither applied psychology nor counselling have fully taken on board the case for a clinical practice informed by serious attention to the social causes of mental distress and an implied need for a 'mass psychology' and even a revolutionary psychology. (Titles like *Radical Psychology* (Brown, 1973) do not characterize psychology course lists today.) Ironically, the social justice claims of women, black people, gays and disabled people have further fragmented any collective will and psychology's field of attention. There is ample scope and need for a new form of applied, coherent, *political* psychology. To some extent, critical psychologists – in their critique of traditional psychology and focus on local activist psychologies – are moving in this direction (for example, Sloan, 2000), yet their products still seem curiously, unhelpfully overintellectualized and psychology-fettered.

Alongside this political impatience with conventional applied psychology, there are a few signs of psychologists focusing on what (I think) is most important. One of these is Baumeister's (1991) excellent *Meanings of Life* book. I single this out because it seems so rare: an accessibly written book, by a psychologist, that looks at the quest for identity, at the meaning of work, religion, relationships, parenthood, death. What I would like to see is just such a promotion of attention to the big questions of human suffering, purpose, spirituality and political justice (Feltham, 2001).

Now the crucial problem here is what place psychology has, if any, in a broad counselling studies discipline. To some extent psychology replaced at least aspects of philosophy and theology, but psychology perhaps assumes its own primacy and immortality. It cannot be assumed that the clinical applications of psychology will last for ever. Currently it is fashionable to engage in varieties of postmodernist discourse and psychology itself is becoming partly infused with poststructuralism, constructivism, narratology and so on. Meanwhile, we have failed to demonstrate quite what the application of theory is *at all* to counselling practice (Feltham, 1999). Meanwhile, critics such as Tallis (1999) point out that the proliferation of 'theorrhoea' in universities is all too easy but probably ineffective for pressing, painful personal concerns in a finite lifetime with limited resources.

As well as having no satisfactory *grand theory of suffering* (I call this 'anthropathology' – something envisaged as more comprehensive than so-called abnormal psychology or psychopathology), psychology lacks a sense of social urgency. Also, in spite of counselling's obvious focus on the suffering of unique *individuals*, psychology lacks any real understanding of highly individual differences, usually moving only between the 'abnormal' and the 'normal' (Offer and Sabshin, 1991). There may be some notable exceptions such as the Myers–Briggs Type Indicator but these are, in my view, still quite limited. It is quite possible to imagine an ambitious discipline paradoxically incorporating both grand theory and attention to individual differences. The genome project leans in this direction of mappable complexity and, for clinical assessment purposes, one can envisage some sort of computer-generated, multispectral individual differences grid being devised, which might usefully suggest to counsellors and their clients where clients' problem clusters are located (or clinical intuition might well be a short-cut towards this!).

So, please let's see more meaning, more meaningful 'realist' theorizing, political psychology, critical thinking, teleology (in the style of archetypal psychologist, James Hillman), more transpersonal psychology, practical preventive psychology and more radical, imaginative and passionate psychology-in-action. Where is the equivalent of psychology's twenty-first century Marx, Darwin or Freud when they're most needed? When, if ever, is psychology finally going to meet the challenge of dropping its dry-as-dust quantitative scientific character (Boyle, 2001) in favour of something ready to stimulate a bit of joy in being alive, justice in social systems and common sense in organizations?

# Sport Psychology

*Ian M. Cockerill*

It is sufficiently arduous for a present-day athlete to maintain a consistently high level of performance without having to cope with the plethora of issues that can lead to 'things going wrong'. In the present context an athlete is either male or female, playing any sport and at a variety of levels. At one end of the continuum there is the full-time professional and, at the other, the occasionally active person. In between, there exists a variety of categories that, broadly speaking, encapsulate the recreational athlete, the serious recreational athlete, the competitive athlete and the serious competitive athlete. What is common to each individual, however, is that all are required to acquire techniques appropriate to the sport, to increase fitness in order to execute that technique, to develop a range of performance strategies and, finally, to possess the necessary psychological attributes that will ensure adherence to the activity over a sustained period.

In this personal perspective, I have drawn upon more than 40 years' experience as a teacher, coach and sport psychologist in an attempt to identify some of the issues that are implicit within sport psychology today. The more one considers what these issues are, the greater the number of paradoxes that are revealed. For example, we know more about training methods, sports medicine, nutrition and mental training than ever before, yet the number of injured athletes is also greater. Why is this? At a fundamental level, the answer must either be that overtraining is endemic, that incorrect training methods are being used by some athletes or that it is a combination of the two – namely, too much inappropriate training. As 400 metres runner, Katharine Merry, prepared to compete for England in the 2002 Commonwealth Games, she wrote of the problems associated with being injured (*The Daily Telegraph*, 7 May 2002). Long experience as an athlete, she said, allowed her to deal with injury, but she referred to many athletes who are unable to cope adequately with injury and who are troubled mentally as a consequence. In just a few sentences, Katharine drew upon several issues that face most sports performers at some time or other and which, increasingly, are being recognized as having at least a psychological antecedent, if not solution.

The following issues are common to most sports in varying degrees. Interestingly, athletes at all levels, from occasionally active amateur to high-profile professional, tend to believe that no one has experienced setbacks in quite the way they have. This is, of course, perfectly true when you think about it. A mistake that we tend to make occasionally when trying to engender empathy with an athlete is to say, 'I know how you feel', but we don't; each person's perception of his or her situation is unique. So what are some of the key psychological issues facing sport psychology at the present time? Aside from injury-related concerns, they include motivation and goal setting, the methods of mental skills training, performance anxiety, player–coach relationships, team cohesion, body image, overtraining and the transition/retirement process, although this list is far from being exhaustive. Rather than refer to specific source material in the text, I have chosen to identify selected further reading at the end that can be referred to according to the interests of the reader. It is evident that while some may be interested in, say, body image, others will be more attuned to retirement issues. The above areas would not be the choice of every sport psychologist, but they are what I consider to be some of the current fundamental concerns at the present time. Also, while some will tend to be on everyone's list, namely motivation, anxiety and mental training, others will be deemed less important by some psychologists.

The importance of *motivation* is self-evident and few would shy from placing it first. Unless an athlete is moved to activity, literally, no progress can be made. We hear about coaches who are 'good motivators' and, while they can perhaps inspire someone to seek to play professional football, compete in an Olympic Games, or complete a marathon, the hard work involved in accomplishing these things must come from within. It is often said that the coach's principal objective is to become redundant and, although some coaches would disagree strongly with that premise, it is fundamentally true. Today's sportsmen and women are often rewarded highly for their performances, but none has achieved high status by merely drifting to the top. The right kind of genetic endowment that leads to the potential for becoming skilled at a given sport counts for little unless qualities like determination, commitment and dedication are part of the equation and some would argue that each of these is largely an inherited characteristic. Closely allied to motivation is *goal setting*. It is interesting that, while players of individual sports such as golf and tennis are well aware of the importance of goal setting, few footballers, for example, consider it to be important. In saying few, there are some that do and they tend to be those who are able to extend their careers by careful planning, recognizing that a good coach can only take you so far. Without a personal plan of action progress will be limited; hence the many underachievers evident in sport.

*Mental training* or *psychological skills training* is exceedingly popular and incorporates goal setting alongside training in the use of mental imagery. Research suggests that mental training has a part to play in the enhancement of athletic performance, but it has been argued recently that programmes should be tailored more precisely to the needs of the individual and that 'one size does not fit all'. This is perfectly logical if we recognize that each athlete is unique. Visualization techniques are highly popular with many athletes and it can be demonstrated that, with consistent practice of certain techniques, it is possible to enhance confidence for the execution of closed-type skills such as putting in golf, serving in badminton and taking a penalty in football. In open skills where the environment is constantly changing, for example open play in a team game, the procedure may be less efficacious.

*Performance anxiety* is evident among most competitive athletes but it is usually possible to control it to the extent that it does not become disruptive. While accepting that anxiety is largely a disruptive state, there are some who would suggest that it can also be facilitative. The arguments for and against perhaps hinge on the level of anxiety, its nature – is it cognitive or somatic? – and the nature of the event where it occurs. Moreover, there is plenty of anecdotal evidence to suggest that the effects of anxiety among coaches should be afforded greater consideration than hitherto in order to examine how an anxious coach can affect an anxious player, or even an entire team.

The *player–coach relationship* is an important issue and one that deserves greater investigation. Today, coaching is, for many, a career, and in most sports it is difficult to obtain a full-time appointment without having undertaken a prescribed course of training. The days when players could become coaches or managers without further education are more or less gone. However, notwithstanding the possession of a coaching qualification, it is still essential for coaches to recognize that formulating the right kind of relationship with an athlete or player does not come neatly wrapped in a coaching certificate! As with most things in life, it has to be worked at. Likewise, *team cohesion* is a precious commodity, but it is not always evident, even in a team with highly skilled players and an experienced coach or manager. Interestingly, there appears to be a move to what the media sometimes refers to as the 'cerebral coach', perhaps describing one who attempts to understand that each player in a team is unique, making an individual contribution to team success. I recall one player saying of his coach: 'He has much experience at the highest level and has achieved success, but he doesn't know what makes me tick.'

For today's athlete it is important to look the part as well as to play it and *body image* is a relatively new area for the sport psychologist to address. Associated with body image are not only issues such as eating disorders and the use of physique-enhancing substances but, for those who compete at a high level, also the perceived importance of projecting an appropriate media image. The increasing number of elements that a full-time athlete has to deal with compared with those of just 10 years ago can mean that he or she may struggle to maintain a proper focus on training and performing. Financial remuneration for an athlete can be great and, given the importance placed upon winning, it is unsurprising that the sporting careers of some individuals can be relatively brief. *Overtraining* is an issue for participants at all levels. If performance outcomes are not what are expected, the answer may not be to train harder, which is what some will advocate. Often it is better to train differently, as overtraining can lead to burnout and to physical illness.

Finally, it is surprising that there are few professional sportsmen and women who, in advance of retirement, consider seriously what they might do after their sporting career ends. It will normally occur somewhere in the mid-30s, when they are still only half-way through what most people believe to be the duration of their working life. True, some can afford to stop earning altogether, but that number is quite small and psychological problems associated with transition from sport have been shown to bring problems for many.

It is evident that there are several key areas which have not been discussed here – for example, issues associated with specific populations such as children, the elderly and those with a disability. Also, the focus has been principally upon sport per se, and there is now a separate area of study called exercise psychology, which is closely related to sport psychology. It is concerned more with exercise promotion and a healthy lifestyle rather than competitive sport, although there are other ways of differentiating between the two. It is hoped that this very brief overview affords an insight into what is developing into a new and exciting field for both research and applied work. Of course, there is still a long way to go, as they say, before sport psychology becomes fully established in all sports. However, it is true to say that research in the various areas of sport psychology is now well established, with a range of good academic journals publishing a variety of interesting work of both a fundamental and an applied nature. Listed below is a selection of further reading that provides an insight into some of the issues that are presently being explored in sport psychology research and practice. It is hoped that this literature will encourage some to consider which important issues are next on the list for investigation and to move forward in this exciting area of psychology.

## Further reading

Balaguer, I., Crespo, M. and Duda, J.L. (eds) (1996) in *Motivation in Sport and Exercise*. Champaign, IL: Human Kinetics.

Bamber, D., Cockerill, I.M. and Carroll, D. (2000) 'The pathological status of exercise dependence', *The British Journal of Sports Medicine*, 34: 125–32.

Cockerill, I. (ed.) (2002) *Solutions in Sport Psychology*. London: Thomson.

Fairburn, C.G. and Beglin, S.J. (1994) 'Assessment of eating disorders: interview or self-report questionnaire?' *International Journal of Eating Disorders*, 16: 363–70.

Jowett, S. and Cockerill, I. (2002) 'Incompatibility in the coach–athlete relationship', in I. Cockerill (ed.) *Solutions in Sport Psychology*. London: Thomson, pp. 16–31.

Junge, A. (2000) 'The influence of psychological factors on sports injuries', *The American Journal of Sports Medicine*, 28: 10–15.

Kreider, R.B., Fry, A.C. and O'Toole, M.L. (eds) (1998) *Overtraining in Sport*. Champaign, IL: Human Kinetics.

Kremer, J. and Scully, D. (2002) 'The team just hasn't gelled', in I. Cockerill (ed.) *Solutions in Sport Psychology*. London: Thomson, pp. 3–15.

Lavallee, D., Nesti, M., Borkoles, E., Cockerill, I. and Edge, A. (2000) 'Intervention strategies for athletes in transition', in D. Lavallee and P. Wylleman (eds) *Career Transitions in Sport: International Perspectives*. Morgantown, WV: Fitness Information Technology, pp. 111–30.

Medvec, V.H, Madey, S.F. and Gilovich, T. (1995) 'When less is more: counterfactual thinking and satisfaction among Olympic medallists', *Journal of Personality and Social Psychology*, 69: 603–10.

Moran, A. (1993) 'Conceptual and methodological issues in the measurement of mental imagery skills in athletes', *Journal of Sport Behaviour*, 16: 156–70.

# Health Psychology

*Paula Nicolson*

The contemporary origins of health psychology (HP) lead back to Matarazzo (1980) who saw it as a discipline involved in research and professional practice to explain, maintain, treat and promote health. HP was also charged with championing the role of the *mind* in the cause and reduction of physical ill-health. As Jane Ogden (2000: 4) proposes, HP challenges the 'mind–body split by suggesting a role for the mind in both the cause and treatment of illness but differs from psychosomatic medicine, behavioural health and behavioural medicine in that research within health psychology is more specific to the discipline of psychology'.

But what is the discipline of psychology itself? It has suffered over recent years from a decrease in creativity, imagination and critical reflexivity exacerbated by linking formal processes of research quality assessment and funding streams. Mainstream HP has evolved as an inherently conservative branch of the discipline, adopting the biomedical model and eschewing a critical reappraisal of its own practice. HP seems unprepared to be self-reflexive. Opportunities have been missed to challenge the status quo in medicine and health care and, if HP is to remain an enterprise in its own right rather than become integrated into the swelling ranks of PAMs (professions allied to medicine), we need to reflect and rethink without delay.

There is no reason for HP to continue to support the status quo. HP in the UK is an intentionally, self-proclaimed *humanistic* enterprise. It is:

> the practice and application of psychological research to: the promotion and maintenance of health, the prevention and treatment of illness, the identification of key factors in the causes of illness and management of health and illness, and the analysis and improvement of the health care system and health policy formation (BPS, 2000).

The aims and purposes of HP are geared towards the enhancement of the health of *individuals* through the application of empirically based knowledge. There is no *overt* declaration of any priority given to the medical model. Furthermore, while HP takes the *individual* as its baseline it recognizes the importance of the '*ecological context* of these psychological aspects of health . . . such as families, workplaces, organisations, communities, societies and cultures' (Marks et al., 1999: 8).

Health psychologists have also given themselves a broad remit, which includes a variety of methods and interpretive and conceptual frameworks. These offer the potential to take one or more of the individual, group, organization, community and cultural contexts as its unit(s) of analysis and challenge pre-existing assumptions about their constitution.

## New Directions: The Role of Qualitative Research

I want to say that HP *can* achieve reflexive and critical competence through using qualitative methods of data collection and analysis. But this is not so. The method itself is not enough – an ideology or standpoint by the researcher is required as part of the research process. It is the standpoint that takes account of the status of knowledge in context.

Qualitative research itself, in some hands, far from challenging the context of human health and illness, has become an adjunct to the status quo (Nicolson, 2001; Collins and Nicolson, 2002). To move forward in any significant way, researchers need to identify to themselves and their peers that they are challenging accepted wisdom.

The substance of my own early research was postnatal depression – I chose to study this qualitatively, in the 1980s when this was anathema to the psychology establishment, and the results of my work led me to take a 'radical' and feminist standpoint. I came to understand that not only do psychologists need to be reflexive and take account of the subjective experience of their respondents in a respectful and ethical manner but they also need to identify and challenge explicit and implicit power structures that shape respondents' experiences. That is dangerous from a 'scientific' point of view.

Qualitative research is not objective – nor is it intended to be. What should matter to the qualitative researcher interviewing women about their postnatal experience is the way that women's explanations for their experiences are seen (often by themselves) as *their* personal problem – as an integral part of women's lives.

Giving a voice is but a small component of the project of qualitative and critical health psychology. Critical health psychologists can use data to argue the case for structural change and reconceptualization of the 'problem'. The respondents whose voices are given a platform can only take their case so far. Indeed, they are unlikely to have the skills to make sense of their experience in a political and social context. Why should they? That is the role of critical health psychologists, who in this case need to ask: is it women or the context of contemporary motherhood, in all its guises, that is at issue here? Women are seen within the mainstream biomedical model as the victims of their bodies. Raging female hormones are seen to plague their lives from adolescence to late middle age. Science, clinical experts and popular myths portray women as emotionally and intellectually unreliable, unpredictable, deficient and a psychological puzzle – all because, for some of their adulthood, women have the capacity to ovulate. Postnatal depression is part of that belief system. For centuries women have been dying from childbirth and experiencing severe ill-health caused by the stresses and strains of motherhood. So why is depression in the weeks and months following birth perceived as 'atypical'? Women's capacity and determination to bear and nurture children under adversity seem endless; but it is not their resilience that interests scientists and clinicians. It is their failure.

Traditional research has deliberately and systematically denied the value of women's experience of the transition to motherhood. There are the 'legitimate' scientific takes on the ways to effective motherhood and these see all women as potential failures. Evidence which takes women's accounts seriously, suggesting postnatal depression to be other than pathological, is dismissed as subjective and anecdotal by those whose major focus is upon using the positivist model in the context of qualitative research.

Publishing data that challenge biomedical and patriarchal power is not necessarily easy or acceptable for those with careers in mind. It is though much easier to do so now at the start of the twenty-first century than it was 20 years ago. Clinical psychologists have managed to incorporate radical alternatives into *some* of their work with vulnerable groups – critical health psychology might assist their efforts by radical interpretation of research findings. Power structures in the organization of health care need to be identified and challenged, and the research and development agenda in health needs to be changed so that continuing inequalities in health care can be challenged. It is not an in-built feature of either qualitative or quantitative research to be either radical or conservative – they answer different orders of questions. The interpretation and implementation of results, however, are a matter for the reflexive or non-reflexive researcher. If a health psychologist demonstrates that only 10% of women in a large-scale study experience premenstrual distress, what should be asked next? Should the focus be on the underlying *cause of their pathology* or should the researcher turn their attention to challenging the efficacy of the operational definition of the concept of PMS (premenstrual syndrome) and the social stereotypes that apply? The choice here has nothing to do with how the data were collected. It depends on whether the researcher takes a conservative or radical/critical perspective to his or her research.

Qualitative research, in its fight for legitimacy in health psychology, is in danger of turning its back on the need for an ongoing analysis of power, precisely because it seeks a share of that power. Chapter 6 identified the need for health psychology to take account of reflexivity in practice. Health psychologists are all in a position to challenge conservative practice on individual, interpersonal, organizational and political levels. However until they choose to do this as a major part of their remit, health psychology (and particularly qualitative research in health psychology) will at best continue to be seen as a complement to the real action – which is the maintenance of the biomedical model.

# Lecturing in Psychology

*Stephen Newstead*

I did my PhD in the late 1960s and started lecturing in the early 1970s. In the 30 years that have passed since then I have seldom regretted my decision, and still enjoy the job I do. However, the job has changed enormously in that time and mostly for the worse.

One of the most dramatic, though fairly gradual and insidious, changes has been in the amount of external control. Lecturers now have their research assessed nationally on a quinquennial basis through a process of peer review known as the Research Assessment Exercise (RAE). All the signs are that this process will be changed next time round, though nobody knows quite what the changes will be. Everyone is agreed, however, that researchers need to be accountable for the way they spend the research money allocated by the funding councils. Research assessment is here to stay.

One knock-on effect of the RAE is that research is becoming more concentrated in certain institutions. The research money available has been awarded disproportionately to the small group of leading research universities, leaving the rest to survive as best they can. Universities are likely in future to define their missions more narrowly, with some focusing on teaching, some on research and some on the local community. Personally, I do not feel comfortable with this move. For me, a university is a place where teaching and research take place hand in hand. I cannot really come to terms with a university in which some kind of research (or other leading-edge practice) does not take place.

Teaching, too, has become much more accountable. The notion of degrees needing to be recognized by the BPS has been with us for several years, though a number of academics still object to the constraints this imposes. In my view, however, this recognition has largely been beneficial, ensuring that courses do not run without adequate resources. More recently a whole raft of other accountability exercises has been introduced. Institutions are regularly inspected by the Quality Assurance Agency (QAA); benchmarking statements have been produced by the QAA for all disciplines and institutions are expected to conform to these in designing their programmes; and the funding councils periodically examine psychology courses to see whether they should be designated as science or social science.

It would be nice to think that this age of inspection is just a passing phase, but this is unlikely to be the case. The nature of the inspection of teaching and research may change, but they will not go away. There is an unfortunate side-effect of all this accountability: the flexibility and freedom associated with lecturing decrease. It is now less easy to carry out blue-skies research since this may not attract funding and may have too long a delivery time. Teaching is expected to follow certain broad guidelines which may inhibit the coverage of new topics or the use of novel teaching techniques. Increasingly, both teaching and research are likely to be constrained by the needs of commerce, business and government.

Would I go into lecturing if I had my time again? The pay is not good and has been declining in real terms over the last couple of decades, so I would not go in it for the money. However, I think I *would* do it again; the friends and colleagues are like minded people, there is an intellectual buzz about being an academic and, despite all the constraints, there is still more freedom in what one does than in many other careers.

# Higher Education

*John Radford*

On the day I write this it is announced that the Millennium Dome has cost 28.4 million pounds during the past year *in which it has been standing empty*. This single wastage would go a long way towards transforming the research underfunding of the most impoverished half of the English universities. The fact is that all education and training of applied psychologists must take place within the national educational system, itself determined mainly by central government (both elected and non-elected). Such a senior academic as Professor Graham Zellick, Vice-Chancellor of the University of London and hardly a revolutionary firebrand, recently pronounced that government policy on higher education for the past two or three decades had been 'little short of disastrous'. The most significant issue, therefore, is the apparent lack of a coherent and credible national policy for higher education, which must of course include a sustainable method of paying for it. As the system becomes ever larger, due to a combination of demand and government action, so it becomes more pressing to consider new approaches. Much of what is currently done appears to assume that a system devised for a upper 10 or 15% can simply be expanded to embrace 50. Furthermore, that elite system itself suffered from a peculiarly British assumption that 'real' education is somehow quite distinct from any practical application.

I have tried to suggest some of the underlying reasons for the present state of affairs and the possibility of learning from the educational systems of other times and places. Specifically with regard to academics, I have urged that to function satisfactorily, higher education depends upon what may be generally characterized as professionalism. Academics badly need to be trained in the range of skills and knowledge they need in a mass system. But more than this, they need to be organized in professional mode, not as 'workers in the knowledge factories'. They need to function, and be rewarded, as autonomous experts at a high level. They need to understand the underlying scientific principles, the history and the philosophical justification of their profession. There are very powerful forces ranged against any such developments and only a few hopeful signs.

Psychologists, I have argued for some time, ought to be at the forefront of a professional approach to higher education, and one of the few positive developments is the creation of the Division for Teachers and Researchers in Psychology within the BPS, with its accompanying formal qualification and route to the status of chartered psychologist.

If academics, and academic psychologists in particular, could develop into fully educated professionals, they might be in a slightly stronger position to influence national educational policy. At least, they might be better able to deal with the problems that policy creates. Among these for psychology specifically is the gender imbalance in recruitment. Psychology has become around 80% female, the result mainly simply of women, belatedly, gaining full access to higher education. Once there is a relatively free choice, gender-associated preferences become evident and appear to be very robust, as is seen when GCE A-level choices follow after the constraints of the National Curriculum. Some may not see this as a problem but it can also be argued that a more even balance would be more desirable. Perhaps a broader approach to what psychology has to offer is needed. This applies even more so to the discrepancy between the large numbers entering first degrees in psychology and the relatively small proportion that can become professional psychologists. With a still larger take-up for higher education this imbalance is likely to increase. It seems to me important to think out both what psychology can offer to the mass of students and what really is the most appropriate preparation for professional courses. This must be in the light both of general educational aims and of what the large majority of students want, which is a useful qualification from a career point of view.

A mass system of higher education demands new approaches to what the nature of that education should be. I would strongly reject the distinction between 'real' and applied education, which appears to me to be particularly inappropriate for psychology. Phrases such as the 'scientist-practitioner' have been around for some time, and even 'metaphysician-scientist-practitioner' (O'Donohue, 1989), pointing to the need for applied psychologists to be aware of the methodological assumptions and social context of their work. I would also reject the assumption that research, at least if defined narrowly, is a necessary condition of higher education. This only became the norm within the last hundred years and within psychology, as I have pointed out elsewhere, largely due to the influence of F.C. Bartlett, who created a model admirable for its purpose of advancing scientific psychology but not necessarily appropriate for mass higher education.

I have tried to address some of the broader issues of applied psychology education and training not, admittedly, proposing many solutions, but in the hope that they will not be neglected among the wide range of specific and technical matters dealt with by others in this volume.

# Ethics

*Geoff Lindsay*

For many years ethics has not received its due attention in applied psychology, especially in the UK. The BPS itself had a Code of Conduct, but no ethical code, or even an ethics committee.

This has been changing over the past five to ten years, partly a result of events and partly because of professional developments. The former have included concerns about the use of treatment programmes, including those on vulnerable clients. A second major area has been the increasing concern, and indeed awareness, of inappropriate relationships, especially between psychologists and clients. Values, opinions and behaviours of psychologists (and others, for example, psychotherapists) have been researched to identify typologies of appropriateness and conflicts and to explore the nature of ethical dilemmas and how these are addressed. For example, ethical questions regarding psychologists and others have been investigated and analysed with respect to power (formal and informal), roles and gender. This has allowed greater clarity with respect to the ethical principles involved and their interpretation and enactment in various situations.

Developments in ethics have been evident in the USA, where the American Psychological Association has continued to revise its ethical principles and code of conduct. In the UK, the BPS has developed an efficient and effective investigatory and disciplinary system which can lead to a member being removed from membership and/or struck off the register of chartered psychologists. An ethics committee is also now in existence and is producing an ethical code to supplement the code of conduct, which is also to be revised. The European Federation of Psychologists Associations Standing Committee on Ethics has developed a meta-code of ethics. This has guided constituent members to ensure their codes are comprehensive and address the four principles of integrity, respect for the person, responsibility and competence. This has been particularly useful for developing associations, including those from eastern Europe.

These developments are important for two main reasons. First, they provide increasing protection for the public and others with whom psychologists interact professionally. This includes practice with client groups and as researchers. Secondly, they add to the standing and integrity of the discipline and its application. One hallmark of a profession is its adherence to ethical standards and education of its members to optimize their behaviour, to regulate and to discipline where there are breaches. While greater commercialism and interest in complaints and litigation may be drivers, psychology should embrace these developments because they are inherently right and appropriate.

What new directions should there be? I would like there to be a greater input on ethics throughout training, including the first-degree and postgraduate professional training. This should reflect knowledge of the principles and codes but also help new practitioners to appreciate that applied psychology also frequently throws up ethical dilemmas, where ethical principles conflict. Secondly, I would like to see more active consideration of ethical issues by practitioners, during training events, staff meetings and supervision. Thirdly, we need more research and conceptual analysis, particularly as new challenges arise – for example, 'reality' television.

Finally, there is the move to statutory registration of psychologists. Regulation by law will help protect the public but must be driven by the profession. We can learn from, but also help, other professions in developing ethics for the twenty-first century. Psychology is particularly well placed to develop ethical thinking and behaviour in its members: by researching the influence and application of ethical principles, and how psychologists and other practitioners recognize and deal with ethical dilemmas. In this sense, ethics is central to the development of applied psychology as a discipline itself, and as an influence on other disciplines.

## Further reading

Francis, R.D. (1999) *Ethics for Psychologists*. Leicester: British Psychological Society.

Lindsay, G. and Clarkson, P. (1999) 'Ethical dilemmas of psychotherapists', *The Psychologist*, 12: 182–5.

Lindsay, G. and Colley, A. (1995) 'Ethical dilemmas of members of the society', *The Psychologist*, 8: 214–17.

Pryzwansky, W.B. and Wendt, R.N. (1999) *Professional and Ethical Issues in Psychology*. London: W.B. Norton.

# Personality

*Michael W. Eysenck*

It has been argued that scientific research first of all needs to address issues of taxonomy or classification before attention is focused on more complex theoretical issues. In other words, we need to know what we should be studying before we can explain it. This is very much the case with personality research. Indeed, it could reasonably be argued that personality researchers have devoted an excessive amount of time to taxonomic issues relating to the structure of human personality. It took approximately 60 years for a consensus to be reached that there are probably five major personality factors (the so-called Big Five), and that they probably consist of extraversion, neuroticism, agreeableness, conscientiousness and openness.

What has been (and remains) the most significant issue in personality research concerns the provision of a detailed account of the internal processes and mechanisms that underlie individual differences on each of these personality dimensions. There is by now a consensus that this is, indeed, a key issue. However, there are fundamental disagreements about the kinds of internal processes that are of most importance. Theorists investigating the Big Five personality factors have assumed that individual differences on each personality factor can be accounted for to some extent in terms of genetic factors. The evidence from twin studies confirms this assumption, but it appears that genetic factors account for only approximately 35% of individual differences in each of the five personality factors (see Eysenck, 2000).

The notion that genetic factors play a role in producing individual differences in personality is a valuable one. However, the route from genetic differences to personality and behavioural differences is likely to be long and tortuous and, so far, there is little understanding of the ways in which genes impact on personality. In addition, the fact that well over half individual differences do *not* depend on genetic factors means that we clearly need to develop an understanding of the precise ways in which environmental factors influence the development of personality. This is hard to achieve because it would ideally require the use of longitudinal studies that are both expensive and time-consuming.

There are other reasons why relatively little progress has been made with the significant issue of understanding the internal processes associated with individual differences in the Big Five personality factors. Probably the most important one is that only a relatively small fraction of personality research is actually concerned with the Big Five factors at all! It would seem appropriate for researchers to develop a good level of understanding of the most important personality factors *before* devoting their efforts to other, less consequential, factors.

In my opinion, what is really needed is a much more comprehensive approach to an understanding of human personality. For example, some theorists focus almost exclusively on individual differences in behaviour, others emphasize individual differences in cognitive processes and still others concentrate on individual differences in physiological functioning. What is needed is research in which all these various kinds of measures are obtained so as to maximize the probability of developing an overall understanding of personality.

Some of the above points can be exemplified with respect to some of my research on the personality dimension of trait anxiety (see Eysenck, 2000). In essence, self-report, physiological and behavioural measures of anxiety were all obtained in a number of studies, and it was found that there were systematic discrepancies among these measures. For example, individuals high in trait anxiety had relatively higher levels of self-reported anxiety than of physiological activation or of behavioural anxiety. Of course, such discrepancies could not have been discovered unless we had taken the unusual step of obtaining all three kinds of measures in the first place.

The use of this comprehensive approach suggested various possible explanations as to why individuals high in trait anxiety showed this pattern. In essence, research carried out by different groups of researchers has indicated that those high in trait anxiety have a number of cognitive biases which lead them to exaggerate the threateningness of the environment, their own internal physiological state and their own behaviour (Eysenck, 2000). More specifically, they show a selective attentional bias (devoting excessive attention to threat-related stimuli) and they show an interpretive bias (producing threatening interpretations of ambiguous stimuli and situations).

There are other ways in which the approach to personality research can be made more comprehensive. For example, there have been exciting developments in cognitive neuroscience in recent years (see Eysenck and Keane, 2000), and the temporal and spatial resolution of the available techniques is improving all the time. Of particular importance, neuroimaging research is rapidly becoming more theoretically driven and is finally providing answers to key theoretical issues. Neuroimaging might help researchers to address an issue such as whether some individuals claiming to be low in trait anxiety are being deliberately dishonest. Neuroimaging could also be used to chart the time course of various forms of processing in response to threat-related stimulation, which might clarify why some individuals experience much more anxiety than others.

In sum, personality research has tended to be too divorced from other areas of psychology. Developments in cognitive psychology, cognitive neuroscience, physiological psychology and so on are all of potential relevance to personality research, and it is to be hoped that personality researchers in the future will make use of these developments in their theoretical and empirical research.

# The Dynamism of Modern Applied Psychology

*Nicky Hayes*

In my view, the most significant new issue or direction in applied psychology today is the way that psychology has opened out, developing and welcoming new areas of expertise and application. Applied psychology has never been as dynamic as it is right now. In recent years, many new areas of psychology have been opened up, and many older but less well recognized areas have strengthened and grown in popularity. This has happened for several reasons. One of them is the effect of the huge expansion of teaching of psychology at general education levels during the past two decades, which has produced a significantly greater general awareness of what psychology has to offer on the part of other professionals, managers and the public as a whole, creating a climate which is far more receptive to contributions and innovation from psychologists than was the case in previous decades.

Another is the way that psychologists themselves have changed. We have become far more confident about interacting with the media and putting ourselves in the public view; and also more confident generally about the value of our discipline and its relevance to both everyday and special problems. This in turn has stimulated an increased respect for the psychologist as a professional and a readiness on the part of the media and other professionals to consult psychologists on a wider range of issues, and that in turn has led to the recognition and institutionalization of several new areas of professional practice. Health psychology is one of the clearest examples of this, but applied psychologists in many other fields are making their presence felt and sharing their professional innovations with other psychologists – a process which directly facilitates the emergence of new areas of applied psychology.

The third reason for the dynamism of modern applied psychology has to do with the way that psychology itself has changed over the past two decades. Psychological methodology has broadened out: two decades ago, laboratory research in psychology was venerated while field-based research was generally regarded as inferior; but in the modern context both types of research are seen as equally valid contributors to psychological knowledge. Similarly, the balance between quantitative and qualitative approaches to data collection has become more even in that both are now acknowledged as playing an important role in psychological research. These changes have resulted in a discipline which is much more at home with the complexities and diversity of the modern world, and much better equipped to address real-world challenges and questions.

Other challenges still remain, not least of which is our need to capitalize on new approaches and methodologies and on the insights obtained from applied research, in the form of integrative theory-building of value to a wide range of psychologists. But the breadth and diversity of applied psychology, and the number of applied psychologists who are exploring new issues and opening up new areas, are indicators of a healthy dynamism right across the spectrum of applied psychology.

## New Directions

I would like to see psychology involved in even more aspects of everyday living: in design, in architecture, in public communication, in transport and planning, in our everyday understandings of human relationships and ideas and – perhaps most of all – in the understandings of decision-makers.

It is right and proper that specialized fields of applied psychology should grow up and be maintained by the psychological profession. But there is also a need for a more general type of applied psychology – for the flexibility to apply psychology as and where it appears to have relevance. This can range from something as trivial as the locations of street crossings to something as wide-ranging as the decisions of politicians.

Several of my own experiences of applied psychology have been in fairly unexpected areas. My first experience of consultancy in industry, for example, was solicited by IBM research laboratories and concerned a problem wherein trainees were underachieving on their day-release courses at local colleges. The result was a programme of workshops, consultations and individual exam counselling, drawing on well-established psychological knowledge. This was a relatively new way of approaching the problem at that time, but it ultimately contributed to the development of the BPS Diploma in the Applied Psychology of Teaching and Learning in the mid-1980s.

In 2000, I attended a series of seminars at the International Congress of Psychology in Stockholm, in which Miles Hewstone and other social psychologists were demonstrating the relevance of modern social psychological insights for political diplomacy and conflict resolution. The diplomats also involved in these sessions were extremely interested and saw considerable potential in this area.

Another example, in which I am still involved, concerns the understanding of interactive science exhibits and how they engage people. An increased psychological understanding of the social and motivational aspects of these exhibits has shown itself to be of direct use to those commisssioning exhibits, to those evaluating them and, in some cases, to the designers themselves.

These are illustrations, but they show how broad ranging applied psychology can be. Sometimes, as in my first example, initiatives may link with others and eventually grow into a new area of applied psychology. But many other examples remain as stand-alone instances of applied psychology, as far as professional structure is concerned. But they also become integrated into the knowledge base and experience of other professional groups and that, in my view, is also a positive thing.

I would like to see generic applied psychologists consulted routinely, whenever a project has relevance for people and doesn't fall into an established area of applied psychology. I'm not claiming that we know everything there is to know – but I am claiming that we have insights which are useful. In my experience psychologists can work positively with just about any other professional group, and to our mutual benefit. If psychological knowledge can help those engaged in decision-making, planning or design to avoid some of the glaringly obvious stupidities which are so common in modern day-to-day living – and I firmly believe it can – we will have made a positive contribution to society.

# References

Adcock, C. and Newbigging, K. (1990) 'Women in the shadows: feminism and clinical psychology', in E. Burman (ed.) *Feminists and Psychological Practice*. London: Sage.

Agnew, S., Carson, J. and Dankert, A. (1995) 'The research productivity of clinical psychologists and psychiatrists: a comparative study', *Clinical Psychology Forum*, 86: 2–5.

Ahmed, B. (1996) 'Reflexivity, cultural membership and power in the research situation: tensions and contradictions when considering the researcher's role', *Psychology of Women Section Newsletter*, 17: 35–40.

Ahmed, B. (1997a) 'Feminist psychology and professionalism: some comments on theory and method', in *Proceedings of the BPS Annual Conference*. Edinburgh: British Psychological Society.

Ahmed, B. (1997b) 'The social construction of identities and intergroup experiences: the case of second generation Bangladeshis in Britain.' Unpublished thesis, University of Sheffield.

Ahmed, B., Nicolson, P. and Spencer, C. (2000) 'The social construction of racism: the case of second generation Bangladeshis', *Journal of Community and Applied Social Psychology*, 10: 33–48.

Ahn, H. and Wampold, B.E. (2001) 'Where oh where are the specific ingredients? A meta-analysis of component studies in counselling and psychotherapy', *Journal of Counselling Psychology*, 48 (3): 251–7.

Alban-Metcalfe, R.J. and Alimo-Metcalfe, B. (2000) 'An analysis of the convergent and discriminant validity of the Tranformational Leadership Questionnaire', *International Journal of Selection and Assessment*, 8 (3): 158–75.

Aldrich, R. (1982) *An Introduction to the History of Education*. London: Hodder & Stoughton.

Alimo-Metcalfe, B. and Alban-Metcalfe, R.J. (2000) 'A new approach to assessing transformational leadership', *Selection and Development Review*, 16 (5): 15–17.

Allen, M. (1988) *The Goals of Universities*. Milton Keynes: SRHE and Open University Press.

Allen, S. (1999) 'Careers after an MSc in health psychology', *Health Psychology Update*, 35: 33.

Altbach, P.G. (1991) 'The academic profession', in P.G. Altbach (ed.) *International Higher Education: An Encyclopaedia*. New York, NY: Garland Publishing.

Altbach, P.G. (ed.) (1996) *The Academic Profession: An International Study*. Princeton, NJ: Carnegie Foundation for the Advancement of Teaching.

Altbach, P.G. and Ogawa, Y. (eds) (2002) 'Special issue on Japan: reform and change in the 21st century', *Higher Education*, 43: 1–155.

American Psychological Association (APA) (1995) *Reforming America's Schools: Psychology's Role*. Washington, DC: APA Books.

Anderson, I. (2002) 'Gender, psychology and law: studies in feminism, epistemology and science – review essay', *Feminism and Psychology*, 12 (3): 379–88.

Anderson, I. and Doherty, K. (1997) 'Psychology, sexuality and power: constructing sex and violence', *Feminism and Psychology*, 7: 549–54.

Anderson, N., Herriot, P. and Hodgkinson, G.P. (2001) 'The practitioner–researcher divide in industrial, work and organizational (IWO) psychology: where are we now and where do we go from here? Centenary issue: emerging issues and future trends in work psychology', *Journal of Occupational and Organizational Psychology*, 74 (4): 391–412.

Arthur, M.B., Hall, D.T. and Lawrence, B.S. (1989) *Handbook of Career Theory*. Cambridge: Cambridge University Press.

Ashworth, J.M. (1993) 'Universities in the 21st century: old wine in new bottles or new wine in old bottles? Higher education foundation lecture', *Reflections on Higher Education*, 5: 46–61.

Atkinson, M., Wilkin, A., Stott, A., Doherty, P. and Kinder, K. (2002) *Multi-agency Working: A Detailed Study*. Slough: NFER.

Aubery, C. (2001) 'Questioning comparative approaches: context and the role of international comparison in policy-making', in T. David (ed.) *Promoting Evidence-based Practice in Early Childhood Education: Research and its Implications. Volume 1*. Oxford: Elsevier Science.

BAC (1996) *Code of Ethics and Practice*. Rugby: BAC.

BACP (2001) *Ethical Framework for Good Practice in Counselling and Psychotherapy*. Rugby: BACP.

Badley, G. (1999) 'Improving teaching in British higher education', *Quality Assurance in Education*, 7: 35–40.

Ball, C. (1992) 'Teaching and research', in T.G. Whiston and R.L. Geiger (eds) *Research and Higher Education: The United Kingdom and the United States*. Buckingham: SRHE and Open University Press.

Ball, C. (1994) *Start Right: The Importance of Early Learning*. London: Royal Society of Arts.

Banister, P., Burman, E., Parker, I., Taylor, M. and Tindall, C. (1994) *Qualitative Methods in Psychology: A Research Guide*. Buckingham: Open University Press.

Barlow, C. (1999) 'Employment experiences of a health psychologist', *Health Psychology Update*, 35: 45–6.

Barlow, D.H., Hayes, S.C. and Nelson, R.O. (1984) *The Scientist Practitioner: Research and Accountability in Clinical and Educational Settings*. New York, NY: Pergamon Press.

Barnes, S.V. (1996) 'England's civic universities and the triumph of the Oxbridge ideal', *History of Education Quarterly*, 36: 271–305.

Barnett, C. (2001) *The Verdict of Peace: Britain between her Past and her Future*. London: Macmillan.

Barnett, R. and Middlehurst, R. (1993) 'The lost profession', *Higher Education in Europe*, 18: 110–28.

Baron-Cohen, S. (ed.) (1997) *The Maladapted Mind: Classic Readings in Evolutionary Psychopathology*. Hove: Psychology Press.

Bartram, D. (1997) 'Distance assessment: psychological assessment through the Internet', *Selection and Development Review*, 13: 10–14.

Bartram, D. (1999) 'Testing and the Internet: current realities, issues and future possibilities', *Selection and Development Review*, 15: 3–12.

Bartram, D. (2000) 'Internet recruitment and selection: kissing frogs to find princes', *International Journal of Selection and Assessment*, 8 (4): 261–74.

Baruch, Y. and Hind, P (1999) 'Perpetual motion in organizations: effective management and the impact of the new psychological contracts on "survivor syndrome"', *European Journal of Work and Organizational Psychology*, 8 (2): 295–306.

Bath, J. (2001) 'Supervising health psychology in the National Health Service (NHS)', *Health Psychology Update*, 10 (3): 9–11.

Baty, P. (2002) 'Academic life is hell – official', *The Times Higher Educational Supplement*, 15 March.

Baumeister, R. (1991) *Meanings of Life*. New York, NY: Guilford Press.

Bayne, R. (1995) *The Myers-Briggs Type Indicator: A critical review and practical guide*. Cheltenham: Nelson Thornes.

Bayne, R. (2000) 'Stress', in C. Feltham and I. Horton (eds) *Handbook of Counselling and Psychotherapy*. London: Sage.

Bayne, R., Horton, I., Merry, T., Noyes, L. and McMahon, G. (1999) *The Counsellor's Handbook. A Practical A–Z Guide to Professional and Clinical Practice*. (2nd edn.) Cheltenham: Stanley Thornes.

Bearman, C. (2002) 'How to apply for a PhD', *The Psychologist*, 15 (7): 340–1.

Beaumont, G. (2001) 'Clinical neuropsychology and health psychology', *Health Psychology Update*, 10 (2): 30–3.

Beech, D. (2000) 'The search conference (continued): adding value at a strategic level', *The Occupational Psychologist*, 40: 21–5.

Bergin, A.E. and Garfield, S.L. (1994) *Handbook of Psychotherapy and Behaviour Change* (4th edn). Chichester: Wiley.

Bimrose, J. (1996) *Counselling and Guidance for Higher Education*. Cheltenham and Strasbourg: UCAS and the Council of Europe.

Bimrose, J. (2000) 'Theoretical perspectives on social context', in C. Feltham and I. Horton (eds) *Handbook of Counselling and Psychotherapy*. London: Sage.

Bleier, R. (1984) *Science and Gender*. London: Pergamon Press.

Bligh, D., Thomas, H. and McNay, I. (1999) *Understanding Higher Education: An Introduction for Parents*. Exeter: Intellect Books.

Bond, M. (1986) *Stress and Self-Awareness: A Guide for Nurses*. London: Heinemann.

Bond, T. (2000) *Standards and Ethics for Counselling in Action* (2nd edn). London: Sage.

Booth, D. (2002) 'Responsibilities of psychologists who support learning in psychological science', *Newsletter of the Division for Teachers and Researchers in Psychology of the British Psychological Society*.

Bowlby, J. (1944) 'Forty-four juvenile thieves: their characteristics and home life', *International Journal of Psychoanalysis*, 25: 19–53.

Bowlby, J. (1951) *Maternal Care and Mental Health*. Geneva: World Health Organization.

Boyer, E., Altbach, P.G. and Whitelaw, M.J. (1994) *The Academic Profession: An International Perspective*. Princeton, NJ: Carnegie Foundation for the Advancement of Teaching.

Boyle, D. (2001) *The Tyranny of Numbers: Why Counting Can't Make us Happy*. London: Flamingo.

Boyle, M. (1999) 'Diagnosis', in C. Newnes et al. (eds) *This is Madness: A Critical Look at Psychiatry and the Future of Mental Health Services*. Ross-on-Wye: PCCS Books.

Boyle, M. (2002) *Schizophrenia: A Scientific Delusion?* (2nd edn). London: Routledge.

Boyle, M., Baker, M., Bennett, E. and Charman, A. (1993) 'The selection of ethnic minority and majority applicants for clinical psychology training courses', *Clinical Psychology Forum*, 56: 9–13.

Bracken, P. and Thomas, P. (2000) 'Putting ethics before effectiveness', *Open Mind*, 102: 22.

Brady, J.L., Healy, F.C., Norcross, J.C. and Guy, J.D. (1995) 'Stress in counsellors: an integrative research review', in W. Dryden (ed.) *The Stresses of Counselling in Action*. London: Sage.

Braithwaite, D. and Meloni, S. (2001) 'PhD training in health psychology: some issues and future directions', *Health Psychology Update*, 10 (3): 76–7.

Brammer, L., Alcorn, J., Birk, J., Gazda, G., Hurst, J., Lafromboise, T., Newman, R., Osipow, S., Packard, T., Romero, D. and Scott, N. (1988) 'Organizational and political issues in counselling psychology: recommendations for change', *The Counselling Psychologist*, 16: 407–22.

Brennan, J., Fredericks, M. and Shah, T. (1997) *Improving the Quality of Education: The Impact of Quality Assessment on Institutions*. London: Quality Support Centre of the Open University.

Briner, R.B. (1998) 'What is an evidence-based approach to practice and why do we need one in occupational psychology?' in *British Psychological Society Occupational Psychology Conference Book of Proceedings*. Leicester: British Psychological Society.

British Association for Counselling (1996) *Code of Ethics and Practice*. Rugby: BAC.

British Psychological Society (1989) *Style Guide: Information and Advice to Authors*. Antrim: British Psychological Society/Greystone Press.

British Psychological Society (1995) *Professional Psychology Handbook*. Leicester: BPS Books.

British Psychological Society (1998) *National Occupational Standards in Applied Psychology* (*Generic*). Leicester: BPS.

British Psychological Society (2000) *What is Health Psychology?* Leaflet from the Division of Health Psychology.

British Psychological Society (2001) *The Directory of Chartered Psychologists*. Leicester: BPS.

British Psychological Society (2002a) *The Directory of Chartered Psychologists and the Directory of Expert Witnesses*. Leicester: BPS.

British Psychological Society (2002b) *The Register of Psychologists as Psychotherapists: Principles and Procedures*. Leicester: BPS.

British Psychological Society/Committee on Training in Clinical Psychology (2001) *Criteria for the Accreditation of Post-graduate Training Programmes in Clinical Psychology* (draft). Leicester: BPS.

British Psychological Society/Division of Clinical Psychology (2000a) *Policy and Guidelines on Supervision in the Practice of Clinical Psychology*. Draft to DCP Committee for consultation.

British Psychological Society/Division of Clinical Psychology (2000b) *Recent Advances in Understanding Mental Illness and Psychotic Experiences*. Leicester: BPS.

British Psychological Society/Division of Clinical Psychology (2001) *The Core Purpose and Philosophy of the Profession*. Leicester: BPS.

British Psychological Society/Division of Educational and Child Psychology (undated, circa 1999) *The Professional Practice of Educational Psychologists*. Leicester: BPS.

Bromley, D. (1986) *The Case Study Method in Psychology and Related Disciplines*. Chichester: Wiley.

Brotherton, C. (1999) *Social Psychology and Management: Issues for a Changing Society*. Buckingham: Open University Press.

Brown, J. (1998) 'Helping the police with their inquiries', *The Psychologist*, 11 (11): 539–42.

Brown, P. (ed.) (1973) *Radical Psychology*. London: Tavistock.

Brownmiller, S. (1975) *Against Our Will: Men, Women and Rape*. New York, NY: Simon & Schuster.

Burden, R.L. (1981) 'Systems theory and its relevance to schools', in W. Gillham (ed.) *Problem Behaviour in the Secondary School*. London: Croom-Helm.

Burgess, R.G., Band, S. and Pole, C. (1998) 'Developments in postgraduate education and training in the UK', *European Journal of Education*, 33: 145–59.

Burgess, T., Locke, M., Pratt, J. and Richards, N. (1995) *Degrees East: The Making of the University of East London 1992*. London: Athlone Press.

Burley, A. (2001) 'Letter', *Clinical Psychology*, 2: 5–6.

Burman, E. (1990) 'Differing with deconstruction: a feminist critique', in I. Parker and J. Shotter (eds) *Deconstructing Social Psychology*. London: Routledge.

Burman, E. (1994) 'Experience, identities and alliances: Jewish feminism and feminist psychology', in K.-K. Bhavnani and A. Phoenix (eds) *Shifting Identities Shifting Racisms*. London: Sage.

Burt, C. (1925) *The Young Delinquent*. London: University of London Press.

Burt, C. (1969) 'Psychologists in the Education Service'. *Bulletin of the British Psychological Society*, 22: 1–11.

Cameron, R.J., Gersch, I.S., M'gadzah, S. and Moyse, S. (1995) 'Educational psychologists and post-trauma stress management', *DECP Newsletter*, 12 (3): 5–20.

Campbell, D. and Stanley, J. (1963) 'Experimental and quasi-experimental designs for research in teaching', in N. Gage (ed.) *Handbook of Research on Teaching*. Chicago, IL: Rand-McNally.

Cann, A., Calhoun, L.G. and Selby, J.W. (1979) 'Attributing responsibility to the victim of rape: influence of information regarding past sexual experience', *Human Relations*, 32: 57–67.

Careers Research and Advisory Centre (1998) *Developing a Research Culture in Career Education and Guidance: Report on Invitational Policy Consultation*. Cambridge: CRAC.

Carpenter, B. (2000) 'Sustaining the family: meeting the needs of families of children with disabilities', *British Journal of Special Education*, 27 (3): 135–44.

Carr, A. (1990) 'Doctoral degrees in clinical psychology', *Clinical Psychology Forum*, 25: 35–7.

Carroll, M. (1996) *Counselling Supervision – Theory, Skills and Practice*. London: Cassell.

Carson, D. (1995) 'Law's premises, methods and values', in R. Bull and D. Carson (eds) *Handbook of Psychology in Legal Contexts*. London: Wiley.

Carswell, J. (1985) *Government and the Universities in Britain: Progress and Performance 1960–1980*. Cambridge: Cambridge University Press.

Castells, M. (1997a) *The Information Age: Economy, Society and Culture. Volume 1. The Rise of the Network Society*. Oxford: Blackwell.

Castells, M. (1997b) *The Information Age: Economy, Society and Culture. Volume 2. The Power of Identity*. Oxford: Blackwell.

Castells, M. (1998) *The Information Age: Economy, Society and Culture. Volume 3. End of the Millennium*. Oxford: Blackwell.

Chambless, D.L. and Ollendick, T.H. (2001) 'Empirically supported psychological interventions: controversies and evidence', *Annual Review of Psychology*, 52: 685–716.

Chaplin, M. (1978) 'Philosophies of higher education, historical and contemporary', in A.S. Knowles (ed.) *The International Encyclopaedia of Higher Education*. London: Jossey-Bass.

Cherrington, D. (1998) *Organizational Behaviour: The management of individual and organizational performance*. Boston: Allyn & Bacon.

Cheshire, K. (2000) 'Clinical training in the 1990s: trainees' perspectives', *Clinical Psychology Forum*, 145: 37–41.

Cheshire, K. (2002) 'Reality shock: the transition from trainee to qualified practitioner', *Clinical Psychology*, 11: 31–5.

Chmiel, N. (1998) *Jobs, Technology and People*. London: Routledge.

Clarke, B.R. (1997) 'Small worlds, different worlds: the uniqueness and troubles of American academic professions', *Daedalus: Journal of the American Academy of Arts and Sciences*, 126: 21–42.

Clarke, B.R. (2001) 'The entrepreneurial university: new foundations for collegiality, autonomy and achievement', *Higher Education Management*, 13: 9–24.

Clearing House for Postgraduate Courses in Clinical Psychology (2001) *Handbook for 2002 Entry*. Leeds: Clearing House for Postgraduate Courses in Clinical Psychology.

Clegg, J. (1998) *Critical Issues in Clinical Practice*. London: Sage.

Clifford, B.R. (1995) 'Psychology's premises, methods and values', in R. Bull and D. Carson (eds) *Handbook of Psychology in Legal Contexts*. London: Wiley.

Clifford, B.R. (1997a) 'Hugo Munsterberg: American psychology's enigma', in A. Chapman et al. (eds) *Biographical Dictionary of Psychology*. London: Routledge.

Clifford, B.R. (1997b) 'Expert evidence: probative or problematic', *International Digest of Law and Psychology*, 5 (4): 140–3.

Clifford, B.R. (2002) 'Methodology: law's adaption to and adoption of psychology's methods and findings', in D. Carson and R. Bull (eds) *Handbook of Psychology in Legal Contexts* (2nd end). London: Wiley.

Coate, K., Barnett, R. and Williams, G. (2001) 'Relationships between teaching and research in higher education in England', *Higher Education Quarterly*, 55: 158–74.

Cobban, A.B. (1975) *The Mediaeval Universities: Their Development and Organization*. London: Methuen.

Coleridge, S.T. (1830) *On the Constitution of Church and State According to the Idea of Each* (reprinted 1972). London: J.M. Dent.

Collin, A. and Watts, A.G. (1996) 'The death and transfiguration of career – and career guidance?' *British Journal of Guidance and Counselling*, 24 (3): 385–98.

Collin, A. and Young, R.A. (1986) 'New directions for theories of career', *Human Relations*, 39: 837–53.

Collins, K. and Nicolson, P. (2002) 'The meaning of "satisfaction" for people with dermatological problems: re-assessing approaches to qualitative health psychology research', *Journal of Health Psychology*, 7: 615–29.

Cook, T.D. and Shadish, W.R. Jr (1986) 'Program evaluation: the worldly science', *Annual Review of Psychology*, 37: 193–232.

Cooke, A., Harper, D. and Kinderman, P. (2001) 'Reform of the Mental Health Act: implications for clinical psychologists', *Clinical Psychology*, 1: 48–52.

Coolican, H. (1998) 'Research methods', in M.W. Eysenck (ed.) *Psychology: An Integrated Approach*. New York, NY: Longman.

Coolican, H., Cassidy, A., Cherchar, A., Harrower, J., Penny, G., Sharp, R., Walley, M. and Westbury, A. (1996) *Applied Psychology*. London: Hodder & Stoughton.

Cooper, D. (1998) *Improving Safety Culture: A Practical Guide*. Chichester: Wiley.

Corrie, S. and Callanan, M.M. (2000) 'A review of the scientist-practitioner model: reflections on its potential contribution to counselling psychology within the context of current health care trends', *British Journal of Medical Psychology*, 73: 413–27.

Corrie, S. and Callanan, M.M. (2001) 'Therapists' beliefs about research and the scientist-practitioner model in an evidence-based health care climate: a qualitative study', *British Journal of Medical Psychology*, 74: 135–49.

Costello, M. and McHugh, D. (2002) 'Joint Conference in Educational Psychology in Dundalk, Ireland, October 9th and 10th 2001', *The Irish Psychologist*, February: 75–6.

Cushway, D. (1992) 'Stress in clinical psychology trainees', *British Journal of Clinical Psychology*, 31: 169–79.

Dale, F. (1997) 'Stress and the personality of the psychotherapist', in Varma, V. (ed.) *Stress in Psychotherapists*. London: Routledge.

Damrosch, S.P. (1985) 'How perceived carelessness and time of attack affect nursing students' attributions about rape victims', *Psychological Reports*, 56: 531–6.

Danzinger, K. (1985) 'The methodological imperative in psychology', *Philosophical Science*, 15: 1–13.

David, T. (ed.) (2001) *Promoting Evidence-based Practice in Early Childhood Education: Research and its Implications. Volume 1.* Oxford: Elsevier Science.

Davies, S. (1992) 'Binary systems of higher education', in B.R. Clarke and G.R. Neave (eds) *The Encyclopaedia of Higher Education. Volume II. Analytical Perspectives.* Oxford: Pergamon Press.

Day, A. (2001) 'An investigation into the impact of the introduction of multi-skilled, semi-autonomous work groups on groups and individuals in two "brownfield" manufacturing sites: the impact of multi-skilled, semi-autonomous work groups in a manufacturing environment: a longitudinal field study.' Unpublished thesis for the Professional Doctorate in Occupational Psychology, University of East London.

Denzin, N.K. and Lincoln, Y.S. (1994) 'Introduction: entering the field of qualitative research', in N.K. Denzin and Y.S. Lincoln (eds) *Handbook of Qualitative Research.* Thousand Oaks, CA: Sage.

Department for Employment (1995) *Competitiveness: Forging Ahead.* Cmnd 2867. London: HMSO.

Department for Trade and Industry (1994) *Competitiveness: Helping Business to Win.* Cmnd 2563. London: HMSO.

Department of Health (1999a) *National Service Framework for Mental Health.* London: Department of Health (www.doh.gov.uk/nsf/mentalhealth.htm).

Department of Health (1999b) *Saving Lives: Our Healthier Nation.* London: Department of Health.

Department of Health (1999c) *Smoking Kills: A White Paper on Tobacco.* London: HMSO.

Department of Health (2000) *The NHS Plan.* London: Department of Health.

Department of Health (2001a) *Choosing Talking Therapies.* London: DH Publications.

Department of Health (2001b) *Treatment Choice in Psychological Therapies and Counselling.* London: DH Publications.

DfE (1968) *The Summerfield Report.* London: DfE Publications.

DfEE (1997a) *Excellence for all Children.* Nottingham: DfEE Publications.

DfEE (1997b) *Excellence in Schools.* Cm 3681. London: HMSO.

DfEE (1998) *Programme of Action.* Nottingham: DfEE Publications.

DfEE (2000a) *Educational Psychology Services (England): Current Role, Good Practice and Future Directions. Report of the Working Group.* Nottingham: DfEE Publications.

DfEE (2000b) *Connexions: The Best Start in Life for Every Young Person.* Nottingham: DfEE Publications.

DfEE (2001) *Connexions: A Consultation on the Draft Quality Standards for the Connexions Service.* London: Department for Education and Employment (http://www.connexions.gov.uk).

DfES (2001) *Special Educational Needs Code of Practice*. Nottingham: DfES Publications.

Division of Counselling Psychology (2001) 'Chartered counselling psychologists' training and areas of competence. Statement from the Division of Counselling Psychology', *Counselling Psychology Review*, 16(4): 41–3.

Dixon, K. (1973) *Sociological Theory: Pretence and Possibility*. London: Routledge & Kegan Paul.

Dryden, W. (1994) 'Possible future trends in counselling and counsellor training: a personal view', *Counselling*, August: 194–7.

Dryden, W., Horton, I. and Mearns, D. (1995) *Issues in Professional Counselling Training*. London: Cassell.

Dryden, W. and Thorne, B. (1991) *Training and Supervision for Counselling in Action*. London: Sage.

Earll, L. and Holmes, T. (2001) 'Development of guidelines on the clinical management and support of people affected by motor neurone disease', *Health Psychology Update*, 10 (2): 25–9.

Ebbesen, E.B. and Konecni, V.J. (1996) 'Eyewitness memory research: probative v. prejudicial value', *Expert Evidence: International Digest of Law and Psychology*, 5 (1/2): 2–28.

Edelstein, B.A. and Brasted, W.S. (1991) 'Clinical training', in M. Hersen et al. (eds) *The Clinical Psychology Handbook*. New York, NY: Pergamon Press.

Edwards, D. and Potter, J. (1992) *Discursive Psychology*. London: Sage.

Eley, A. (1994) 'Management training for the university head of department', *International Journal of Educational Management*, 8: 20–2.

Ellenberger, H. (1994) *The Discovery of the Unconscious. The History and Evolution of Dynamic Psychiatry*. London: Fontana.

Ellinson, L. (2000) 'Rape and the adversarial culture of the courtroom', in M. Childs and L. Ellison (eds) *Feminist Perspectives on Evidence*. London: Cavendish.

Elliott, J. and Waterhouse, R. (2002) 'Why Oxford is going begging', *The Sunday Times*, 31 March.

Ellis, W. (1994) *The Oxbridge Conspiracy: How the Ancient Universities have Kept their Stranglehold on the Establishment*. London: Michael Joseph.

Elton, L. (1989) *Teaching in Higher Education: Appraisal and Training*. London: Kogan Page.

Elton, L. (1992) 'Research, teaching and scholarship in an expanding higher education system', *Higher Education Quarterly*, 46: 252–68.

Elton, L. (2000) 'The UK Research Assessment Exercise: unintended consequences', *Higher Education Quarterly*, 54: 274–83.

Enders, J. and Teichler, U. (1997) 'A victim of their own success? Employment and working conditions of academic staff in comparative perspective', *Higher Education*, 34: 347–72.

Engel, A.J. (1983) *From Clergyman to Don: The Rise of the Academic Profession in Nineteenth-century Oxford*. Oxford: Clarendon Press.

Engel, G. (1977) 'The need for a new medical model: a challenge for biomedicine', *Science*, 196: 129–36.

Engeström, Y. (1994) *Training for Change: New Approach to Instruction and Learning in Working Life*. Geneva: International Labour Office.

Engeström, Y., Engeström, R. and Kärkkäinen, M. (1995) 'Polycontextuality and boundary crossing in expert cognition: learning and problem solving in complex work activities', *Learning and Instruction*, 5: 319–36.

Eraut, M. (1989) 'Initial teacher training and the NVQ model', in J.W. Burke (ed.) *Competency Based Education and Training*. London: Falmer Press.

Eraut, M. (1994) 'Implication for standards development', *Competence and Assessment*, 21, 14–17.

Eraut, M. (1994) *Developing Professional Knowledge and Competence*. London: Falmer.

Eustace, R. (1992) 'United Kingdom', in B.R. Clarke and G.R. Neave (eds) *The Encyclopaedia of Higher Education. Volume I. National Systems of Higher Education*. Oxford: Pergamon Press.

Evidence for Policy and Practice Information and Co-ordinating Centre (2001) *EPPI Information leaflet*. London: EPPI (www.eppi.ioe.ac.uk. e-mail: eppi.edinfo@ioe.ac.uk).

Eysenck, H.J. (1964) *Crime and Personality*. London: Paladin.

Eysenck, M.W. (2000) 'A cognitive approach to trait anxiety', *European Journal of Personality*, 14: 463–76.

Eysenck, M.W. and Keane, M.T. (2000) *Cognitive Psychology: A Student's Handbook* (4th edn). Hove: Psychology Press.

Falk, G. (1990) *The Life of the Academic Professional in America: An Inventory of Tasks, Tensions and Achievements. Mellen Studies in Education. Volume 15*. Lewiston, NY: Erwin Mellen Press.

Faulkner, A. and Thomas, P. (2002) 'User-led research and evidence-based medicine', *British Journal of Psychiatry*, 180: 1–3.

Fearnley, S. (1995) 'Class size: the erosive effect of recruitment numbers on performance', *Quality in Higher Education*, 1: 59–65.

Feltham, C. (1995) *What is Counselling?* London: Sage.

Feltham, C. (1997) *Time-limited Counselling*. London: Sage.

Feltham, C. (1999) 'Against and beyond core theoretical models', in C. Feltham (ed.) *Controversies in Psychotherapy and Counselling*. London: Sage.

Feltham, C. (2000a) 'Types of goal', in C. Feltham and I. Horton (eds) *Handbook of Counselling and Psychotherapy*. London: Sage.

Feltham, C. (2000b) 'Settings and opportunities for employment', in C. Feltham and I. Horton (eds) *Handbook of Counselling and Psychotherapy*. London: Sage.

Feltham, C. (2001) 'Counselling studies: a personal view', *British Journal of Guidance and Counselling*, 29 (1): 111–19.

Feltham, C. (2002) 'Starting in private practice', in J. Clark (ed.) *Freelance Counselling and Psychotherapy*. Hove: Brunner-Routledge.

Feuerstein, R., Rand, Y., Hoffman, M. and Miller, R. (1980) *Instrumental Enrichment: An Intervention Programme for Cognitive Modifiability*. Baltimore, MD: University Park Press.

Field, J. and Leicester, M. (eds) (2000) *Lifelong Learning: Education across the Lifespan*. London: Routledge/Falmer.

Finn, S.E. (1996) *Manual for Using the MMPI-2 as a Therapeutic Intervention*. Minneapolis, MN: University of Minnesota Press.

Fish, D. (1991) *Promoting Reflection: Improving the Supervision of Practice in Health Visiting and Initial Teacher Training*. London: West London Institute of Higher Education.

Fleming, I. and Taylor, J.D. (1998) *The Coaching Pocketbook*. Carmathen, Wales: Management Pocketbooks.

Fox, D. and Prilleltensky, I. (eds) (1997) *Critical Psychology: An Introduction*. London: Sage.

Frederickson, N., Osborne, L.A. and Reed, P. (2001) 'Teaching experience and educational psychologists' credibility with teachers: an empirical investigation', *Educational Psychology in Practice*, 17 (2): 93–108.

Freeman, L. and Miller, A. (2001) 'Norm-referenced, criterion-referenced, and dynamic assessment: what exactly is the point?' *Educational Psychology in Practice*, 17: 3–16.

Friedman, A., Durkin, C., Phillips, M. and Voltsinger, E. (2000) *Strategic Directions for UK Professional Associations*. Bristol: University of Bristol, Professional Associations Research Network.

Funder, D.C. (2001) 'Personality', *Annual Review of Psychology*, 52: 197–221.

Furnham, A. (1992) 'Prospective psychology students' knowledge of psychology', *Psychological Reports*, 70: 375–82.

Furnham, A. (1997) *The Psychology of Behaviour at Work: The Individual in the Organization*. Hove: Psychology Press.

Gaskins, S. (1997) 'Independent candidates undertaking the society diploma', *Counselling Psychology Review*, 12 (2): 66–9.

Gersch, I.S. (1986) 'Behaviour modification and systems analysis in a secondary school: combining approaches', *Educational and Child Psychology*, 3 (2): 61–7.

Gersch, I.S. (1990) 'The pupil's view', in M. Scherer et al. (eds) *Meeting Disruptive Behaviour: Assessment Intervention and Partnership*. Basingstoke: Macmillan Education.

Gersch, I.S. (1992) 'Pupil involvement in assessment', T. Clive (ed.) in *The Assessment of Special Educational Needs: International Perspectives*. London: Routledge.

Gersch, I.S. (1995) *The Pupil's View: Council for Disabled Children. School's Educational Needs Policy Pack. Discussion Paper* 1. London: National Children's Bureau.

Gersch, I.S. (1996) 'Applying psychology to school effectiveness', in I.S. Gersch and A. Holgate (eds) *Psychology in Practice, with Young People, Trainees and Schools*. London: London Borough of Waltham Forest.

Gersch, I.S. (2000) 'Listening to children: an attempt to increase the involvement of children in their education by an educational psychology service.' A commissioned reading for the Open University on the professional development of SENCOs.

Gersch, I.S. (2001a) 'Keynote address to the annual conference of the Association of Educational Psychologists. The future of educational psychology: our part in determining the shape of the profession.' Newport, Wales.

Gersch, I.S. (2001b) 'Educational psychology: a crystal gaze into the future. Keynote address to the June conference in educational psychology' (summarized in Costello, M. and McHugh, D. (2002), *The Irish Psychologist*, February: 75–6.

Gersch, I.S. and Holgate, A. (eds) (1991) *The Student Report*. London: London Borough of Waltham Forest.

Gersch, I.S., Kelly, K., Cohen, S., Daunt, S. and Frederickson, N. (2001) 'The Chingford Hall School Screening Project – can we have more EP time please?' *Educational Psychology in Practice*, 17 (2): 135–56.

Gersch, I.S., with Moyse, S., Nolan, A. and Pratt, G. (1996) 'Listening to children in educational contexts', in R. Davie et al. (eds) *The Voice of the Child – A Handbook for Professionals*. London: Falmer.

Gersch, I.S. and Noble, J. (1991) 'A systems project involving students and staff in a secondary school', *Educational Psychology in Practice*, 7 (3): 140–7.

Giddens, A. (1976) *New Rules of Sociological Method: A Positive Critique of Interpretative Sociology*. London: Hutchins.

Gilbert, P. and Bailey, K.G. (eds) (2000) *Genes on the Couch: Explorations in Evolutionary Psychotherapy*. London: Brunner-Routledge.

Gill, R. (1995) 'Relativism, reflexivity and politics: interrogating discourse analysis from a feminist perspective', in S. Wilkinson and C. Kitzinger (eds) *Feminism and Discourse: Psychological Perspectives*. London: Sage.

Goldberg, D. and Huxley, P. (1992) *Common Mental Disorders*. London: Routledge.

Green, F. (2002) 'A measure of myopia', *The Times Higher Educational Supplement*, 12 April.

Greenberg, K. (2001) 'Attending to hidden needs: the cognitive enrichment advantage perspective', *Educational and Child Psychology*, 17: 51–69.

Greenhalgh, T. (1999) 'Narrative based medicine in an evidence based world', *British Medical Journal*, 18: 323–5.

Griffin, C. (1986) 'Qualitative methods and female experience: young women from school to the job market', in S. Wilkinson (ed.) *Feminist Social Psychology*. Milton Keynes: Open University Press.

Griffin, C. (1995) 'Feminism, social psychology and qualitative research', *The Psychologist*, 8: 111–14.

Gutkin, T.B. and Curtis, M.J. (1990) 'School-based consultation: theory, techniques and research', in T.B. Gutkin and C. Reynolds (eds) *The Handbook of School Psychology* (2nd edn). New York, NY: Wiley.

Gutkin, T.B. and Reynolds, C. (eds) (1990) *The Handbook of School Psychology* (2nd edn). New York, NY: Wiley.

Hajek, P. (1989) 'Helping smokers to overcome withdrawal: background and practice of withdrawal-orientated therapy', in R. Richmond (ed.) *Intervention for Smokers*. London: Williams & Wilkins.

Halgin, R.P. (1999) 'Clinical training: challenges for a new millennium', *Journal of Clinical Psychology*, 55: 405–9.

Hallas, C. (2001) 'Understanding heart failure and transplantation: the role of a health psychologist', *Health Psychology Update*, 10 (3): 34–9.

Halsey, A.H. (1992) *The Decline of Donnish Dominion: The British Academic Professions in the 20th Century*. Oxford: Clarendon Press.

Halsey, A.H. and Trow, M.A. (1971) *The British Academics*. London: Faber & Faber.

Hammersley, D. (2003) 'Training and professional development in counselling psychology', in R. Woolfe et al. (eds) *Handbook of Counselling Psychology* (2nd edn). London: Sage.

Harari, H., Harari, O. and White, R. (1985) 'The reaction to rape by American male bystanders', *The Journal of Social Psychology*, 125: 653–8.

Harding, S. (ed.) (1987) *Feminism and Methodology: Social Science Issues*. Milton Keynes: Open University Press.

Hardman, C. (2001) 'Using personal construct psychology to reduce the risk of exclusion', *Educational Psychology in Practice*, 17: 41–51.

Hargreaves, D.H. (1996) 'Teaching as a research-based profession: possibilities and prospects.' Teacher Training Agency annual lecture, London.

Harold, F. (2000) *Be your Own Life Coach*. London: Hodder & Stoughton.

Harper, D.J. (in press) 'Introducing social constructionist psychology into clinical psychology training', in G. Larner and D. Paré (eds) *Collaborative Practice in Psychology and Therapy*. New York: Haworth Press.

Harré, R. and Secord, P.F. (1972) *The Explanation of Social Behaviour*. Oxford: Blackwell.

Hattie, J. and Marsh, H.W. (1996) 'The relationship between research and teaching: a meta-analysis', *Review of Educational Research*, 66: 507–42.

Hatton, C., Gray, I. and Whittaker, A. (2000) 'Improving the selection of clinical psychologists: the clearing house research project', *Clinical Psychology Forum*, 136: 35–8.

Hawkes, N. (2002) 'Unhappy doctors cannot stomach modern medicine', *The Times*, 5 April.

Hawthorn, R. and Butcher, V. (1992) *Guidance Workers in the UK: Their Work and Training.* Cambridge: CRAC.

Haward, L.R.C. (1981) *Forensic Psychology.* London: Batsford.

Henkel, M. (2000) *Academic Identities and Policy Change in Higher Education.* London: Jessica Kingsley.

Hepburn, A. (2000) 'On the alleged incompatibility between relativism and feminist psychology', *Feminism and Psychology*, 10: 91–106.

Hodgins, S. (1997) 'An overview of research on the prediction of dangerousness', *Nordic Journal of Psychiatry*, 51 (Suppl. 39): 33–8.

Hodkinson, P. and Issit, M. (eds) (1995) *The Challenge of Competence: Professionalism through Policies for Vocational Training in England and Wales.* London: Cassell.

Hodkinson, P., Sparkes, A.C. and Hodkinson, H. (1996) *Triumphs and Tears: Young People, Markets and the Transition from School to Work.* London: David Fulton.

Hollin, C. (2001) *Handbook of Offender Assessment and Treatment.* Chichester: Wiley.

Hollway, W. (1989) *Subjectivity and Method in Psychology: Gender Meaning and Science.* London: Sage.

Home Office (1999) *What Works. Reducing Re-offending: Evidence-based Practice.* London: Home Office (www.homeoffice.gov.uk/cpd/probu/wworks.pdf).

Horton, I. (2002) 'Regulation, registration and accreditation: some issues' in J. Clarke (ed) *Freelance Counselling and Psychotherapy.* Hove: Brunner – Routledge.

Hoshmand, L.T. and Polkinghorne, D.E. (1992) 'Redefining the science–practice relationship and professional training', *American Psychologist*, 47: 55–66.

Houghton, K. (1996) 'Critical incidents involving school children – research update: the response from school psychological services', *Educational and Child Psychology*, 13: 59–75.

House, R. and Totton, N. (eds.) (1997) *Implausible Professions: Arguments for Pluralism and Autonomy in Psychotherapy and Counselling.* Ross-on-Wye: PCCS Books.

Howarth, C.I. (1993) 'Assuring the quality of teaching in universities', *Reflections on Higher Education*, 5: 69–89.

Howitt, D. and Owusu-Bempah, J. (1994) *The Racism of Psychology.* New York, NY: Harvester-Wheatsheaf.

Hubble, M.A., Duncan, B.L. and Miller, S.D. (eds) (1999) *The Heart and Soul of Change. What Works in Therapy?* Washington, DC: American Psychological Association.

Hyland, T. (1994) *Competence, Education and NVQs: Dissenting Perspectives.* London: Cassell.

Institute of Career Guidance (ICG) (2002) *Constructing the Future. Social Inclusion: Policy and Practice.* Stourbridge: ICG.

Jacobs, M. (1995) 'Contribution to I. Horton, R. Bayne and J. Bimrose (eds) New direction in counselling: a roundtable', special issue of *Counselling*, 6 (1): 34–40. Reprinted in S. Palmer, S. Dainow and P. Milner (eds) *Counselling. The BAC Counselling Reader.* London: Sage.

Jaspers, K. (1960) *The Idea of the University.* London: Peter Owen.

Jelly, M., Fuller, A. and Byers, R. (2000) *Involving Pupils in Practice: Promoting Partnerships with Pupils with Special Educational Needs.* London: David Fulton.

Jenkins, S. (1995) *Accountable to None: The Tory Nationalisation of Britain.* London: Hamish Hamilton.

John, I. (1998) 'The scientist-practitioner model: a critical examination', *Australian Psychologist*, 33: 24–30.

Johnstone, L. (2001) *Users and Abusers of Psychiatry* (2nd end). London: Routledge.

Jones, A. (1998) 'What's the bloody point? More thoughts on fraudulent identity', *Clinical Psychology Forum*, 112: 3–9.

Jones, D.R. (1988) *The Origins of Civic Universities: Manchester, Leeds and Liverpool*. London: Routledge.

Jones, F. and Bright, J. (2001) *Stress: Myth, Theory and Research*. London: Prentice Hall.

Jordanova, L. (1989) *Sexual Visions: Images of Gender in Science and Medicine between the Eighteenth and Twentieth Centuries*. Hemel Hempstead: Harvester.

Kane, E. (2002) The Policy Perspective: What Evidence is Influential? In S. Priebe and M. Slade (eds) *Evidence in Mental Health Care*. London: Brunner-Routledge. (pp. 215–225).

Kaplan, A. (1964) *The Conduct of Enquiry*. San Francisco, CA: Chandler.

Kelly, D. and Gray, C. (2000) *Educational Psychology Services (England). The Research Report*. Nottingham: Department for Education and Employment.

Kennedy, P. and Llewelyn, S. (2001) 'Does the future belong to the scientist-practitioner?' *The Psychologist*, 14: 74–8.

Kerlinger, F. (1970) *Foundations of Behavioural Research*. New York, NY: Holt, Rinehart & Winston.

Kerr, C. (1990) 'The American mixture of higher education in perspective: four dimensions', *Higher Education*, 19: 1–19.

Killeen, J. and White, M. (1992) *The Economic Value of Careers Guidance*. London: Policy Studies Institute.

Kitzinger, C. (1989) 'Interview with Derek Mowbray', *The Psychologist*, 12: 440–1.

Kitzinger, C. (1995) 'Social constructionism: implications for lesbian and gay psychology', in A.R. D'Agnelli and C.J. Patterson (eds) *Lesbian, Gay and Bisexual Identities over the Lifespan*. New York, NY: Oxford University Press.

Kitzinger, C. and Wilkinson, S. (1995) 'The challenge of experience for feminist psychology: false consciousness, invalidation and denial', in *Proceedings of the Women and Psychology Conference*, University of Leeds.

Kolb, D.A. (1984) *Experiential Learning: Experience as the Source of Learning and Development*. London: Prentice Hall.

Kolb, D.A., Rubin, I.M. and McIntyre, J.M. (1974) *Organizational Psychology: An Experiential Approach*. Englewood Cliffs, NJ: Prentice Hall.

Kutchins, H. and Kirk, S.A. (1997) *Making us Crazy: DSM: The Psychiatric Bible and the Creation of Mental Disorders*. New York, NY: Free Press.

Lago, C. and Thompson, J. (1996) *Race, Culture and Counselling*. Buckingham: Open University Press.

Larner, G. (2001) 'The critical-practitioner model in therapy', *Australian Psychologist*, 36: 36–43.

Lave, J. (1991) 'Situated learning in communities of practice', in L. Resnick et al. (eds) *Perspectives on Socially Shared Cognition*. Washington, DC: American Psychological Association.

Legg, C. (1998) *Psychology and the Reflective Counsellor*. Leicester: BPS Books.

Leitner, E. (1998) 'The pedagogical qualifications of the academic teaching staff and the quality of teaching and learning', *Higher Education in Europe*, 23: 339–49.

Leong, F.T.L. (1995) *Career Development and Vocational Behavior of Racial and Ethnic Minorities*. Mahwan, NJ: Erlbaum.

Levine, A. (1997) 'How the academic profession is changing', *Daedalus: Journal of the American Academy of Arts and Sciences*, 126: 1–20.

Light, G. and Cox, R. (2001) *Learning and Teaching in Higher Education: The Reflective Professional*. London: Paul Chapman.

Lincoln, Y. and Guba, E. (1985) *Naturalistic Inquiry*. Beverly Hills, CA: Sage.

Lindow, V. (2001) 'Survivor research', in C. Newnes et al. (eds) *This is Madness Too: Critical Perspectives on Mental Health Services*. Ross-on-Wye: PCCS Books.

Llewelyn, S.P. and Kennedy, P. (2001) 'A Delphi study of the future of British clinical psychology training', *The Psychologist*, 14: 74–8.

Locker, J. (2001) 'Opportunities in smoking cessation for psychology graduates', *Health Psychology Update*, 10 (3): 29–31.

Long, C.G. and Hollin, C.R. (1997) 'The scientist-practitioner model in clinical psychology: a critique', *Clinical Psychology and Psychotherapy*, 4: 75–83.

Lunt, I. (1998) 'Education and training for psychology in Europe: an overview', *Psychology Teaching Review*, 7: 4–10.

Macdonald, G. and Roberts, H. (1996) *What Works in the Early Years?* Barkingside: Bernardo's Publications.

Macdonald, G. and Williamson, E. (2002) *Against the Odds: An Evaluation of Child and Family Support Services*. Edinburgh: London: National Children's Bureau.

Mackay, T. (1999) *Quality Assurance in Education Authority Psychological Services*. Edinburgh: Scottish Executive Education Department.

Mackin, T. (2002) 'Training for Essex EPs in information and communication technology: an assessment of future needs.' Doctorate in educational psychology thesis, School of Psychology, University of East London.

Macran, S. and Shapiro, D.A. (1998) 'The role of personal therapy for therapists: a review', *British Journal of Medical Psychology*, 17: 13–25.

Maliphant, R. (2000) 'Quality and quantity demands in educational psychology: strategic objectives for the 21st century', *Educational and Child Psychology*, 17 (2): 16–26.

Malamuth, N. and Check, J. (1980) 'Sexual arousal to rape and consenting depictions: the importance of the woman's arousal', *Journal of Abnormal Psychology*, 89: 763–6.

Maracek, J., Fine, M. and Kidder, L. (1997) 'Working between worlds: qualitative methods and social psychology', *Journal of Social Issues*, 53: 631–44.

Marks, D.F. (1996) 'Health psychology in context', *Journal of Health Psychology*, 1: 7–21.

Marks, D.F., Brucher-Albers, C., Donker, F.J.S., Jespen, Z., Roriquez Marin, J., Sidot, S. and Wallin-Backman, B. (1999) 'Health Psychology 2000: the development of a professional health psychology', *Health Psychology Update*, 35: 4–16.

Martin, C. (2001) *The Life Coaching Handbook*. Arlesford, Hants: Crown House Publishing.

Martinez, M., Gros, B. and Romaña, T. (1998) 'The problem of training in higher education', *Higher Education in Europe*, 23: 483–95.

Martinson, R. (1974) 'What works? Questions and answers about prison reform', *Public Interest*, 10: 22–54.

Matarazzo, J.D. (1980) 'Behavioral health and behavioural medicine: frontiers for a new health psychology', *American Psychologist*, 35 (9): 807–17.

Matarazzo, J.D. (1982) 'Behavioral health's challenge to academic, scientific and professional psychology', *American Psychologist*, 37 (1): 1–14.

Maynard, M. (1994) 'Methods, practice, and epistemology: the debate about feminism and research', in M. Maynard and J. Purvis (eds) *Researching Women's Lives from a Feminist Perspective*. London: Taylor & Francis.

McAdams, D.P. (1995) 'What do we know when we know a person?' *Journal of Personality*, 63 (3): 365–96.

McDermott, M.R. (2001a) 'Redefining health psychology: Matarazzo revisited', *Health Psychology Update*, 10 (1): 3–10. Also republished in Marks, D.F. (ed.) (2002) *The Health Psychology Reader*. London: Sage.

McDermott, M.R. (2001b) 'On redefining health psychology as "behavioural health" ', *Health Psychology Update*, 10 (3): 59–62.

McKenzie, D. (1987) 'Teaching students who already know the truth', *Cultic Studies Journal*, 4: 61–72.

McKey, H.R., Condelli, L., Ganson, H., Barrett, B., McConkey, C. and Plantz, M. (1985) *The Impact of Headstart on Children, Families and Communities*. Washington, DC: CSR.

McLeod, J. (1998) *An Introduction to Counselling*. Buckingham: Open University Press.

McLeod, J. (2001) *Counselling in the Workplace*. Rugby: BACP.

McMahon, G. (1994) *Setting up Your Own Private Practice*. Cambridge: National Extension College.

McMahon, G. (1995) *Setting up Your Own Private Practice in Counselling and Psychotherapy*. Cambridge: National Extension College.

McMahon, G. (1997) 'Counselling in private practice', in G. McMahon and S. Palmer (eds) *Handbook of Counselling*. London: Routledge.

Mead, G.H. (1934) *Mind, Self and Society*. Chicago, IL: University of Chicago Press.

Medawar, P. (1972) *The Hope of Progress*. London: Methuen.

Mellor-Clark, J. (2000) *Counselling in Primary Care in the Context of the NHS Quality Agenda. The Facts*. Rugby: BACP.

*Memorandum of Good Practice on Video-recorded Interviews with Child Witnesses for Criminal Proceedings* (1992) Issued by the Home Office and Department of Health. London: HMSO.

Meyrick, J. (2001) 'From psychology degree to the Health Development Agency in three easy moves', *Health Psychology Update*, 10 (3): 27–8.

Michie, S. (2001) 'Issues in health psychology: the UK debate', *Health Psychology Update*, 10 (3): 54–7.

Middlehurst, R. (1993) *Leading Academics*. Buckingham: SRHE and Open University Press.

Miller, G.A. (1969) 'Psychology as a means of promoting human welfare', *American Psychologist*, 24: 1063–75.

Miller, J., Taylor, B. and Watts, A.G. (1983) *Towards a Personal Guidance Base*. London: Further Education Unit.

Mills, J.S. (1874) *A System of Logic*. New York, NY: Harper.

Milne, D. (1990) 'The scientist-practitioner in practice', *Clinical Psychology Forum*, 30: 27–30.

Milne, D. (1999) 'Editorial: important differences between the "scientist-practitioner" and the "evidence-based practitioner" ', *Clinical Psychology Forum*, 133: 5–9.

Milne, D., Britton, P. and Wilkinson, I. (1990) 'The scientist-practitioner in practice', *Clinical Psychology Forum*, 30: 27–30.

Milne, D. and Paxton, R. (1998) 'A psychological reanalysis of the scientist-practitioner model', *Clinical Psychology and Psychotherapy*, 5: 216–30.

Misra, G. (1993) 'Psychology from a constructionist perspective: an interview with Kenneth J. Gergen', *New Ideas in Psychology*, 11: 399–414.

Moncrieff, J., Wessely, S. and Hardy, R. (1998) 'Meta-analysis of trials comparing antidepressants with active placebos', *British Journal of Psychiatry*, 172: 227–31.

Moorman, A., Ball, M. and Henricson, C. (2001) *Understanding Parents' Needs: A Review of Parents' Surveys*. London: National Family and Parenting Institute.

Morse, J.M. (ed.) (1992) *Qualitative Health Research*. Newbury Park, CA: Sage.

Mortimer, H. (2001) *Special Needs and Early Years Provision*. London: Cassell.

Moses, I. and Roe, F. (1990) *Heads and Chairs*. Kensington, NSW: University of Queensland Press.

Moss, P. (2001) 'Policies and provisions, politics and ethics', in T. David (ed.) *Promoting Evidence-based Practice in Early Childhood Education: Research and its Implications*. Volume 1. Oxford: Elsevier Science.

MPAG (1990) *Clinical Psychology Project: Full Report*. London: Department of Health.

Mulvey, M.R. (2002) 'Ethical practice in guidance: do the right thing', in Institute of Careers Guidance (ed.) *Constructing the Future. Social Inclusion: Policy and Practice*. Stourbridge: ICG.

Munafo, M. (1999) 'Careers after an MSc in health psychology', *Health Psychology Update*, 35: 33.

Munsterberg, H. (1908) *On the Witness Stand: Essays on Psychology and Crime*. New York, NY: Clark Boardman.

Murray, R. (2002) *How to Write a Thesis*. Buckingham: Open University Press.

Myers, M.B., Templer, D.I. and Brown, R. (1984) 'Coping ability of women who become victims of rape', *Journal of Consulting and Clinical Psychology*, 52: 73–8.

National Committee of Enquiry into Higher Education (1997) *Higher Education in the Learning Society (the Dearing Report)*. London: HMSO.

Neenan, M. and Dryden, W. (2002) *Life Coaching: A Cognitive-Behavioural Approach*. London: Brunner-Routledge.

Nelson-Jones, R. (1999) 'On becoming counselling psychology in the society: establishing the Counselling Psychology Section', *Counselling Psychology Review*, 14(3): 30–7.

Newman, J.H. (1857) *The Idea of a University* (reprinted 1960). San Francisco, CA: Rinehart Press.

Newstead, S.E. (1992) 'The use of examinations in the assessment of psychology students', *Psychology Teaching Review*, 1: 22–33.

Newstead, S.E. (2000) 'Silk purse or sow's ear? A psychological perspective on recent developments in higher education', *Psychology Teaching Review*, 9: 1–10.

Nichols, K., Cormack, M. and Walsh, S. (1992) 'Preventative personal support: a challenge for training courses', *Clinical Psychology Forum*, 45: 29–31.

Nicolson, P. (1994) 'Reflexivity and the experience of the research interview: women's identity, self-awareness and the case of postnatal depression', in *Proceedings of the 2nd International Qualitative Health Research Conference, Hershey, Pennsylvania, USA*.

Nicolson, P. (2001) 'Critical health psychology: a radical alternative to the "mainstream"?' *Psychology, Health and Medicine*, 6 (3): 258–61.

Niemeyer, G.J. and Diamond, A.K. (2001) 'The anticipated future of counselling psychology in the United States: a Delphi poll', *Counselling Psychology Quarterly*, 14(1): 49–65.

Noble, K.A. (1994) *Changing Doctoral Degrees: An International Perspective*. Buckingham: SRHE and Open University Press.

Nolan, A. and Sigston, A. (1993) *Where Do I Go from Here? A Booklet for Students who have been Excluded from School*. London: London Borough of Waltham Forest.

Norcross, J.C., Brust, A.M. and Dryden, W. (1992) 'British clinical psychologists. II. Survey findings and American comparisons', *Clinical Psychology Forum*, 40: 25–9.

Oakeshott, M. (1990) *Educational Guidance and Curriculum Change: A Project Report*. London: Further Education Unit.

O'Donohue, W. (1989) 'The (even) bolder model: the clinical psychologist as metaphysician-scientist-practitioner', *American Psychologist*, 44: 1460–8.

Offer, D. and Sabshin, M. (eds) (1991) *The Diversity of Normal Behavior: Further Contributions to Normatology*. New York, NY: Basic Books.

Ogden, J. (2000) *Health Psychology: A Textbook*. Milton Keynes: Open University Press.

Organization for Economic Co-operation and Development (1995) *Educational Research and Development: Trends, Issues and Challenges*. Paris: OECD.

Osipow, S.H. and Fitzgerald, L.F. (1996) *Theories of Career Development* (4th edn). Needham Heights, MA: Allyn & Bacon.

Osipow, S.H. and Littlejohn, E.M. (1995) 'Toward a multicultural theory of career development: prospects and dilemmas', in F.T.L. Leong (ed.) *Career Development and Vocational Behavior of Racial and Ethnic Minorities*. Hillsdale, NJ: Lawrence Erlbaum Associates.

Palmer, S. and Szymanska, K. (1996) 'Cognitive therapy and counselling', in S. Palmer et al. (eds) *Counselling: The BAC Counselling Reader*. London: Sage.

Parker, I. (1994) 'Reflexive research and the grounding of analysis: social psychology and the psy-complex', *Journal of Community and Applied Social Psychology*, 4: 239–52.

Parker, I. and Burman, E. (1993) 'Against discursive imperialism, empiricism and constructionism: thirty-two problems with discourse analysis', in E. Burman and I. Parker (eds) *Discourse Analytic Research: Repertoires and Readings of Texts in Action*. London: Routledge.

Parker-Rees, R. (1997) 'Making sense and made sense: design and technology and the playful construction of meaning in the early years', *Early Years*, 18: 5–8.

Patel, N. (1999) *Getting the Evidence: Guidelines for Ethical Mental Health Research Involving Issues of 'Race', Ethnicity and Culture*. London: MIND/Transcultural Psychiatry Society.

Patel, N., Bennett, E., Dennis, M., Dosanjh, N., Mahtani, A., Miller, A. and Nadirshaw, Z. (eds) (2000) *Clinical Psychology, 'Race' and Culture: A Training Manual*. Leicester: BPS.

Perkin, H.J. (1987) 'The academic profession in the United Kingdom', in B.B. Clark (ed.) *The Academic Profession*. Berkeley, CA: University of California Press.

Perkin, H.J. (1991) 'History of universities', in P.G. Altbach (ed.) *International Higher Education*. New York, NY: Garland Publishing.

Perkin, H. (1996) *The Third Revolution: Professional elites in the modern world*. London: Routledge.

Perkins, R. (2001) 'What constitutes success?' *British Journal of Psychiatry*, 179: 9–10.

Phillips, A., Hatton, C. and Gray, I. (2001) 'Which selection methods do clinical psychology courses use?' *Clinical Psychology*, 8: 19–23.

Phillips, A., Hatton, C., Gray, I., Baldwin, S., Burrell-Hodgson, G., Cox, M., Hoy, J., McCormick, R., Rockliffe, C. and Wilson, J. (2001) 'Core competencies in clinical psychology: a view from trainees', *Clinical Psychology*, 1: 27–32.

Phillips, E.M. and Pugh, D.S. (1994) *How to Get a PhD. A Handbook for Students and their Supervisors* (2nd edn). Buckingham: Open University Press.

Phillips, M. (2001) 'The professions must resist being Blair's scapegoats', *The Sunday Times*, 11 March: 17.

Pilgrim, D. (1993) 'Objections to private practice', in W. Dryden (ed.) *Questions and Answers on Counselling in Action*. London: Sage.

Pilgrim, D. (1997) *Psychotherapy and Society*. London: Sage.

Pilgrim, D. (2000) 'Psychiatric diagnosis: more questions than answers', *The Psychologist*, 13 (6): 302–5.

Pilgrim, D. and Treacher, A. (1992) *Clinical Psychology Observed*. London: Routledge.

Pilling, S. (2001) 'BPS Centre for Outcomes Research and Effectiveness (CORE)', *Health Psychology Update*, 10 (3): 32–3.

Pollard, P. (1992) 'Judgements about victims and attackers in depicted rapes: a review', *British Journal of Social Psychology*, 31: 307–26.

Porteous, M. (1997) *Occupational Psychology*. London: Prentice Hall.

Potter, J. (1982) ' "Nothing so practical as a good theory." The problematic application of social psychology', in P. Stringer (ed.) *Confronting Social Issues*. London: Academic Press.

Powicke, F.M. and Emden, A.B. (1936) *The Universities of Europe in the Middle Ages by the Late Hastings Rashdall. New Edition in Three Volumes* (1st edn 1895). Oxford: Oxford University Press.

Prochaska, J.O. and Norcross, J.C. (1999) *Systems of Psychotherapy. A Transtheoretical Analysis* (4th edn). Pacific Grove, CA: Brooks/Cole.

Putnam, R. (1993) 'The prosperous community: social capital and public life', *The American Prospect*, 13: 35–42.

Raaheim, K., Wankowski, J. and Radford, J. (1991) *Helping Students to Learn: Teaching, Counselling, Research*. Buckingham: SRHE and Open University Press.

Race, P. (2001) *The Lecturer's Toolkit: A Practical Guide to Learning, Teaching and Assessment* (2nd edn). London: Kogan Page.

Radford, J. (1992) 'The undergraduate curriculum in psychology', *The Psychologist*, 15: 273–6.

Radford, J. (1994) 'Remote and ineffectual? The background to the profession of academic psychologist', *Psychology Teaching Review*, 3: 29–45.

Radford, J. (1997) 'Academic psychologists: parasites, priests, proletariat or professionals?' *Psychology Teaching Review*, 6: 170–89.

Radford, J. (ed.) (1998) *Gender and Choice in Education and Occupation*. London: Routledge.

Radford, J. (1999 unpublished) 'A subject of some importance: a personal view of teaching psychology.'

Radford, J. (2001) 'Doctor of what?' *Teaching in Higher Education*, 6: 527–9.

Radford, J. (2002) 'Examining higher education: an English perspective', in A. Raaheim and K. Raaheim (eds) *Examining: An Academic Headache*. Bergen: Sigma Forlag International.

Radford, J. and Govier, E. (eds) (1980) *A Textbook of Psychology*. London: Routledge.

Radford, J. and Holdstock, L. (1993) 'What students want: objectives of first year psychology students in Ireland, Norway, Portugal, Spain and the United Kingdom', *Psychology Teaching Review*, 2: 39–49.

Radford, J. and Holdstock, L. (1996) 'Academic values rule', *New Academic*, 5: 10–11.

Radford, J. and Holdstock, L. (1997) 'Higher education: the views of parents of university students', *Journal of Further and Higher Education*, 20: 81–93.

Radford, J., Holdstock, L. and Raaheim, A. (1999a) 'Academic attitudes: an Anglo-Norwegian comparison.' Internally circulated report, University of Bergen, Norway, and University of East London.

Radford, J., Holdstock, L. and Wu, R. (1999b) 'Psychology as a subject, compared to other subjects: views of pre-university students', *Psychology Teaching Review*, 8: 26–36.

Radford, J., Raaheim, K., deVries, P. and Williams, R. (1997) *Quantity and Quality in Higher Education*. London: Jessica Kingsley.

Radford, J. and Rose, D. (eds) (1980) *The Teaching of Psychology. Method, Content and Context*. Chichester: Wiley.

Radford, J. and Rose, D. (eds) (1989) *A Liberal Science. Psychology Education, Past, Present and Future*. Buckingham: Open University Press.

Randle, K. and Brady, N. (1997) 'Managerialism and professionalism in the "Cinderella service"', *Journal of Vocational Education and Training*, 49 (1): 121–39.

Ratey, J.R. and Johnson, C. (1997) *Shadow Syndromes*. New York, NY: Bantam.

Ravenette, T. (ed.) (1999) *Personal Construct Psychology Theory in Educational Psychology*. London. Whurr.

Reason, J. (1997) *Managing the Risks of Organizational Accidents*. Aldershot: Ashgate.

Reason, J. (2000) 'The Freudian slip revisited', *The Psychologist*, 13 (12): 610–11.

Redondo, S., Sanchez-Meca, J. and Garrido, V. (2002) 'Crime treatment in Europe: a final view of the century and future perspectives', in J. McGuire (ed.) *Offender Rehabilitation and Treatment: Effective Programmes and Policies to reduce Re-offending*. Chichester: Wiley.

Reese, J.T. (1995) 'A history of police psychological services', in M.I. Kirke and E.M. Scrivner (eds) *Police Psychology into the 21st Century*. Hillsdale, NJ: Lawrence Erlbaum Associates.

Rice, M. (2000) 'Age of the flex exec', *Management Today*, August: 47–52.

Richardson, J., Felder, G., Eldridge, S., Shan Chung, W., Coid, J. and Moorey, S. (2001) 'Women who experience domestic violence and women survivors of childhood sexual abuse: a survey of health professionals' attitudes and clinical practice', *British Journal of General Practice*, 51: 468–70.

Ridgeway, C.C. (2000) 'Eight years on: what's so special about chartered occupational psychologists?' *The Occupational Psychologist*, 41: 13–15.

Rigby, S. (2001) 'Living with multiple sclerosis: the potential role of health psychology', *Health Psychology Update*, 10 (2): 14–17.

Roberts, G.A. (2000) 'Narrative and severe mental illness: what place do stories have in an evidence-based world?' *Advances in Psychiatric Treatment*, 6: 432–41.

Robson, C. (2002) *Real World Research* (2nd edn). Oxford: Blackwell.

Rogers, E.S., Chamberlin, J., Ellison, M.L. and Crean, T. (1997) 'A consumer-constructed scale to measure empowerment among users of mental health services', *Psychiatric Services*, 48: 1042–7.

Rose, D. and Radford, J. (eds) (1984) *Teaching Psychology. Information and Resources*. Leicester: BPS.

Rose, H. and Rose, S. (eds) (2000) *Alas, Poor Darwin: Arguments against Evolutionary Psychology*. London: Jonathan Cape.

Roth, A. (1995) 'Getting on clinical training courses', *The Psychologist*, 11: 589–92.

Roth, A. and Fonagy, P. (1996) *What Works for Whom? A Critical Review of Psychotherapy Research*. London: Guilford Press.

Roth, A. and Leiper, R. (1995) 'Selecting for clinical training', *The Psychologist*, 8: 25–8.

Roth, T. (1999) 'Evidence-based practice: is there a link between research and practice?' *Clinical Psychology Forum*, 133: 37–40.

Rothblatt, S. (1991) 'The American modular system', in R.O. Berdahl et al. (eds) *Quality and Access in Higher Education: Comparing Britain and the United States*. Buckingham: SRHE and Open University Press.

Rudkin, A. (2000) 'Having the courage to lack conviction', *Clinical Psychology Forum*, 141: 47–8.

Salmi, J. (2001) 'Testing education in the 21st century: challenges and opportunities', *Higher Education Management*, 13: 105–30.

Salter, B. and Tapper, T. (1994) *The State and Higher Education*. London: Woburn Press.

Sampson, E.E. (1993) 'Identity politics: challenges to psychology's understanding', *The American Psychologist*, 48: 1219–30.

Sanders, C. (2002) 'Debt grows ever bigger and ever more painful', *The Times Higher Supplement*, 1 February.

Savickas, M.L. (1993) 'Career counseling in the postmodern era', *Journal of Cognitive Psychotherapy*, 7 (3): 205–15.

Savickas, M.L. (1995) 'Current theoretical issues in vocational psychology: convergence, divergence, and schism', in W.B. Walsh and S.H. Osipow (eds) *Handbook of Vocational Psychology: Theory, Research and Practice* (2nd edn). Mahwah, NJ: Lawrence Erlbaum Associates.

Scaife, J. (1995) *Training to Help: A Survival Guide*. Sheffield: Riding Press.

Schön, D.A. (1983) *The Reflective Practitioner: How Professionals Think in Action*. New York, NY: Basic Books.

Schön, D.A. (1987) *Educating the Reflective Practitioner*. San Francisco, CA: Jossey-Bass.

Scott, P. (2001) 'Conclusion: triumph and retreat', in D. Warner and D. Palfreyman (eds) *The Shape of UK Higher Education: Managing Change and Diversity*. Buckingham: SRHE and Open University Press.

Seligman, M.E.P. (1997) 'Prevention is the theme of the '98 presidential year', *The Monitor*, December: 35.

Shapiro, S. (2000) *Choosing a Counselling or Psychotherapy Training*. London: Routledge.

Sharf, R.S. (1997) *Applying Career Development Theory to Counseling*. Pacific Grove, CA: Brooks/Cole.

Shaw, T.F. (1992) 'What's so special about chartered occupational psychologists?' *The Occupational Psychologist*, April: 10–12.

Shinn, C.H. (1986) *Paying the Piper: The Development of the University Grants Committee, 1919–1946*. Lewes: Falmer Press.

Shotland, R.L. and Goodstein, L. (1983) 'Just because she doesn't want to doesn't mean it's rape: an experimentally based causal model of the perception of rape in a dating situation', *Social Psychology Quarterly*, 46: 220–32.

Sigston, A., Curran, P., Labram, A. and Wolfendale, S. (eds) (1996) *Psychology in Practice with Young People, Families and Schools*. London: David Fulton.

Silver, H. (1990) *A Higher Education: The Council for National Academic Awards and British Higher Education, 1964–1989*. London: Falmer Press.

Sinclair, R. (1998) 'Developing evidence-based policy and practice in social interventions with children and families', *International Journal of Social Research Methodology*, 1 (2): 169–76.

Slade, M. and Priebe, S. (2001) 'Are randomised controlled trials the only gold that glitters?' *British Journal of Psychiatry*, 179: 286–7.

Sloan, T. (ed.) (2000) *Critical Psychology: Voices for Change*. Basingstoke: Palgrave.

Smail, D. (1993) *The Origins of Unhappiness: A New Understanding of Personal Distress*. London: HarperCollins.

Smail, D.J. (1998) 'What's it all about?' *Clinical Psychology Forum*, 119: 22–4.

Smail, D. (2001) *The Nature of Unhappiness*. London: Robinson.

Smith, A. (1776) *The Wealth of Nations* (reprinted 1986). Harmondsworth: Penguin Books.

Smyth, J. (ed.) (1995) *Academic Work: The Changing Process in Higher Education*. Buckingham: SRHE and Open University Press.

Social Exclusion Unit (1999) *Bridging the Gap: New Opportunities for 16–18 Year Olds*. CD-ROM in education, employment and training. Cm 4405. London: HMSO.

Sparrow, J. (1967) *Mark Pattison and the Idea of a University*. Cambridge: Cambridge University Press.

Spinelli, E. (2001) *The Mirror and the Hammer. Challenges to Therapeutic Orthodoxy*. London: Continuum.

Stainton Rogers, W. and Stainton Rogers, R. (2001) *The Psychology of Gender and Sexuality*. Milton Keynes: Open University Press.

Standing Conference of Associations for Guidance in Educational Settings (1991) 'Statements of Principles and Definitions' (mimeo). Stourbridge: SCAGES.

St Ather, T. (1999) 'Where do we go from here...again?' *The Occupational Psychologist*, 38: 59–61.

Stephenson, W. (1953) *The Study of Behavior: Q Technique and its Methodology*. Chicago, IL: University of Chicago Press.

Stevens, A. and Price, J. (1996) *Evolutionary Psychiatry: A New Beginning*. London: Routledge.

Stoker, R. (2002) 'Educational psychology: diversity led, context sensitive and process driven – a view of the future. Debate: Division of Educational and Child Psychology, the British Psychological Society', *DECP Newsletter*, 101 (March).

Swann, C. (2001) 'Health psychologists in practice? A view from public health', *Health Psychology Update*, 10 (3): 23–6.

Sweet, P.R. (1978–80) *Wilhelm von Humboldt: A Biography*. Columbus, OH: Ohio State University Press.

Sylva, K. (1994) 'School influences on children's development', *Journal of Child Psychology and Psychiatry and Allied Professions*, 35: 135–70.

Syme, G. (1994) *Counselling in Independent Practice*. Buckingham: Open University Press.

Szymanska, K. (2002) 'Trainee expectations in counselling psychology as compared to the reality of training experiences', *Counselling Psychology Review*, 17 (1): 22–7.

Tallis, R. (1999) *Theorrhoea and After*. Basingstoke: Palgrave.

Tallman, K. and Bohart, A.C. (1999) 'The client as a common factor: clients as self-healers', in M.A. Hubble et al. (eds) *The Heart and Soul of Change*. Washington, DC: American Psychological Association.

Taylor, P.G. (1999) *Making Sense of Academic Life: Academics, Universities and Change*. Buckingham: SRHE and Open University Press.

Terkel, S. (1972) *Working*. New York, NY: Avon Books.

Thomas, G.V., Turpin, G. and Meyer, C. (2002) 'Clinical research under threat', *The Psychologist*, 15: 286–9.

Thorne, B. (1992) 'Psychotherapy and counselling: the quest for differences', *Counselling*, November: 244–8.

Thorne, B. (1995) 'Contribution to I. Horton, R. Bayne and J. Bimrose (eds): New direction in counselling: a roundtable', *Counselling*, 6 (1): 34–40.

Thorne, B. (1999) 'The move towards brief therapy: its dangers and its challenges', *Counselling*, February: 7–11.

Thorne, B. (2002) 'Regulation – a treacherous path', *Counselling and Psychotherapy Journal*, March: 4–5.

Tight, M. (1996) 'University typologies re-examined', *Higher Education Review*, 29: 577.

Triandis, H.C. (1989) 'Cross-cultural industrial and organizational psychology', in H.C. Triandis et al. (eds) *Handbook of Industrial and Organizational Psychology. Volume 4* (2nd edn). Palo Alto, CA: Consulting Psychologists Press.

Triandis, H.C. and Brislin, R.W. (1984) 'Cross-cultural psychology', *The American Psychologist*, 39: 1006–17.

Trow, M. (1987) 'Academic standards and mass higher education', *Higher Education Quarterly*, 41: 268–98.

Tudor, K. and Merry, T. (2002) *Dictionary of Person-centred Psychology*: London: Whurr.

Tweed, R.G. and Lehman, D.R. (2002) 'Learning considered within a cultural context: Confucian and Socratic approaches', *The American Psychologist*, 57: 89–99.

Ussher, J.M. (1989) *The Psychology of the Female Body*. London: Routledge.

Ussher, J.M. (1991) *Women's Madness: Misogyny or Mental Illness*. Hemel Hempstead: Harvester Wheatsheaf.

Ussher, J.M. and Nicolson, P. (eds) (1992) *Gender Issues in Clinical Psychology*. London: Routledge.

Van Deurzen-Smith, E. (1993) 'Does being a psychologist help a counsellor in his or her work?' in W. Dryden (ed.) *Questions and Answers in Counselling in Action*. London: Sage.

Van Laar, D.L. and Sherwood, S.J. (1995) 'Where do all the psychologists go? First destinations of psychology graduates 1989–1991', *Psychology Teaching Review*, 4: 40–51.

Vansina, L.S. (1998) 'The individual in organizations: rediscovered or lost forever?' *European Journal of Work and Organizational Psychology*, 7 (3): 265–82.

Walkerdine, V. and the Girls and Mathematics Unit (1989) *Counting Girls Out*. London: Virago.

Wallace, L. (1998) 'Consultancy in health psychology to health services', *Health Psychology Update*, 34: 42–7.

Wallace, L. (2000) 'What did this course do for you? The employability of masters graduates in health psychology', *Health Psychology Update*, 39: 4–10.

Walsh, S. and Cormack, M. (1994) ' "Do as we say and not as we do": personal, professional and organisation barriers to the receipt of support at work', *Clinical Psychology and Psychotherapy*, 1: 101–10.

Walsh, S., Nichols, K. and Cormack, M. (1991) 'Self-care and clinical psychologists – a threatening obligation?' *Clinical Psychology Forum*, 37: 5–7.

Walsh, S. and Scaife, J. (1998) 'Mechanisms for addressing personal and professional development in clinical training', *Clinical Psychology Forum*, 115: 21–4.

Ward, C. (1995) *Attitudes toward Rape: Feminist and Social Psychological Perspectives*. London: Sage.

Wardle, J. (2000) 'Editorial – public health psychology: expanding the horizons of health psychology', *British Journal of Health Psychology*, 5: 329–36.

Wardle, J. (2001) 'Health psychology in Britain: past, present and future', *Health Psychology Update*, 10 (3): 43–7.

Warnock, M. (1989) *Universities: Knowing our Minds*. London: Chatto & Windus.

Warren Piper, D. (1992) 'Are professors professional?' *Higher Education Quarterly*, 46: 145–56.

Watkins, C. (2000) Introduction to articles on consultation. *Educational Psychology in Practice*, 16 (1): 5–8, and seven other articles in the same journal on consultation by Wagner; Dickinson; Kerslake and Roller; Gillies, Christie, Hetherington and Parkes; Watkins and Hill; Munro (all in *Educational Psychology in Practice*, 16 (1).

Watt, G. (1996) *The Role of Adult Guidance and Employment Counselling in a Changing Labour Market: Final Report on EUROCOUNSEL: An Action Research Programme on Counselling and Long-term Unemployment*. Dublin: European Foundation for the Improvement of Living and Working Conditions.

Watts, A.G. (1991) 'The impact of the "New Right": policy challenges confronting careers guidance in England and Wales', *British Journal of Guidance and Counselling*, 19 (3): 230–45.

Watts, A.G., Guichard, J., Plant, P. and Rodriguez, M.L. (1994) *Educational and Vocational Guidance in the European Community: The Synthesis Report of a Study Carried out on Behalf of the Commission of the European Communities*. Luxembourg: Office for Official Publications of the European Communities.

Widdicombe, S. (1993) 'Autobiography and change: Rhetoric and authenticity of Gothic style', in E. Burman and I. Parker (eds.) *Discourse Analytic Research: Repertoires and readings of texts in action*. London: Routledge.

Wilkinson, J. (2002) Letter to *The Psychologist*, 15 (4): 168.

Wilkinson, R. (ed.) (1969) *Governing Elites: Studies in Training and Selection*. New York, NY: Oxford University Press.

Wilkinson, S. (1988) 'The role of reflexivity in feminist psychology', *Women's Studies International Forum*, 11: 493–502.

Wilkinson, S. (1997) 'Feminist psychology', in D. Fox and I. Prilleltensky (eds) *Critical Psychology: An Introduction*. London: Sage.

Williams, D.D.R. and Garner, J. (2002) 'The case against "the evidence": a different perspective on evidence-based medicine', *British Journal of Psychiatry*, 180: 8–12.

Williams, D.I. and Irving, J.A. (1996) 'Counselling psychology: a conflation of paradigms', *Counselling Psychology Review*, 11 (2): 4–6.

Williams, J.E. (1984) 'Secondary victimisation: confronting public attitudes about rape', *Victimology: An International Journal*, 9: 66–81.

Willig, C. (2001) *Introducing Qualitative Research in Psychology: Adventures in Theory and Method*. Milton Keynes: Open University Press.

Winter, R. (1989) *Learning from Experience: The Practice of Action Research*. Lewes: Falmer Press.

Winter, R. (1991) *Outline of a General Theory of Professional Competences*. Chelmsford: The Anglia/Essex Accreditation of Social Services Experience and Training (ASSET) Programme.

Wolf, A. (1995) *Competence-based Assessment*. Buckingham: Open University Press.

Wolfendale, S. (1995) 'The code of practice and parents: a stimulus for re-appraisal for EPs' work with parents', *Educational and Child Psychology*, 12 (3): 73–9.

Wolfendale, S. (1997) 'The child in the context of the family: implications for the practice of EPs', *Educational and Child Psychology*, 14 (3): 77–83.

Wolfendale, S. (1998) *All About Me*. Nottingham: NES-Arnold.

Wolfendale, S. (1999) 'Parents as partners in research and evaluation: methodological and ethical issues and solutions', *British Journal of Special Education*, 26 (3): 164–8.

Wolfendale, S. (ed.) (2001) 'Report of an updated national survey of professional/practitioner doctorates in educational psychology.' Contact author at School of Psychology, University of East London.

Wolfendale, S. (ed.) (2002) *Parent Partnership Services for Special Educational Needs: Celebrations and Challenges*. London: David Fulton.

Wolfendale, S. and Bastiani, J. (eds) (2000) *The Parental Contribution to School Effectiveness*. London: David Fulton.

Wolfendale, S. and Corbett, J. (eds) (1996) *Opening Doors. Learning Support in Higher Education*. London: Cassell.

Wolfendale, S. and Einzig, H. (eds) (1999) *Parenting Education and Support: New Opportunities*. London: David Fulton.

Wolfendale, S. and Robinson, M. (eds) (2001) 'Educational psychologists working with the early years: a framework for practice.' Contact the authors at the School of Psychology, University of East London.

Woodhead, C. (2002) 'Trouble in the trades', *The Times Higher Educational Supplement*, 29 March.

Woolfe, R. (1996) 'Counselling psychology in Britain: past, present and future', *Counselling Psychology Review*, 11 (4): 7–18.

Woolfe, R. (2002) Letter to *The Psychologist*, 15 (4): 168.

Woolgar, S. (1988) *Knowledge and Reflexivity: New Frontiers in the Sociology of Knowledge*. London: Sage.

Worrall, L. and Cooper C.L. (1997–ongoing) *IM/UMIST: Quality of Working Life Survey*. London: Institute of Management.

Wray, J. (2001) 'Health psychologists in paediatric cardiology – is there anybody (else) out there?' *Health Psychology Update*, 10 (3): 4–8.

Wright, A. (1998) 'The move to three year training: opportunities, threats and challenges. A service perspective in professional training in educational psychology: the next 50 Years. Special issue', *DECP Newsletter*.

Yardley, L. (2000) 'Dilemmas in qualitative health research', *Psychology and Health*, 15: 215–28.

Yardley, L. (2001) 'Qualifying as a chartered health psychologist: the stage 2 qualification', *Health Psychology Update*, 10 (3): 63–6.

Yarmey, A.D. (1997) 'Probative v. prejudicial value of eyewitness memory research', *Expert Evidence: International Digest of Law and Psychology*, 5 (3): 89–97.

Young, R.A. and Collin, A. (2000) 'Introduction: framing the future of career', in A. Collin and R.A. Young (eds) *The Future of Career*. Cambridge: Cambridge University Press.

# Index